MATTHEW SPENDER

Within Tuscany

VIKING

VIKING

Published by the Penguin Group
Penguin Books USA Inc., 375 Hudson Street, New York, New York 10014, USA
Penguin Books Ltd, 27 Wrights Lane, London W8 5TZ, England
Penguin Books Australia Ltd, Ringwood, Victoria, Australia
Penguin Books Canada Ltd, 10 Alcorn Avenue, Toronto, Ontario, Canada M4V 3B2
Penguin Books (NZ) Ltd, 182–190 Wairau Road, Auckland 10, New Zealand

Penguin Books Ltd, Registered Offices: Harmondsworth, Middlesex, England

First published 1992
3 5 7 9 10 8 6 4 2

Printed in the United States of America
Set in 12/14pt Lasercomp Bembo

ISBN 0-670-83836-5

FOR MARO

CONTENTS

Contents

ACKNOWLEDGEMENTS

I have changed the names of one or two friends in cases where I felt that the written word might offend. For complicated reasons two of the places visited have been camouflaged, making this a most peculiar travel book. To add to the confusion, some of the characters are imaginary.

The request of John Ferro Sims and Colin Webb of Pavilion Books for some captions to John's photos started me off. John also very kindly helped me to print my own photographs, after this book, so unlike the one he asked for, had been finished.

I would like to thank Marco and Giuseppe Maccari for having read the chapter on their father Mino, and for giving their permission to reprint some of the illustrations Maccari made for the magazine *Il Selvaggio*.

Notes and bibliography are mixed together at the end of the book, to make both look more substantial. If I included a proper bibliography, I would have to cheat and insert the many volumes I have not read. All the translations from the Italian are mine.

Without the persistent help of Antonia Till and Peter Carson I would never have learned to turn rambling individual passages into a narrative. Esther Sidwell edited the copy, Justin Harris gave minute attention to the final proofs, and Caroline Muir saw the book through the press.

Within Tuscany

I would like to thank all those who gave me ideas:
Lisa Alì, Marisa Anichini, Sandra Bianchi Bandinelli,
Andrea Barzini, Bernardo Bertolucci, Carla Bonelli,
Ginevra Bompiani, Umberto Calò, Francesca Marzotto
Caotorta, Neri Capponi, Patrizia Cavalli, Don Giuseppe
Celai, Thekla Clark, Ettore Fallani, Magouch Fielding,
Caio Fonseca, Urbano Fontana, Luciano Fosi, Cesare
Furini, Giorgio Giannelli, Mary Hollingsworth, Giovanni
Kezich, Alessandro Marchini, Libero Mugelli, Bruno Parri,
Marjorie Reeves, Don Osvaldo Secciani, Mata Spinola,
Emanuela Stucchi, Alberto Trapassi, Luca Verdone, Anna
Vivante, Alessio Vlad, Georgina Van Weylie, Kimiko
Watanabe, Elizabeth Wipp.

My daughters, my parents, my wife.

1 · SAN SANO

We came to live near Siena on a whim, tired of the thin blue light of London town. A year or two, we said, not more, or else the hayseed will germinate in our hair and the red corpuscles in our blood will become silted with wine lees.

We must have had feet that rooted easily. The house had been abandoned for twenty years and still looked friendly. Outside the back door the vines spread from tree to tree in the old style, and we met workmen in the village who could remember who planted them. The sun came through gap-toothed holes in the roof and floors, right down to the stables below. So we latticed them with chestnut rafters, re-tiled and made good, largely with our own hands. The garden grew cabbages and beans, and in the autumn the olives along the dry-stone walls produced fruit that had to be picked and taken to the mill.

Without thinking much about it we acquired two great wheels with which to support the otherwise wholly interior preoccupations of artists. The first was the annual repetition of agricultural duties, shaped by habits that went back to Roman times and punctuated not so much by seasons as by the changing moon and the recurring name-days of saints. Certain things could be seeded on Candlemas, but never before, and a strange piece of doggerel I've now forgotten told you so. This agrarian culture has almost gone, now that the peasants are salaried workers and the eyes of the young are turning to the bright lights of the industrial towns in the valleys.

The second wheel was to have children here, our first daughter, Saskia, and then our second daughter, Cosima, and see the countryside through their eyes, join in the drama of schooling and upbringing, amid a whole flock of once raucous fledglings who are now grown up.

Ghosts surrounded our first years. We were used to ghosts. In London we had lived in a ramshackle old flat, where Maro, my wife, once saw a red-haired young man staring down at her as she was drifting off to sleep. He proved to be a rare but demanding visitor, this spirit with a hand half raised, like one who has something important to say. (Low corridor, late-eighteenth-century ceiling.)

Here in Tuscany there was the ghost of a malignant sprite, 'Like the eye of a chicken,' said the bowed man who came to see the house a year or two after we had settled in. 'And it followed you from room to room, never left you alone. You'd see it there in front of you, unblinking, just when you'd thought it had gone away! And at night, *una bara*, a coffin, high on the wall in your bedroom. There! See!'

We looked, and saw nothing. Truly, we assured him, we have never lived in a house less filled with anxiety, whatever the weather or season. The old man seemed perplexed. He was down from Montevarchi with his granddaughter, who was evidently bored by country matters. She took his arm to lead him away, but he longed to see every room, searching for the ghosts which had, in the end, driven him from the house, twenty years previously.

'You see,' he said, explaining perhaps more to himself than to us, 'two families lived here in those days. Fifteen people! And three oxen for the ploughing, seven pigs in the courtyard outside, many sheep on the hill. And so many children! Those animals . . . '

'Maybe it was the ghost of a malevolent chicken,' said Maro, and the granddaughter sniggered.

He smiled from politeness, wearily, as if we could never understand. 'Were we certain that never . . . ?', and so I took him patiently through the house twice over to make sure that the ghosts were really gone; and then through the garden, where rosemary planted as an ornamental shrub filled him with wonder at the decadence of modern times.

We were Protestants, I told him, and perhaps these ghosts came only to Catholics. A foolish thing to say, but it satisfied him at last. Of course! Protestants! He made it sound as if we had protested against everything, good spirits and bad.

Rebuilding the house retrieved the language for me, first learned up on Lake Garda during summer holidays as a child. I now acquired new words appropriate only to masons. The odd collapsible scaffolds they used were called *'caprette'*, or little goats, as they had small iron horns to stop planks falling off the ends. To do a job quickly, you urged the masons on with the words *'quanto prima'*, a purely Tuscan construction coming straight from the Latin *'quam celerrime'*.

And I learned about Tuscan workmen themselves, with their quiet way of moving about the building site, high on humour, low on anger. The image of a long-dead workman comes to mind as I write, who put his feet together like a cricketer when cutting stones. And another who was so terrified of thunder that he went to hide in the cellar during a storm, with his head in his arms. Nobody teased him. In some of those spring tempests, the rain comes rattling over the hills like cavalry on cobbles and the sky for a while seems much too close to the earth.

On a tip from a peasant in the village, I dug for treasure in the cowshed, but found none. The worn stones from its floor were placed in the courtyard around a second-hand ornamental drain. They were of *albarese*, a precipitate limestone that can be cut like flint, with just a hammer, and they came from a pit in the hillside a hundred yards off.

We altered the structure of the house as little as possible. It had no 'original state' to which one could refer. There was supposed to have been an ancient convent on the site, and some bits were definitely older than other bits. But to me the date 1750 carved on the chimney-piece seemed correct: the moment when it became fashionable for Florentines to invest in a new estate in the wilds between Florence and Siena, with tax benefits for those who took up the challenge.

In their decline, these buildings were rightly protected. For hygienic reasons it was now illegal to keep cattle in the stalls downstairs, yet it was also illegal to change the stalls to living quarters. In the conversions, which took place twenty-three years ago, these contradictory messages were simply ignored. And recently a law of *condono*, or forgiveness, was passed, allowing illegal alterations to be accepted by the government upon payment of a symbolic self-assessed fine – a mystical process that combined repentance from sin with an obol to the government, rather like the sale of indulgences in the sixteenth century, which paid for the Sistine Chapel.

Our only major innovation was a back staircase, rebuilt from a nineteenth-century cowshed we had dismantled. As we were building the staircase, who should come by but Otello, at that time the foreman of Public Works at the local *Comune*. He was just the man the builders most wanted not to see, as of course we had no official permission to build. 'Well,' he said, 'what are you up to here?' Each workman froze in whatever movement he happened to be doing, one with a trowel in mid-air, another with slippy-slop cement in a barrow halfway up a ramp. Silence. 'Oh well,' I said blushing, 'you see this staircase was – ah – falling down.' Otello acquired a strange interior look of serious doubt, then consulted the sky, consulted the ground, and went away. An interesting man, he seldom intervened in life around him, but had an infallible instinct for finding out what went on.

Our nearest neighbour was a sharecropper, or *mezzadro*, called Vittorio Fosi. He told me, in 1968, that the previous year for him had been a good one. He had sold half a *vitellino*, a calf sprung from one of the plough-team, bred for slaughter and kept for most of its brief life in the half-dark of a stall; and the halves of four pigs. The other halves of these animals belonged to the landowner. These sales gave him all the cash he ever needed, he said. He bought shoes and tobacco, and salt from the state monopoly. A little petrol for the motor bike perhaps. Material from the market for his wife to make into clothes. This was as close to self-sufficiency as one could ever imagine in Europe of the late twentieth century.

That first year he ploughed our kitchen garden using the team of white oxen, mother and aunt of the *vitellino*. I remember him talking to them, using odd cow-words to make them start and stop. When I complimented him on their beauty, their patience, their remarkable obedience, he said, 'they understand everything: they only lack the power of speech', a remark I found beautiful at the time, as subtle as love, but which I have since discovered was a ritual reply centuries old.

Vittorio and I planted a walnut together in the back garden. Six inches below the surface, we came across a huge rock. Vittorio was delighted. You pull it out, and the hole is made. So the oxen pulled, the tree ten inches high was planted, and today in spring its fragile globe shimmers at the edges for a week or two, before the huge branches fill out with green.

Trees touch their extremities today that I was not even aware I had planted in the same field, twenty years ago.

Looking out at the huge bowl of the walnut yesterday, I heard an echo of long-dead Vittorio's voice, telling me that snakes like its shade, and climb into the branches of walnut trees to mate. This danger could be mitigated by burning at its feet old shoes and rubber tyres.

From Vittorio I learned about the difficult soil I gradually desired to cultivate. When wet, you didn't touch it; you were 'better off staying in bed'. Shrubs or vegetables planted out in such conditions would bake in a clay pot of your own making, airless in the hardening soil. So we learned to glance at the ground constantly, gauging the state of abrasion or friability as it dried out. When the conditions were perfect, you dropped everything and ploughed – except of course if you had a painting coming along, in which case you postponed it, and then down would come the rain, and away would fly another fortnight while you looked at the ground, waiting.

Eventually I acquired a tractor, but I was never any good at ploughing. The fresh bark of young olives would peel from the trunk as easily as pith off an orange whenever I passed near by. I would postpone the job and it would rain, and when finally I got down to it the couch grass and wild rye would pack the ploughshare at the very moment the furrow was to tip over, clogging the bar that held the brace. Or the far ploughshare would catch some protruding stone from the eighteenth-century terraces and dump a heap of shale and decayed stone oh-so-neatly on to the ploughed earth.

Expressionless, or indeed with slight respect, Vittorio would advise me to keep my hand near the clutch, to disengage if I were to be so unfortunate as to plough a spur of the living rock just beneath the topsoil.

Ancestral frugality tinged Vittorio's life. A year after we met I came across him carving a new yoke for the ox-team from an oak cut down in the wood. We were restoring the roof at the time, and, taking advantage of my wonder at his skill as a carpenter, he came up smilingly to talk of little birds, *gli uccellini*, asking me some favour. Thinking vague thoughts of St Francis, I agreed. Whereupon he followed me back to the house, got out on the roof, and carefully removed from under the tiles all the young sparrows that were nesting there, tweaking their necks to make them lie still for the spit.

'Beware of the salamander,' said Vittorio. 'He is immune to fire, and his bite is poison.'

To feed the family or the animals had the same word: *governare*. By contrast, the government, according to Vittorio, did not 'govern', being too busy doing all the eating itself.

From Vittorio we learned how much could be taken from the hillside, rather than bought in cardboard boxes at the local store. *Pungitopo*, a small holly, would clean your chimney if hauled up and down on a rope or stout string. Acacia was good for the handles of picks, hoes and *bidenti*, two-pronged mattocks, mentioned in old Latin texts. Pruned trees of *Acer campestre*, the field maple, could be turned into a living support for the vines. A weed they called *vetrilla* could be used to polish glass. Some peasants even grew their own hemp, to make ropes with.

Two years after we came, Vittorio's land was bought by an industrialist from Brescia who turned him into a salaried worker. The oxen were sold, the stalls downstairs were closed in accordance with the appropriate regulation on hygiene, and he was told to work from eight to five every day on a specified wage.

Before this happened, a benevolent government offered him the chance to buy the house he lived in and the land he worked, at an artificially low evaluation, with a loan repayable over forty years, at 2 per cent. In spite of my insistence, he turned this offer down. Forty years, he said, was too long for him to commit himself to an obligation, as he was already fifty years old. He would not die leaving his son in debt.

Too surprised to continue the argument at the time, for a long while I wondered whether this extraordinarily long loan had been offered by the government to *discourage* the survival of a peasant class, while apparently seeming to promote its survival.

Vittorio went into a decline, a kind of culture shock. He had a hunting dog called Whiskers, which, by unfortunate coincidence, was stolen from him about the same time. He went for endless walks in what was to him an apparently vast free time, looking for this dog. I would meet him miles from home, looking miserable.

He survived and became reconciled to his new position, earned much more money than before, lived in the urban metropolis of Gaiole, all one thousand and fifty souls, bought a car. I would see him driving around, always with a good Sunday hat on even inside the car. And if he passed me on the road, I would read his lips saying '*Buon giorno, Signor Matteo,*' as if we had met in the open air, and he behind a pair of white oxen.

When Vittorio died, the postman smiled complacently and told me he had been '*un po' all'antica*', by which he meant 'old-fashioned'.

Our elder daughter Saskia was born in Florence, in 1970.

I remember trundling through the night in a very small Fiat, stopping every ten minutes for Maro's labour pains, while the cars piled up behind us hooting in protest.

The obstetrician had an urgent appointment on the ski slopes, and our daughter emerged slightly mauled about the head. She was a nervy infant, flinching if I laughed in the small room, which I did quite often for she was my first child, and I had never imagined the event could be so exciting.

Our second daughter Cosima was born at home, the last child in the *Comune* to be born outside hospital more or less on purpose. Odd things happened to my wife as she was carrying out the tea things to the local midwife and my mother-in-law, one warm afternoon in August. The midwife had got it wrong by a month, and was planning a short trip to Paris. She had just come round to check up and say goodbye.

'And are you going to beat the pavements, when you get there?' asked my mother-in-law politely as they sipped, meaning 'Are you going to go window-shopping?'

'*O Signora,*' said the dear lady, 'I'm much too old to do *that!*'

Maro laughed so much that the tea things came crashing down, and the midwife had no time to go home and get her 'nice new little bag' of gloves, rubbing alcohol and string.

At dusk, the electricity failed. I was told to boil water, lots of it, and refused, thinking it a ploy to get rid of useless husbands. We lit candles.

'What nice candles,' said the midwife cheerfully, as she smoked a cigarette with her left hand and explored the child, still inside her mother, with her right. 'It looks just like a funeral.'

Her name was Azzurrini, and indeed for me she had for evermore the pragmatic aura of the Blue Fairy in *Pinocchio*, whenever I read this masterpiece to the children, before bed.

Cosima was born neatly, in subdued light (courtesy wild-cat strike at Enel), a mere half-hour after labour began, in a bed carved and joined by my own hand, surrounded by a remarkable number of unmarried aunts, there to see how childbirth went.

When the doctor came he disapproved of everything. Such a risk, these days, having a baby at home. We stood to attention like good soldiers in front of their sergeant. Afterwards, we had a party, midwife, baby and all.

Still smoking, the midwife kept flipping over the newborn child. 'What shoulders!' she said admiringly, though it was not a part of her that the rest of us found particularly interesting. Signora Azzurrini compared Cosi's anatomy to that of an adult hare.

2 · SCHOOL

Time passed, and the moment when the young needed schooling caught up with us. The garden was still full of legumery and the light of London still seemed unattractive to this 'alternative nuclear family', as an Italian would have called us in the early seventies. Once immersed into the educational system it seemed just too hard to return to London and the dull tubercular north.

The village school had one classroom for everyone. There were only seven pupils, all of different sizes. The teacher was a very gifted woman and all the children learned to read and write between September and Christmas.

Our elder daughter's first day of school was unforgettable. She rode her tiny bicycle to the end of the drive, turned, waved and then took off down a short cut through the vines. Blue bike, blue raincoat, wet leaves. She was five.

In winter the whole school, all eight of them if one included the teacher, huddled round a stinking stove with a leaky and illegal outlet right through the window. There was no question of getting this fixed. The stove and the classroom belonged to the industrialist from Brescia, Vittorio's employer, who wanted to evict them so that he could fill their hall of learning with farm equipment. He was perfectly prepared to risk finding all the scholars asphyxiated one day, their grammar books still clutched in their hands, one collective past participle.

★

The little room had a hat rack by the window, benches and a closed cupboard called *Biblioteca*. I looked inside once, to check their collection of books. It was entirely filled with empty beer cans.

The existence of the school itself was eventually threatened by the central authorities, who decided to close all the outlying village schools and bus the children to larger premises where they could enjoy the benefits of efficient plumbing in a haven of white tiles, under the eye of a watchful beadle during break.

We protested, held stormy meetings, confronted a small sad official sent out from Siena, who suddenly decided to let us run the place ourselves if we could. For three months I taught English at the school in the next village but one, while my wife taught art in ours. Her class was neat and orderly. Mine was hell. At one point, I descended so low as to poke a little boy in the bum with a Biro, to make some point concerning the pronunciation of the definite article. I said to myself, now perhaps this is not the gesture of a true professional, and gave up.

But the school that was taught art by Maro flourished in the creativity which comes from innocence. She claimed that puberty brought with it non-artistic aims, like the Vespa and the disco on Saturdays, the lure to drive to hot spots like Montevarchi and San Giovanni. Pending this moment she taught a quiet, respectful group, male voices teetering on the brink of sudden baritone, female chests still more or less flat. A couple of years later these beautiful children had vanished, leaving behind animated statues worked over by a later hand.

Our children also grew up, and faced the trauma of moving from Gaiole to Siena. For me this was triggered when Cosi came back one day with a report beginning with the words, '*contenutisticamente possibilista, però* . . . ', meaning roughly, 'She's got some good ideas, but . . .' How can this poor child, I asked myself, go through life with a language so pompously fluffed out with Ciceronian constructions? Bullied by dog Latin? So we sent them south to a better school in Siena.

I followed, by becoming the parents' rep. There was not a great deal of competition for the job. The teachers were polite, and listened to any kind of didactic argument, but as far as I could tell they never changed their curriculum for anything a parents' representative ever said.

In theory we had some power. We could choose the textbooks and veto the history course if it failed to coincide with our own high standards. We could dictate the flavour of religious studies and re-route the annual school outing. All interesting problems – especially the school outing, that fascinating rite of passage where the kids discover cigarettes and French kissing, and the notion that love can be a public spectacle carried out among an audience of ululating peers. For thousands of Italian school-children the Leaning Tower of Pisa or the Uffizi is a warm primal memory, far from the small historical point the teacher might have wanted to make at the time. Be patient, tourist, as you thread your way among them.

As for the right to veto the school books, we annually attended a meeting where parents, teachers and books were lumped together and stirred.

Italian schools used to arrange their own curricula according to a series of cautious negative parameters laid down by the state, dictating that each theme should have not less than x and not more than y pages devoted to it. As long as these parameters were observed, publishers were free to give the subject what bias they wished. Often it was not clear what line a history textbook might be following; working out the political flavour of a book could involve counting pages rather than analysing content.

We were seldom presented with the mayhem of selection. The teacher would have brought it down to a choice of two, which was kind, but once you had sat down in the middle of the hum and gaggle and put a finger in one ear trying to read, to emerge hot and sweaty and breathing hard three quarters of an hour later, having plumped for one particular pile, as like as not the teacher would smilingly point out the attractions of the books remaining on the table. It was after all a choice of one.

Sometimes a left-wing history book might have more (for instance) on the life of Christ than a Catholic one. The reasons for this were complicated. There was a moment when the Italian Communist Party claimed Christ as a forebear; and meanwhile there was always the problem of the Hour of Religion in class.

I always fought for more study of the Bible in class, unsuccessfully, but as usual I missed the point. The fight was whether or not there should be a Scripture class at all. There were deeply anticlerical socialist teachers who would teach the life of Christ in Marxist terms during the history lesson, but who would refuse to teach anything about him in the *Ora di Religione*. There were Catholics who would teach anything to keep the Hour going – Buddha, Confucius, Zoroaster – avoiding for the moment the problems of discussing Christ.

There is no state religion in Italy, and in theory any child was free to opt out of the Hour of Religion. But it was rare that any child claimed this right. For a while the Liceo Classico of Siena enjoyed the paradox that, while their father fought for better teaching in the Hour of Religion in every parents' meeting, Saskia and Cosima alone in all Siena sat quietly in the corridor for the duration, saying politely they were atheist if ever a passing teacher asked.

They had not always been atheists. The elder went through a passionate Catholic phase at the age of seven, though her theology had been strangely tinged by a recent visit to Iran, where a friend of ours was working. There, left in the cook's apartment while we toured the sites, she had emerged a passionate Shiite.

Back in Italy her view of the Mass involved a fat padded carpet and carefully chosen wardrobe. The plastic babies kept in a row in the bookshelf acquired turbans and incense, though the actual ceremonies took place (as in Tehran) behind carefully shut doors. There was an occasional wail or throb of a drum, heard from the floor below. The empty feel of the desert perceived through a clean tent wall, the beating of a soft childish forehead against the unresilient tiles. A sudden demand for the compass reference for Mecca. Younger sister coopted to a subsidiary role holding Armenian slippers, practically strangled by a loose chador. Garbled bits of what one hoped was classical Arabic followed by references to '*Il Re del Toro*' ('the King of the Bull'), which came from '*il Redentore*', the Redeemer. Her Catholicism was what you might call ecumenical, if ecumenical means shoving in a bit of everything for the greater glory of God.

Every Sunday I would take this eclectic daughter to Mass, on condition that she left her shroud behind.

After a while I decided that I very much liked our parish priest, a man younger than myself, and remarkably straightforward and unsentimental in his sermons. On one particular saint's day he was required to touch the throats of his parishioners with a pair of crossed candles, to save them from sore throats during the ensuing winter. Don Osvaldo, fired by the revolutionary whiffs of the early seventies, gave his parishioners a speech on the foolishness of superstition. Touching their throats would never protect them against bugs, he said, and if they had flu they should see the doctor. He said it well, and the little flock listened in respectful silence. Then they all queued up to be touched by the candles anyway.

Osvaldo soon became a close friend of the family. We even painted portraits of him, one from each side. Neither Maro's nor mine was successful – he did fidget so, chain-smoking in embarrassment at being looked at for himself alone. If he talked, he could relax, which meant that the sittings usually went on through supper and all night, with many interesting discussions of a cosmological kind.

He was the second parish priest since we had come to live near the village. The first had been there for years, a large and extraordinarily short-sighted man with a soft voice, who would stare up from under at you through glasses like the bottoms of two bottles.

There is an annual ritual just before Easter, in which the parish priest goes round all the houses in the village to bless the walls and beasts therein. A good excuse to evict the spiders and mice accumulated over the winter, beat the carpets, scream at the children for the state of their toy cupboards, etc. When we arrived, strangers in every sense, this worthy gentleman appeared as usual, buoyed by an ample curiosity about our ways and with the perfect excuse to examine them at close quarters.

'My, what a lot of books,' he said, after he had admired our comatose angels in their tiny cots and absent-mindedly sprinkled each room with holy water. He took down a book at random. *The Erotic Drawings of Auguste Rodin.* 'Ah,' he said, 'what art!' He took down another. *Frescos from Pompei: The Secret Rooms of the Museo Nazionale in Naples.* Ahem!

'Wasn't it lucky these books weren't in Italian,' we said as he rode off – as if there was anything unintelligible about the illustrations.

The following year we had the house nicely scrubbed, walls painted to get rid of the autumnal smoke, and we had meanwhile learned that it was traditional to offer a glass of Vin Santo (from 'Zante', apparently – nothing to do with holy wine) and a few dry biscuits. We were all ready and peering out of the window to see his Vespa trundle through the vines. 'There he is!' The robed figure rode with difficulty, a small wind catching the lace of his clean Easter surplice. At the head of the drive he stopped, as if remembering something, and paused to look at us. We waved, but he couldn't see that far. Thoughtfully he turned his bike round and drove off again, leaving our walls unblessed.

He died the following year, in a tragic but spectacular accident. Turning a corner on his Vespa, he rode between two large oxen, not noticing they were carrying the plough slung upside down between them.

Osvaldo was characteristically reluctant to come to the house for a very different reason. I bless people, not walls, he said. What is the point of blessing walls? So he blessed us instead. But it is always awkward to sprinkle water over the doubtful.

When Saskia was in the midst of her Catholic phase, we took her along to Osvaldo to see if he could stretch a point and baptize her. He looked down at the smiling, temporarily toothless nymph in pantaloons and a veil, clutching a black dolly vaguely done up as a Virgin Mary.

'You see, Matteo,' he said tactfully, 'the thing is that I feel that if you had gone to live in Africa instead of Tuscany, you would have taken her to the witch-doctor with the same serenity with which you now bring her to me.'

And he was not far wrong. Elder daughter, now at university studying anthropology, is miffed that she can't participate in certain Yoruba rites, as she hasn't got a religion of her own. Apparently you have to check in one to get another, and if you haven't already got one, you can't start.

When I told Osvaldo all this in the village post office recently, he gave a quiet sigh and said, 'Well, I am so glad I get some things right.'

3 · SAN GIUSTO

Three years ago Don Osvaldo came round to the studio to see what I was up to. He seemed in a brisk and attentive mood, cheeks pink, hands plump, a man very much in control of himself.

I showed him my work. He had a way of keeping quite still whenever I had to explain something that was in itself flattering. I was engaged on some large carvings in bas–relief showing figures twisting about in tightly flattened dimensions. It seemed he liked them. He examined them carefully and seriously and stroked the wood lightly with the tips of his fingers. Then to my surprise he offered me a commission to make a crucifix for a local church I'd never heard of, called San Giusto in Salcio, off the back road from Lecchi to Radda.

We went off to see it immediately, a coldish October evening with lots of sun. As we drove, Osvaldo told me that San Giusto was an ancient foundation built on the ruins of an Etruscan temple at the junction of two important roads. This was just the right thing to get me interested. I enjoy thinking of my colleagues, the Etruscans.

The church was a beautiful building of the eleventh century. I felt ashamed to have lived near by for so many years and never entered it. A gentle nun lived in the substantial quarters beside it. She came from the north and spoke with an unfamiliar singsong accent. The atmosphere was one of total quiet.

I could hardly speak for excitement. I went outside and cut a tall stick from a clump of scrub oak at the edge of the fields. This I held high in the air inside the church, standing on the altar, as a gauge for the eventual sculpture, with Osvaldo and the nun down below, looking upwards in a deadpan way.

In this hieratic position I was suddenly overcome by a need to explain my own beliefs, and how they might affect the sculpture.

'Although I have a deep admiration for Christ as a man,' I said, 'I am filled with uncertainties concerning the side which has to do with God . . . '

Half a sentence into a long and difficult speech, and they were waving their hands up at me, shocked, shushing me. I lowered the stick. Short silence.

'Perhaps I could express something which stressed his humanity,' I said. I felt quite exhausted.

'The only thing I would like to say,' said the nun in a timid voice, as if to change the subject, 'is that I have to work here for three or four hours a day. [Meaning pray.] I hope very much you won't stress His suffering, as this can get to be a bit depressing.'

I went back to the village feeling undone by simplicity. But I took out a few books and thought of a way of making something appropriate, if it came off. In the late eleventh century there was a period of about fifty years when it was the fashion to depict Christ triumphant over death at the Crucifixion. It would suit the church, and also the needs of the nun.

I made a few drawings, bought wood and laid it out on the asphalt outside Libero's workshop, his plane being considered, by the universal consent of the village woodworkers, to be more 'intelligent' than that of Beppe for joining large planks. I cut a matrix or blank about seven foot high, the figure of Christ in semi-bas-relief. An odd idea, but in the half-dark of a church and with massive undercutting it would have the optical effect of a charcoal drawing.

I took everything home and worked on it for a fortnight before striking that quagmire of doubt that lurks at the heart of every creative adventure. Sometimes this can be worked through, sometimes you just have to lay off for a while. I let my Jesus be.

Then a terrible thing happened. While driving back from Lecchi one afternoon, Don Osvaldo suffered a cerebral haemorrhage which left him paralysed.

He was rushed to hospital, and the news that trickled back to the village seemed very bad. His friends and parishioners kept discreetly away; this was something for his immediate family. After a week, however, it seemed as if he might rally, so I went to visit him in hospital, past the Consorzio Agrario just over the railway track, up a brand new road which seems perfect for cars travelling at two hundred kilometres an hour, to the hospital tucked behind a convenient hill.

The room on the fifth floor was full of his parishioners. Osvaldo looked terrible. He had the quality the dead acquire, of looking quite unlike themselves. Hands were waved as I walked in, the villagers clad in dark colours warding me off, forearms stiff from the elbow up as if participating in some final act of misery, pointing their fingers towards heaven with their mouths open, drowning. Unable to speak I came and left without stopping, bending down to clasp his mother in the passage outside, a small lady mummified by grief.

I returned a couple of days later to find Osvaldo much more himself, and very impatient with his weeping parishioners. As soon as he saw me he tried to sit up, but it was clear he was immobile on one side. 'The cross,' he said, 'the cross.' A wave of contagious anxiety went through the crowd at his bedside. 'I am working hard at it,' I said – which was untrue. But having said this, I was forced to return to it.

Over the next weeks I grew used to the new hospital, with its vertical bias so unlike the old one up in town. A coffee bar would have been nice, and some trees, and something that might re-create the atmosphere of a piazza. People hung around the corridors with little ease, as if the new hospital were something between an airport and a city of the future, a transit lounge for the dispatch of souls. (The old hospital in Siena was one of the great public works of the late middle ages. Until recently you could be ill there in a ward eighty yards long frescoed with scenes of fourteenth-century pathology − a small group of doctors in long robes staring thoughtfully at a red peasant without a leg, in a bed with sheets. But the frescos were dusty, and the Belle Arti refused to have them touched, and the doctors would point up at them, these magnificent works, to say how unhygienic they were.)

The cross, and Don Osvaldo lying there in the new hospital, a freshly built ward halfway to the sky, dominated my days for the next two months. As he slowly improved I talked to him about his illness as best I could.

I said that the brain was like a large empty palace of many rooms, some of which were familiar and others not. In spite of the scientific progress of the last fifty years, we knew as little about the brain today as Europeans knew of America in 1520. The metaphor of the palace and the wilderness helped him to concentrate. There were other rooms which could be opened, I said, other paths through the unknown forests, other parts of the brain which might be woken to take over the parts you have lost. The habit of concentration through prayer would surely help. In such harsh circumstances all we have are words, and I would try never to leave Osvaldo until I had seen his expression change from emptiness to frowning obstinacy to courage, over the days and months.

As I carved in my studio, I inhabited a parallel world of

imagined landscape. I was possessed by the idea of a mountain valley with running water, and a particular tree cut down by a peasant or image-hewer of south Germany, and that was me. I conjured up the strained isolation of life at the edge of the village in this imagined past, the incomprehension of all but the local priest. The language they might have spoken, some old German dialect sounding like a mountainous pile of logs tipped from a stack and avalanching their way into a crevasse.

The end of this fantasy was that I would bring the finished cross into the church of San Giusto on Easter Sunday and Osvaldo in his wheelchair would take one look and rise, miraculously cured. I even told him this as he thrashed around, still often impatient, on the eve of being discharged from hospital. Being Tuscan, he was sceptical. Far from being miraculously cured, he said, 'in the state I'm in I would be far more likely to drop dead'.

I finished the piece just as Don Osvaldo was discharged from hospital. I was eager to bring it to San Giusto as soon as possible, but he seemed reluctant. Easter came and went, then *Mariassunta*, the Assumption of the Virgin, which is in the middle of August. There was a day in September called the Elevation of the Cross – but Osvaldo in his cautious way skipped that one too. He seldom moved from home and was totally engrossed in physiotherapy and the reconquest of his left side.

As he got better, it was my turn to become impatient. One fine day I loaded my Jesus into the van and took it down to the church, where I left it parked among dingy baroque chasubles in the sacristy.

The nun, whose hands seemed permanently folded in front of her in an expression of spiritual self-containment, looked at it with quiet attention.

'It is very beautiful,' she said at last. 'It is impossible that anyone could make such a thing without being inspired by God. But,' she added, 'you have forgotten the Wound.'

'The what? Oh yes – you are absolutely right.'

I went over and drew it on His side, remembering correctly which side it was. Silence, as of remote contemplation.

'That is not quite right,' she said softly. 'It must be like a smile, a smile in the side of Christ.'

I heard nothing more about my crucifix for a month. Then Osvaldo rang me up and said that an unfortunate thing had happened. The *vicario* of the Bishop of Fiesole, who specialized in approving the interiors of churches, had seen it and didn't find it suitable. I was surprised and upset. If Osvaldo had asked me to make a cross, what business was it of the Bishop of Fiesole? Osvaldo talked about the diocesan boundaries, river beds, the legacy of Countess Matilda in 1036, in the tone of one who would soothe an errant child. It would not be easy, he added, to get the bishop to change his mind, as this would put the *vicario* in a difficult position, but as the bishop himself was coming the following month, Osvaldo would try.

'On the other hand,' he added 'we could always try the Belle Arti first.'

A period of precarious intrigue followed, in which I took no part. I was in fact annoyed to discover that not one but two bodies had to give their permission for this Thing to take its place above the altar, and resented not having been informed before. Osvaldo would ring me from time to time, giving the state of play, saying the *vicario* might change his mind or the bishop wasn't coming or the Belle Arti might be favourable or whatever, but I decided that the whole thing had now become too much for me, for a work for which I wouldn't be paid anyway. And one fine day I drove to San Giusto, took my Jesus out of the musty old sacristy and propped it up in the church where all could admire it, on the left as you came in, standing on a piece of an old altar to give it a bit of height, and with a spotlight of anaemic wattage aimed at his chest.

On a nearby pew I left a fat exercise book with a sign above it in three languages, asking all visitors to write their opinion of the new cross, and whether it was worthy to take its place above the high altar.

This was another tactless move. Many friends stopped by to write what a genial piece they thought it was, but many strangers inscribed their horror that such a nice church could be desecrated by such a rotten work of art – modern as it was, with the wood new and the chisel contemporary. Reading these remarks in French and Italian and German, I could feel the breath of some collective spirit of Europe warming the back of my neck.

Christmas came and went, another occasion lost. Then Osvaldo rang me to say that there was now an anonymous letter in circulation protesting at the presence of my cross in San Giusto. What excitement! Had it always been like this in the good old days, I asked my art-historian friends hysterically? And the answer came back, Yes. Read Vasari. Read Condivi. Did you see what Michelangelo said about Raphael? When they tried to get some money back from him for not having finished the Julius tomb? No? Well look it up then!

> . . . All the differences between Pope Julius and myself grew from the jealousy of Bramante and Raffaello of Urbino, and this was the reason why I did not finish the tomb in [Julius's] lifetime. They wanted to ruin me. Raffaello did this on purpose, as whatever he had of art he got from me.[1]

'The Julius tomb took thirty years or so of wrangles and intrigues – count yourself lucky, my boy,' said the wise historian at the end of the telephone. 'And Michelangelo claimed at the end of his life that it cost him personally more money than he ever made from it.'

On a wet February morning the following year I crept down and removed my cross, wrapped it in plastic and drove to Siena to ask the Belle Arti permission to send it off to London.

To my utter amazement they looked at it on the polished floor of the palace frescoed with fish-tailed nymphs and said, 'Why did you take it down? The image of *Christus Triumphans* as opposed to *Christus Dolens* is exactly right for a church of that period. Mind you, strictly speaking, it would look better in polychrome.'

I could not speak, I was so surprised. 'I – you – nobody let me know that you liked it.' They smiled, that an innocent foreigner could take such a direct view. 'Of course we like it. Unfortunately we can't say so in public. We have to wait until somebody else does first. And besides, that anonymous letter was really very annoying.'

So my Jesus went to London to take part in an exhibition called 'Modern Artists Respond to the Challenge of Religious Art'. I was lucky: not many modern artists have a seven-foot Christ in limewood handy. On the other hand the market for a seven-foot Christ in limewood was, I discovered, remarkably small.

When it came back, I once again decided on the direct approach. One day I went down with Stefano di Tosa, the young mason named after the house he lives in, like a twelfth-century nobleman, and, with Don Osvaldo and the nun again watching me from below, we hung my Christ eight foot above the altar, on double chains. I had been terrified by a dream that my piece had fallen on Don Osvaldo's head one Sunday morning, so we used a chain that could have supported a Centurion tank filled with troops and ammunition.

High in the half-dark of the stone church, some distance from the congregation, the deep shadows gave the wooden folds in the robes their necessary softness. Those connoisseurs whose nasty remarks had filled my exercise book asked if it was a different sculpture. Some rare acquaintances gave me an unexpected smile. The anonymous letter-writer, who by that time had been identified, was distracted by a vile court case which he had brought against an extremely nice girl in the village. Sister Isabella complained that it was too high. Perhaps one day I'll risk the life of Stefano and lower it. She says it gives her a crick in her neck, unless she concentrates on his feet.

Against this background of quiet approval, Don Osvaldo and I drove to Florence one damp spring morning to obtain the signature of the Bishop of Fiesole, authorizing a certain English sculptor to suspend his crucifixion above the high altar of San Giusto in Salcio, until such time as either he (the sculptor) or they (the Church) wanted it removed.

Don Osvaldo came out of his uncle's house wearing a hat called a '*kolbacco*', an object supposed to be Russian but in fact resembling an unsuccessful thirteenth-century pudding. He moved with difficulty, but without help, and he had a bright blue car with automatic gears, so that he was once again able to visit the parish.

It was a beautiful drive. Fresh grass in the vineyards, about to be ploughed under, lent colour to the stripes of the hillsides, and the black woods were just beginning to be dusted with green.

We took his car, as Osvaldo said his disabled sticker would give access to that forbidden *piazzetta* in the centre of Florence where the bishop was to be found. He gossiped, I vaguely listened. We talked about the court case of this local girl, which centred on some missing receipts. A foolish, even nasty business which suggested that our anonymous denouncer might be not quite right in the head. Either that, or just not Tuscan.

After a while it began to rain.

Towards the outskirts of Florence Osvaldo became more nervous − irritated, he said, by the squeaking of the windscreen wipers. He was anxious about the traffic. Like an obsequious acolyte I suggested a left or a right whenever he hesitated.

Once in Florence we took the panoramic road past San Miniato and eventually crossed the river. Outside the Biblioteca Nazionale we consulted a wet and irate traffic warden. Flustered, Osvaldo rummaged for his red card with a black wheelchair printed on it. We ended up tucked away in a courtyard not far from the Duomo, grey portico and gravelled ground, between two grand cars with ecclesiastical stickers in the front window.

For a moment nothing was visible except the blank cream walls of the coldly restored Renaissance building, something between a school and a hospital. Then some clerics began to walk through, each greeting Osvaldo with affection and familiarity as he stumbled over the gravel and under the arch.

He managed the dark interior staircase with difficulty, his left shoe worn on top where steps had rubbed it many times before.

The upper floor had a clean and airy feel. One room led to another; a sequence of small rooms became a large corridor. People in grey came and went, holding documents, unhurried but busy. They made way for Osvaldo.

A small group was waiting to see the bishop, from which emerged a vivacious woman accompanying a clean girl, an archetypical niece. For five minutes she buttonholed Osvaldo, talking to my surprise of local village gossip. Then we were summoned by the bishop's secretary, who took us to an office of ordered papers, a photocopying machine and a large safe with gilded angels on it.

The secretary had two expressions, one open and friendly in greeting, one shut and absorbed as he read my document. Two years previously, before it emerged that my crucifix might be rejected, I had taken the trouble to draw up something severely legal. After a minute's study the secretary asked, 'Can San Giusto afford the insurance?' I quickly said that I would be willing to waive the clause, at which he smiled and said, 'That is hardly in your interest.' Puzzled, I kept quiet.

At this point Osvaldo took out a bundle of other documents to be signed and photocopied, after which the secretary took us to see the bishop.

The lady-with-niece was already in congress, and we were left to listen to her chatter through a shadowy pebble-glass door. The ante-room was almost empty, with stiff chairs around the wall and a single print in a mahogany frame high up, with a wisp of olive branch stuck in the top. There was also a Gothic young man with a neat waxed moustache, who went into the corridor to smoke. Osvaldo kept up a running commentary about the lady-with-niece, and said he too would like a cigarette, but he didn't smoke any more, except at home.

The bishop came out in a slight hurry, a tall man eroded by trivial details recently received, very pale, with glasses and fresh brown hair.

We entered his small dark study. I was surprised at his comparative youth. He shared with his secretary the quality of absenting himself totally to read, re-emerging from time to time to ask all the latest news from Don Osvaldo. He wanted to know where I came from, where I fitted in. It emerged that the diocesan boundary lay some few hundred yards from our house, so that I effectively belonged to Arezzo, not Fiesole, a fact which he found amusing.

I was glad that my document was serious and full of heretofores and whithertos. He eventually rang through to the secretary, asked if he could sign, received a formal assent from the keeper of documents, and called for his seal. He then excused himself and rang an abbot, sitting up straighter to accommodate the weightier language that implied the mutual respect of equals. The seal came. I was disappointed to see a rubber stamp, and said so to Osvaldo. The bishop brightened and said he never brought the Renaissance seal of gilded bronze down from Fiesole, although it was much nicer, as it was so heavy. 'Please forgive me, Abbot,' he said into the phone, 'I was not referring to you.'

Afterwards Osvaldo and I went shopping, in some cubbyholes hidden around the courtyard. He needed Hosts, and as the lady wrapped them, struggled to take out his purse from his paralysed side. I stopped him and paid for them, thinking this might be a useful gesture if there actually is a Hereafter.

Round the corner for a cup of coffee and a cigarette, in a bar where American tourists studied the glass case of sandwiches with the attention due to ancient jewels. Osvaldo sat down, ignoring a pair of female legs in leopard tights all of sixty centimetres from his head. He ate a pizza. We drank some coffee.

Osvaldo was ready for home, but I insisted we walk up the road to see the Museo dell'Opera del Duomo. He asked me cautious, almost peasanty questions. Was it far? Were there stairs? What was there to see? Michelangelo, I said, and Luca Della Robbia and Donatello. I was shocked to find he knew nothing of Florence, had never even been to the Uffizi.

Thin crowds hindered our passage in the street, under low cloud strung between the rooftops.

A silence of total awe overcame him in the lower room of

the museum, where the Donatello *Moses* so nearly approaches bas-relief, except for the jittery softness of those intellectual hands and the deep undercutting of the folded cloth.

I started to explain about form and light, the hardness of stone, the softness of shadow.

In a low voice Osvaldo asked who the statue was. Moses, I said.

'Ah,' he murmured. 'Moses.' And he stood for a moment looking at the carved stone; then moved gently on to the Donatello *Magdalene*. He began to talk about her, very quietly, almost to himself: what she had been like as a person, how her life had become posthumously entwined with various legends. How Donatello in a word had been unfair to her.

In the upper room, Osvaldo moved stiffly, whether because his body ached or because he was giving these works his deepest attention, I could not tell. All around him, however, the statues seemed animated, moving, breathing, laughing. The marble frieze of the Della Robbia *Cantoria*, at the level of the floor, had all the frivolity of a school outing, filled with those busy little intrigues that totally exclude the teachers, the shepherds, us.

I padded behind Osvaldo as he followed the works, into the room where the panels from Giotto's tower describe the various works and days of the early fifteenth century, telling us that their epoch, the epoch of Moses, and our own, are as one. Osvaldo named each figure, and told me where they all belonged, in the real narrative of this world. He described what he saw as if it were a fragment of a life, turned to stone.

Eventually we turned left, moving slowly, as the other visitors moved slowly, like fish.

The Michelangelo *Deposition* is placed halfway down a dark flight of stairs. When we were in front of it, I told Osvaldo how the Master had lost his temper with the stone, hit the elbow, thrown away the left leg; how the angel on the left was finished by a pupil. How Michelangelo has this quality of violent impatience, combined with a feeling for softness, the softness of skin.

'Who is the man above?' asked Osvaldo.

'Joseph of Arimathea,' I said, 'although it is also said to be a self-portrait.'

I insisted that we walk round the carving, with Osvaldo clutching the rail, to see its extraordinary back – that unfinished fragment of a mountain where all sense of scale and age is destroyed. It has form, but it is the form that lies innate in the great blocks of marble that still lie in the quarry. Only the hand of the angel among folds impatiently sketched by a chisel, with marks so similar to the charcoal shading of his drawings, brings a human scale almost to the surface – almost but not quite, as if what you see is taking place under the surface of disturbed water.

But Don Osvaldo was not interested in the imagined mountainside. To see this Michelangelo so close dehumanized it, returned it to the natural rock from whence it came. For Osvaldo the human core was its most interesting element. He shuffled round to the front, to look at the Michelangelo face to face, while I muttered and brooded in the dark side of the mountain.

It rained off and on as we drove home. I dozed in a heap, held in place by my seat-belt.

Osvaldo drove well and seemed pleased with the achievement of the morning's signatures, photocopies, receipts. He told me how the garrulous lady-with-niece fitted in to the local landscape, and described his life in the seminary years ago, where he had seen the future bishop officiate at his first Mass. He made no references to sculpture.

The warm ground steamed slightly in the Val di Pesa, where

the factories making tiles and hollow bricks threaten to join one to another, end to end. Then we climbed toward Panzano and the rain came down again, just enough to make the asphalt shine. Going back, the windscreen wipers made less noise.

4 · CRAFTSMEN

Massimo, down at the sawmill by the River Arbia, free on Saturdays to work for perverse foreigners such as myself, helped me with the bodies from the back of the car, set them on the toothed trolley, and phlegmatically cut them all in half, lengthwise. Toes first, then knees, crotch, breasts one each side of the screaming blade, and out through the tangled mass of hair.

I have a thing about hair. The more the better, even in wood.

'What are you going to do with all these women?'

'Oh, they keep me company,' I said.

Then I asked him how much. He smiled through unshaved black stubble and said he liked sawing ladies in half, so it was up to me. He bowed with slight irony when I slipped him a couple of notes, so that I was unsure if I'd given him too much or too little.

The technique is simple. First find a poplar in the forest, the taller the better. Cut down, and reduce to segments two metres tall. In summer the dying tree hisses like a kettle, a strange and disturbing sound. Take the trunks to a flat place and set upright. Remove bark. Look, think, cut.

You will have perhaps a month or two before the saturated trunk begins to dry out. The active outer wood, lighter in colour and quicker to dry, presses against the solid heartwood in the centre, causing cracks to appear. Before this happens, slice the lovely lady lengthwise, hollow her out into two bizarre canoes, and wait for her to dry. Glue back together in six months and start working again, the mood changed, the wood hard, and the statue clapping like a wooden bell as you work.

The moment when the statues are stuck back together again takes place up in the village, at Libero's. I admire Libero. Of all the lads in the local village whom I have seen grow up over the years, his life has been the most coherent and dedicated. He has two lively children and a wife who works in the local health clinic, and an uncomfortable workshop crammed with loved machines.

I like craftsmen. Much of my life is spent with them, some great masters, some just enthusiastic. The ideal, for me, is a quiet man of ritualistic habits who produces what he needs to live, and then potters about the studio thinking of new forms. Sometimes he makes them, and sometimes he tells you about them in a far-off, intimate manner, as something he might get around to, some day.

Workshops, this male environment, have a peculiar cosiness which sometimes can be lacking in the scrubbed and scoured household in the background. Girlie calendars dominate the interiors of the tool-cupboards or odd corners where only the workmen are likely to look. Odd muses of light-industrial machines. She who attempts to garotte a fire-extinguisher with the muscles of her thighs, and she who straddles a many-nozzled fruit-spray, and she who emerges through a rubber tyre triumphantly holding a spanner. What contorted stories must lie behind these odd predicaments! But the effect is strangely relaxing, making one feel a bit more warmly about hub-caps as such. The Japanese girl with the buzz-saw at Mauro the blacksmith's has surgically rounded eyes and a small appendix scar, indicating the cultural influence of the West.

Craftsmen

After the olives are in and the sky flecks over with low cloud like corduroy, in winter, before Christmas, and the air is occasionally filled with dusty flakes of snow that settle on the backs of cats all plumped out for the winter, then I grab my coat and flee the house with the excuse of making some essential piece of furniture that cannot be delayed a moment longer. At home, the hoops that support mosquito-nets in summer are removed and bound with branches from the ornate bay tree in the back garden, and the chimney-piece is laden with branches cut from the young pines. A good moment to abandon the chaos of family life, all ribbon and fairy lights made up of tiny, irreplaceable bulbs.

Libero possesses that cardinal virtue of craftsmen: obstinacy. When last there, I found a new stencil high on the dusty wall, which he had taken himself from a table leg in the Bargello museum, stooping to the floor with cardboard and stubby pencil when the guard's back was turned. I was touched by this appetite to learn. A first-rate Florentine restorer would never use a stencil. A look, a sideways glance, would suffice.

Many years ago I was walking across the Ponte Santa Trinità in Florence with a young artisan, who asked me if I knew who had designed the *palazzo* we were approaching. I guessed a name. Yes, he said. But he died halfway through. Who continued? I did not know. And who designed the windows? And where does that particular bevel come from? And what is the name of the tool with which it is made? I could not answer.

'Ah,' he said with a histrionic sigh, 'you could never imagine the weight of all the geniuses who have worked in this city.'

I was reminded of the nightmare which persecuted De Chirico when he lived in Florence, in which he felt himself gradually suffocated by the descending weight of a huge classical head. But it was unusual to find a craftsman so articulate, and indeed, soon afterwards, I heard that he had left furniture restoration to start a far more lucrative business making picture frames.

The usual Tuscan craftsman is immune to introspection and ambition. His knowledge is absolute, and at the same time remote. In a certain sense it might as well not be there. If for instance an eminent professor writes that Michelangelo used a certain tool to make a certain sculpture, in order to tackle certain difficulties, the argument fits into a total view of Michelangelo as a sculptor. A mason of Carrara, whose knowledge of carving would be infinitely greater, would never even think about Michelangelo's technique – indeed would never discuss him at all, except to say that such and such a piece is beautiful.

No, even that is wrong. He would agree politely with you, if you suggested that this piece or that was beautiful, but he would say '*È!*' in his agreement (a high vowel, pitched on the upbeat), as much as to say that, really, we do not have to go into the question as to whether Michelangelo was or was not a good sculptor.

Last year Libero and I made an ornate neo-baroque cupboard, using planks of cypress that were too full of knots for sculpture. (Indeed, the finished cupboard today has a definite case of the pox, if ever furniture could.)

In the centre of the second plank as we split it, the saw made a thin high shriek, something like the cry of a bird. The Phoenix of cast iron calling to its mate. At this, Libero clapped his hands together sharply once and shouted at the ceiling, '*Budella di Pio Nonaccio*', which being interpreted means, 'By the guts of horrible old Pius the Ninth'. (A datable expletive – Pius the Ninth was the pope who did his absolute best to prevent the unification of Italy.) When the two halves of the plank fell apart, there in the centre lay a jagged shard of shrapnel, souvenir of those weeks when the Allied Front passed through, shelling from hilltop to hilltop, in the summer of 1944.

Craftsmen

Libero knows his instruments by heart, even down to the different blades of the ancient band-saw. These have to be sharp, of course, but they must also make their own way, have the quality of *strada* ('road'), as they cut through the clinging wood. The damage caused by the piece of shrapnel produced from him a fascinating discourse on a new sharpening expert he had found in Siena, whose balance of *strada* with edge was particularly bright. The personal qualities of machines are discussed in the village today, as a century ago we might have discussed oxen.

To see the hand tools of a former period polished and hung on a wall is a terrible thing, like seeing wild animals stuffed and glass-eyed in a museum.

Our partnership consists of me designing and instructing, Libero cutting and executing, with a definite moment when my artistic improvisation encounters a problem that has to be solved – hey presto! – by his remarkable expertise. Until then, he dozes. In the case of this cupboard, I made a crucial mistake in cutting the ornamentation before working out a way for the sides to be fitted together. Suddenly he blinked and woke up. Seen from the end, in profile, the side now resembled a staircase from which one or two steps had been wantonly chewed. Libero's eyes closed, his moustache drooped.

He looked remote, like a Hun regretting some detail of last year's season of pillage. Long silence while I looked about the little shop, my turn to be bored. Dusty fly-blown stencils hung high near dusty fly-blown tits. Finally he took a whirling bevel which had to be mounted on a machine with elbows, and wheels to guide the wood to the sharp teeth of a circular gouge. Maximum drama in getting the thing to work. There emerged a brilliant piece of cutting, the two sides fitted perfectly without my ornaments being affected. I kept a discarded piece for a couple of months as an example of three-dimensional imagination, unlikely to be appreciated by anyone but me, who witnessed it.

Every time I go there, I urge Libero to spend some money on a few safety devices, such as vacuum equipment to clear the dust-ridden air. He cheerfully changes the subject, moustache on the alert, eyes squinting and bright, enjoying my wild sense of humour. The example of Aldo in the next village seems to count for nothing. Aldo, after many years of working in a cubby-hole like Libero's, has contracted cancer of the nose, a horrible thing. Libero shrugs. But then, even Aldo seems to take six months living in the very armpit of death simply as part of the profession. When I saw him last, he was still smoking cigarettes – 'as a challenge to myself,' he said. I didn't understand. 'Oh well, think about it very hard, because I don't really understand it myself. And when you have finished thinking,' he said laughing, 'tell me your conclusions.'

Each machine lives in a halo of latent malevolence. Libero has a mechanical plane consisting of a cylinder with blades which whirl round at high speed. When working, it screams, but when turned off, it goes silent, even though for two minutes it continues moving. I fear that one day I might sit on this monster, after it has been switched off but is still moving, to turn my buttocks into instant *prosciutto crudo*. And the whirling dervish that cut the joins of my cupboard frequently refuses to do what he is told. When that happens, you take your hat and go off to the bar for a quick one. It is dangerous to take risks with a cutting machine.

Giovanni in the village used to work a machine which stamped out metal parts used in the guts of washing-machines. The essential toggle screw which adjusted this thing lay behind a slow-moving, very large, very sharp, flywheel. Of course you were supposed to turn the machine off when fiddling with the screw, but Giovanni used to flick his hand in and out of the spokes of the wheel, until one day it caught and crushed a finger. He refused the firm's offer of compensation. He would hold his finger in the air and look at it, shaking his head, as if he had been deservedly punished. The event and the damage had to be relived until it was absorbed into his idea of himself. To accept personal responsibility for what had happened was essential if he was to retain his pride in being a master craftsman.

All craftsmen are competing with machines, even as they use them. If their prices are too high, the client will prefer the less beautiful machine-made object. In Italy the gap between these two prices appears to be small. A ceramicist in Italy can ask perhaps a third as much again for a hand-made vase as for its machine-made counterpart. In Germany the factor would be double, perhaps triple. In Japan, ten times.

And while the humbler artisans are restrained from overpricing themselves by the competition of machines, the master craftsmen are restrained by the example of their more modest colleagues. Maybe there is no strict line between them. All of which gives Italian craftsmen a cautious modesty which in its way is an attractive and even admirable quality. You talk of skill, they talk of wood. You talk of art, they talk of clay.

Three years ago a Florentine art dealer told me that some time in the early eighties the directors of some leading antique dealers, Wartski, Grauss Antiques, S. J. Phillips of Bond Street among them, met to discuss the sudden flood of fake Italian cameos on the London market. I imagined the scene: green baize table, the manicured hand that reached for the cut-glass decanter. The murmur of preoccupied upper-class voices, the technical backchat with arcane specialized terms, perhaps a map of Europe with lines drawn over it in red. What emerged was that somewhere in Florence was an artisan whose cameos, when mounted upon worn Victorian snuffboxes, would age them by two centuries, quintupling their value.

By chance one wet afternoon Maro and I came across this genius in a small shop not far from the Masaccios. A classic Florentine workshop, with dusty wares in the dull front window of a deep but narrow segment of a building, and a door that rebuffed our attempt to penetrate beyond it. Eventually he came to open up for us, the unacknowledged master, grumbling at being disturbed, eager to dissuade us from looking over his wares.

From behind an old bicycle the eyes of Michelangelo's *David* looked hawk-like into mine, in a plaster cast taken as it were from the life – the indentation of the eyes so deeply and passionately cut, so precise. Shelves of moulds for the reducing machine stood just behind, models that were obviously Victorian, but the reduced lapis lazuli versions looked older. The floor of marble chip tiles was patinated with filth to the texture of bronze. On the walls were rusting metal stencils for mirrors, covered with so much dust that it had accumulated upwards, like iron filings round a magnet. There were workbenches end to end among the machines, and heaps of discarded fragments of mother-of-pearl and lapis lazuli, and black Belgian marble, whose dust is erroneously believed to be poisonous.

He assumed the classic pose of a Florentine artisan, of initial rejection. How his work was unappreciated by the ignorant, neglected by the government and social services. The ritual moan of the neglected craftsman, from which he descended to the specific pleasure of telling us that he was the last of his kind. That his daughter had a nice small shop with two photocopiers and a fax machine and didn't want to know anything about cameos. Still, he said with a grim glee, she had a lovely honeymoon in Texas last month, and it was the cameos that paid for it.

As for him, what could he do but keep going, even though he was so old? Of course, the Germans were in the competition now, but they could only do the poured stone. Cheap stuff, but some of it lovely. Not to be underestimated. Their poured coral, for instance, was quite beautiful. Still, not the real thing. Luckily he had found a young man who was a good finisher. Very talented. Spends a lot of time on it, but the results are remarkable. A real artist.

So saying he tipped out in front of us two plastic bags entirely filled with fresh sixteenth-century cameos.

'But it is you, you who are the real artist,' we told him.

His eyes were bad. He could hardly walk any more. The taxes were terrible – too much paper, not enough hard work, these days.

We told him about the high prices they were getting on the London market, and he was amused. Neither jealous nor resentful, he was firm in his own scales of values and the independence which selling them as reproductions gave him. He would cheat nobody. But after half an hour, sniggering inwardly as if coughing, he pulled out a book of smudgy photographs of things the firm had once made. Photographs that were indistinct, because taken furtively through museum glass.

His machine was beautiful, made in Bremen in 1888. He took me by the arm and dragged me round the corner, to a back room inserted in someone else's building and reached through a lean-to of plastic which had evidently been there for ever. More rotten planks, bags of sawdust, and an abandoned workbench with tools half engaging a piece of rock, like cutlery on a dirty plate. Here there was yet another antique reducing machine, making a happy hum as if engaged in private conversation, busy duplicating in lapis lazuli two nymphs preening a baby with wings.

He raised his palms in worship of this machine. With a tight smile, as if he was nibbling his own upper lip, he described to me its little personal habits as if it had an emotional identity like ours.

'And this,' he said. 'Can you guess what this is?'

He took from a shelf a small length of turned metal with a butterfly-nut at either end. As I examined it, he told me it came from a German land-mine. He had sat on it during the war, he said, when he had worked with the *genio militare* clearing minefields. And the reason why he wasn't dead was that the percussion cap was in upside down. What luck! '*Che culo!*', which means both 'What luck', and, 'What a bottom'. And his friend who works in Scandicci, who was with him in the army, when he sees him in the street, yells at him even today, '*Che culo!*', and he turns, and it is him.

He took from the wall a dim photo of himself and his unit in the war, as healthy and upstanding and outward-looking a young man as he was now bent and sardonically turned inward.

The end of the story is an anticlimax. We ran into some London dealers visiting Florence and sent them to see the old artisan. It was a disaster. They recognized the machines immediately. 'How interesting! Look, John, isn't that the reverse camber they introduced after the Great Exhibition of 1851, the one with gears for the sinister image along with the dexter?' The master tried to sell them the entire shop for a huge sum, and they said they could do better in Manchester. Apparently there was some corner of restructured England that was forever filled with wonderful machines, obtainable for the price of any old iron.

To make a figure in terracotta is technically easy. You start at the big toe and work upwards, leaving the inside hollow as you go up. There, that's the trade secret as Urbano told it to me. Now all you need is to go ahead and do it; but slowly, or it will all fall down.

I came across Urbano about eight years ago and have worked

with him happily ever since. The hillside where he has his workshop was once sheer and grassy; it now has various factories clinging to it as Castellina's Industrial Zone takes off. We share a collective envy of the maker of swimming-pools just opposite. We look at him, busy even in the rain, as we have lunch.

Urbano makes garden pots of terracotta, as his father did before him. The little family originally used a kiln up on the road to Pieve Asciata, not far from our house. The way they lost these premises is extraordinary. One day Urbano's father met the *fattore*, or bailiff, of the big landowner whose kiln it was, riding to market in Siena in his little pony-cart. The two men agreed to race each other, and Urbano's father won. The *fattore* made an offer for his horse, and was turned down.

'That horse is too good for a working man,' said the *fattore*, and the following week Urbano's father was evicted from both house and kiln.

'Horses were very important in those days, you understand,' Urbano said in explanation, as if defending the odious *fattore*. 'It was a way of showing who was the more important figure. Like cars today, only worse.'

The little family moved to Castellina, where they took over a notorious kiln which had never worked efficiently. At this point Urbano would be sidetracked into a discussion of 'Kilns I Have Known', full of interesting details about aperture, vents, height of chimney, etc., etc., and concluding with the story of the wonderful pot which his grandfather once made inside the kiln itself, so big that they had to take out a bit of wall to remove it. This piece won a gold medal in the Artisans' Fair in Impruneta in 1901, and is now buried up to its neck in the back garden of the Carabinieri in Panzano. Moral: if you want to make a tall pot, don't hurry.

Close parentheses. Urbano's father rebuilt the chimney of the dud kiln in Castellina, making the aperture of the exit vent remarkably small, and the chimney tall. Then he packed it with raw tiles in a special way so as to make the heat travel as he wanted, in and out of the pots which were being fired. All the workers in clay for miles around argued passionately about whether all this would work; the hillside was covered with grinning colleagues the first day he used it. It was successful, and the family has been there ever since.

The kiln was inherited by Urbano and his brother, with whom he eventually fell out. In the eight years I've worked with Urbano I have never even seen this brother, who makes almost identical wares on the top floor while we work together down below. From time to time we can hear him moving about upstairs, coughing, dropping an implement, scolding or being scolded by his wife.

In the early days of his marriage, Urbano made a contract to supply a certain amount of wares each month to a man who eventually turned out to be a crook. I don't know quite what went wrong, but in order to get out of this arrangement, Urbano paid off this man, going into debt to do so.

There followed five years of extraordinary heroism. He and his wife contracted to supply a nearby kiln with a certain quantity of clay each week. Which meant digging it out of the hillside by hand, drying it in the sun, breaking up the lumps, running it through the milling machine, and reloading it on to a truck. I forget what huge amount they had to supply each day, but it meant getting up at three in the morning, digging out the hillside by eleven, then recuperation and a big meal, before inverting the morning's labour by shovelling the dried lumps of clay scattered all over the courtyard up and over and into the mountainous, gibbering, clanking, dust-spewing milling machine and into the truck, before collapsing into bed at dusk.

I kept thinking, during this strange story, that he would have done far better to take a loan from the bank and pay off the debt by selling his own wares. Selling clay can't have brought in a wage remotely equivalent to the effort involved, even though after a while they were able to buy a small bulldozer to do the actual digging. But Urbano, like Vittorio, like many craftsmen or small farmers who work entirely within the dimensions of their own family, loathed the idea of debt.

What seems to me typical about Urbano's personal history is the element of passivity, of chance. Life itself seems to have the initiative. If it had not been for the horse-race in 1926, they might still be in the kiln at the top of the short cut to the old Roman road. If life shoves some grotesque obstacle in their way, they simply confront it, almost without blinking. Once through, their initiatives are cautious and low key.

Is the same true of Michelangelo? I suspect it is. He spent much more of his life with workmen and stonecutters than he ever did with pretentious bluestockings like Vittoria Colonna. But in the published papers of Michelangelo, the contracts and letters to chisellers of one kind and another are kept separate from his poems and letters to popes, so you can think of him as an intellectual and not a craftsman, if you like.

When I propose to Urbano Fontana some phantasmagorical plan – supplying a Munich store with crockery, for instance – he replies, 'Yes, I understand, but . . . ' and then there follows some minute but immovable detail, about glazes and body temperatures, the price of *gasolio* for transport or the intricacies of VAT. I protest, say I have a German friend who can give him a *raccomandazione*, and another who can smuggle the pots up there. He smiles, argues gently but persistently for hours.

He seems almost pleased when he has talked me out of it. He turns to walk off among the drying pots with a swagger, whistles, tosses a ball of clay in the air before going back to work. And he greets me with special friendliness at the end of the day, full of compassion in victory for having talked me out of it. Good try, he implies. After all, I have done my best.

5 · SERAVEZZA[2]

As potters are often secretly obsessed not by ceramics but by fire, so sculptors are sometimes obsessed not by carvings but by stone. And the craftsmen who work in quarries do not think about stone, they think of the mountain. In all three cases it is a question of sublimating a mean passion for a grand one. Man makes his little artefacts, but it is the live material as nature brought it forth that remains the challenge.

To love marble you have to imagine how it is made.

The beginning lies in the sea and, in it, thousands of minute organisms living out short lives of frantic animation triggered by nothing more than the quality of sunlight filtering down from above. They swim with fins of waving jelly, with flickering feelers, with emphatic puffs of jet propulsion. They have every conceivable method of protection: by shell, by carapace, by cornucopia, smooth as paper or covered with delicate lances. Their guts are twisted below the shell, or trail above their backs like kites. They hang there in the water in clouds of dazed confetti, above their brothers of the reef who have chosen the sedentary strategy, feet firmly planted in the mountain made from billions of their own dead antecedents.

Countless numbers die over the years and leave microscopic fragments of themselves sparkling downwards to the sea floor. Large bodies of water move over the same area in the same way for millennia and the sea acts as a sieve, precipitating the material into coherent strata. The silt, the mush of bones, the limestone paste, sink to the bottom to form a thick layer of aspiring rock.

Nothing seems more uniform than these millions of square miles of seabed covered with the same promising stuff, below countless tons of water whose weight will eventually create stone. Yet chance punctuates it constantly. Plumes of undersea mineral-bearing spouts shoot up from deep volcanic fissures. Shelves of crust hitch and grind against each other, sift and split. The continental plates never stay still. Mountains are created from folds of stone, generating immense extremes of heat and pressure. *'Il peso non dorme'*, they say in the quarries: 'Weight never sleeps.' Constant ageing affects the skin of the old elephant upon which, transient parasites, we live.

In 1806 Sir James Hall packed a gun barrel with chalk, plugged it securely and heated it to a high temperature. Carbonic acid was produced, creating great pressure within the barrel. When it had cooled the gun was opened and found to contain granular crystals of marble. This demonstrated for the first time that chalk and marble, like other limestones, have the same origin in the sediment of carbonates formed from old bones and shells, and that marble has been made crystalline by the heat and pressure that are generated in the making of the mountains.

I read somewhere that Michelangelo talked of carving a whole mountain into a sculpture, up behind Carrara. It's one of those stories I think about from time to time, as if I were mentally touching a horseshoe for luck.

'It should still be possible to see where he worked, I think,' Vittoria told me years ago, outside the Biblioteca Nazionale in Florence. 'Michelangelo opened one of the mines up behind Pietrasanta; it is in Vasari. I do not know which quarry, and perhaps it is only a legend. But it would be nice to find out, no?'

47

She was combing her hair as she spoke, and her feet were pointed in opposite directions like a dancer at the barre. The day was warm, and I liked these preparations, tidying up her hair for the benefit of ancient manuscripts. I still retain a clear image of the occasion. She was fresh to research, pleased with herself for having come this far already.

'It would be easy to recognize, because he carved his initial – the letter M, no? – high up on the wall. It must be a famous, a well-known thing in Pietrasanta, don't you think?'

I thought about this for a moment. Sometimes Vittoria's sense of irony was too subliminal for me.

'Do you really see Michelangelo carving his initials on a wall?'

'But of course!' she said, hitching up her bag to march off. 'At Sounion Lord Byron carved his name on a column when he visited it. So Michelangelo would have done the same. Surely?'

She left before I could think of an answer. I could see from the way she walked up the steps, zebraed by sunlight, that she was very pleased with herself, for having had the last word.

Pietrasanta is a small town underneath the mountains of marble above Pisa and Lucca. A paradise for sculptors, with a greater concentration of those who carve and those who cast bronze than anywhere else in the world. These days this local population of master craftsmen is heavily salted with young foreigners there to learn the trade, or old masters having their polystyrene mock-ups turned into stone. All meet convivially in the local bar to catch up on recent gossip, and pass the word for new jobs or places to stay.

I had been there a number of times without ever having followed up the question of the quarry of Michelangelo. From time to time, generally late at night, we would talk about the hole in the side of the mountain, and the young apprentices would passionately repeat the rumour that an unfinished statue by Michelangelo was still up there. The locals when pressed were sceptical. No quarry, no square inch of any quarry, could remain unexplored after all these years. There are no secrets, they said.

Then one evening in the piazza with an American sculptor called Caio, I found myself talking about the abandoned mine in the hills. He thought the whole thing absurd, but ran his fingers through his extraordinary black hair and looked behind him into the bar to see if any of the old stonecutters might be there.

He took me by the shoulder and pushed me in. There at the back, among the card-players and under the flickering TV set, a hard old man stood at the bar among his mates, shouting about this and that. Caio with difficulty extracted him, introduced us, and talked about this trace memory of Vittoria's, the letter M, high on the wall of marble in a disused quarry.

Romano nodded, unsurprised. If it existed, he said cautiously, it would be on Monte Altissimo behind Seravezza, the next town along as you skirt the Apuan Alps. He had worked in all the quarries in Seravezza since the age of twelve, he said. I was thrilled to meet him, amazed at his good health, full of admiration for his extraordinary experience. Behind him on the TV among the bottles young girls dressed as butterflies began to disrobe. He accepted a glass of something, put his elbows on the bar and waited for more questions.

Once he spoke, his reply was thorough and precise. 'Michelangelo was working in Carrara, but he did not get on well with the Carraresi. Then the pope ordered him to go to the new mines at Seravezza, because they had found a vein of very fine marble at a place called La Tacca Bianca.'

'What does that mean?' I asked, groping for a pencil.

'*Una tacca* is where you hit it with a chisel. *Tac!*' He mimed a blow. 'They called it this because the very first time a workman hit the rock to test it, a piece of pure white stone came out. Anyway, although it was remote and difficult, Michelangelo worked the mine and took from it the marble he used for the big *Pietà* in Rome. The one attacked by a mad German with a hammer ten years ago. Also the big *Moses*. And the columns for San Lorenzo which he never built, the stone of which was stolen in Rome.'

Caio asked about a road. Wasn't there some road which Michelangelo . . . ? 'Oh yes,' I said excitedly, 'the road was in Vasari too, come to think of it.'

'The road he made to get the stone down from the mountain ran from Riomagno to Malbacco behind Seravezza, near the school, and is called today the Via Michelangelo Buonarotti,' said Romano solemnly. 'Above the bridge it becomes Via Monte Altissimo, and I do not think that Michelangelo built it. He brought down the stones to the head of the road on a *lizza dura*, which is a kind of heavy sledge made from the trunks of two large trees tied together. They came down the river bed. Here and there he had to make short cuts at the side of the river, but most of these do not exist any more.'

A man in a tuxedo on the television congratulated a young lady on being more or less naked, and offered her a silk kimono.

'It must have been here on Monte Altissimo that Michelangelo worked,' said Romano, puffing his cigarette, 'because when they came to make a film about him, they shot it here at Seravezza and not at Carrara. The one with Tsarles Hess.'

'Charlton Heston?'

'*Esatto*: in the part of Moses.'

'You mean in the part of Michelangelo,' said Caio. 'He did Moses too, but that was another film.'

'That I do not know, but the film was made here. I remember because they made me show them all the mines.'

A far-away look came into the eyes of this marvellous old man, and he started talking about the mines. My envelope was not large enough to write them all down. Monte Bardiglio, both the quarry on the coast and the one up at the chapel. Monte Altissimo, where Michelangelo truly was. He even showed the film troupe the mine at Cervaioli where the arabesque marble comes from, which is six miles on the other side and has nothing whatever to do with Michelangelo. 'They saw them all,' said Romano, 'and they never stooped to examine a single stone!'

The television kept up its stylized amateur striptease with the sound turned down. Romano thought for a moment, then became both passionate and secretive. Fragmented extensions of bare legs and arms like vertical smiles glowed in each of the bottles among which the TV stood.

'They say that once, many years ago, a shepherd found a block of lapis lazuli up there. He told no one, but took a small piece to the Medici, hoping for a reward. He died before he could say where he found it, and though they sent down all sorts of experts from Florence, they never discovered the source. Nor has anyone since. So there is still a treasure somewhere up there in the mountains . . . '

At Seravezza the houses went up the side of the hill, and two rivers met by a square of leafy sycamores in the French style. A humpback bridge crossed over one river, where bored young men on bikes tried to decide which side was the right place to be. Caio made me drive through them, against the one-way system, pursued by a tired '*Ao!*' and a raised arm of rejection.

On the other side we hesitated, asked the way in a pretty

piazzetta, and then drove north, joining a road on the left of the branching valley.

This new short piece of road was Michelangelo's, leading to the quarry he revived. The road ran parallel to an empty river bed and the landscape on either side soon became steeper. We went through a little hamlet and crossed over to the eastern bank. Between us and the stream were small factories, where waste fragments were cut into tiles that were stacked between the bus-stops and the telephone poles.

The bed of the stream was dry, filled with white boulders tumbled into spheres by the torrential winter floods. Caio said that there were pools down there, cold but clean, and in summer the sculptors of Pietrasanta often came up here to swim.

Up above us the peaks were fringed with trees against the sky, with a heavy crimping of greenery beneath. There would not be much light in winter, but now the sun was up there somewhere, discouraging the wispy condensation from becoming cloud.

'It's a mountains' mountain,' said Caio semi-seriously. 'As you have a painters' painter, or a poets' poet.'

In the flank of the extraordinarily steep peak which we were approaching there appeared a black hole near the top. The quarry of Michelangelo. The road became narrower and Caio made me sound the horn at every corner. By the side of the road a cheerful woman held up her hand as her husband winched down a stout log recently cut. The woods were blackened just above. It had been a bad summer for fires, and there were cauterized areas all along the coast.

The asphalt came to an end. We took a sharp turn to the right, up the steep shale slopes of a dirt track, the vegetation changing, cluttered with ferns. There was no sign of marble that I could see. The road had been made ready for the winter with gulleys and ramparts dug and thrown up transversely every fifty yards, to catch the run-off in the rainy month of November.

Passing through an untended part of the wood we came to a gully with a ledge on which stood a heavily boarded house. We stopped. The shutters rejected our friendly approach. A Chinese sculptor lived there last year, Caio said. He went to the edge of a balcony set over the chasm and hollered across the valley. Silence, waiting for an echo. To me the place seemed haunted. I said we should go on.

Not far off we came to a green plateau, upon which a grey-haired young man was setting a simple fork beside a knife upon a blue wooden table by a rock. Born bachelor, battered Citroën, mongrel dog. Caio vaguely recognized him. They performed the cowboy greeting of artists, hands poised above imaginary pistols, showing their teeth.

He told us his name was France. His number-plate was Austrian and his bumper had a sticker for the Salzburg festival. He had a little tent and a table, chair and bottle of wine. He also had an altar at the edge, three splayed sticks tied together at the top, with a rope that dangled down between them, ending in a perforated stone. Just to tell the time he told me, seeing my dubious look.

Behind us, where the road forked, was a gaudy shrine to the Madonna, bright blue frame and fresh flowers. The procession had come up two days before, said France. Near by on an abandoned shack I saw a sticker saying 'VIRGIN MARY, PRAY FOR THOSE WHO WORK IN THE QUARRIES.' Crude black letters of supplication or command.

Caio and France chatted about Manhattan.

The abandoned masons' shack was neat and clean, with plates, cutlery, wooden boards, evidently imported recently by France. The ancient lavatory was newly polished, a handmade throne of wood.

One branch of the road went straight on, the other curved to the right, over the hill. A fresh rock-spill of gigantic proportions blocked the straight branch. I could see the truncated path on the other side of the gulley, covered with fresh grass of extraordinary bright green. That, I took it, was Michelangelo's route down from the rock face, from the quarry to where the sledge made of trees waited in the bed of the river.

'They stole my stones,' said France smiling as we got back in the car. 'I collected them last year and now they are gone. Maybe they tipped them back into the valley.'

I told him that Michelangelo had suffered from plundering too.

'Ah well,' he said cheerfully. 'To be in his company . . .'

He said that the worst was over. We drove onwards, leaving the trees behind. The world became still steeper, more remote.

Monk's pepper grew in the shade of deep places in the road where the sun shone rarely. Crags and spills threatened the sides of the car and there were overhangs across the road at the hairpin bends. The sun gave way before the cloud, which accumulated gradually between us and the mine. The hole became a black mouth squarely inserted into the misty scree of the Monte Altissimo.

By and by a truck filled with quarry workers passed us, going down. No one stopped to ask our business, or give us a smile and a wave.

Further up the hill we found the modern quarry, a segment of the mountainside mathematically amputated. A crystal negative of perfect right angles surrounded by blocks of several tons, each the size of a small car. The hole was huge; plastic tape warned strangers not to fall in. There was no one about. One could look down at a huge cross-section of the marble bed, see the wavy striations of grey among the white just as it had been deposited by the tide on the sea floor, the angle of the lines now a sharp diagonal, formed when the mountain was forced upwards. A long fault of sand and shale ran like a line drawn in charcoal through the middle. *'Dino, ti amo'* was sprayed in black upon the beautiful marble face in front of the car, and then cancelled in red: *'Silvia, stronza, mi hai tradito.'*

The road's ending. But across the quarry it seemed that a disused path continued up the hill behind an orderly stack of boulders.

A pioneering mood came over Caio as we started out on foot. There was a rattler upon every rock, injuns in the middle ground, a quest to pursue among those rugged peaks. The road had sections chewed away here and there, and the occasional rockfall created miniature recesses which Caio could fill with imaginary bears.

By and by I got the hang of Caio's humour. The lengths of wire that occasionally lay across the path were the severed stings of giant scorpions. The discarded and rusty bits of old machines were the crampons of lost climbers whose bodies had never received Christian burial. I could hear a faint breeze over the mountains, giving the impression that we were above the level suitable for humans, let alone trees. The clouds were within grasping distance now, forming momentarily and vanishing again some hundred yards vertically above.

Caio was thrilled to find a fresh pile of goat pellets, shiny as olives.

'I knew it. The wildebeest!'

The goats themselves were round the next corner.

'I correct myself. Feral goats. Or is it ferrule?'

'I think they look pretty fat and sleek,' I said. 'Maybe the workers at the mine give them *grissini* at lunch-time.'

'Biscuit-fed goat,' said Caio. 'Nothing tastier!'

Behind a penultimate curve we came across a small landslide, with shelves of rock shuffled like a pack of cards. Below the path the hard scree fell away at an angle of forty-five degrees, right down to the cliff beyond which, on his domestic ledge, stood France, just visible by his tent. A good place from which to let down rock gently towards the river bed; a bad place for an intrepid traveller to fall.

At this point Caio began to tell me how he loathed heights, how once on Machupicchu he had been marooned by his mother with his eyes tight shut for twenty minutes and so on. I looked at him standing there, motionless on a slab of rock, huge shoulders, bronzed, with the chest of a man who daily carved a life-sized marble mastodon out in the yard before breakfast. It took me a moment to realize he was being serious. 'Actually,' he said, 'I do have this, ah, thing about heights.'

I held my hand out across to him and told him not to look down. Thus the heroes managed to get by the rockfall without leaving their battered corpses in the dell. Caio tried not to shake as he stepped down again on to dry land.

The last hundred yards were handsome, like the avenue to a castle, not a road to a hole in a mountain.

Debris of rusted railway-lines at the entrance. Wooden struts engraved with filigree tendrils of moss growing like fur within the soft summer rings of each year's growth, the air of a serious concern abandoned many years before. A winch hut containing roots of iron where an engine had been. From the window, feelers of wire trailed over the edge into the valley. A rotten soapbox, a green spittoon (so it seemed) and the haunches of a motor bike with springs grinning through the saddle. All durable debris, you might say. No matches, cigarette butts or other jetsam of the day-to-day.

The quarry now rose above us like the mouth of a petrified whale. It was hard to look at it. Indeed we did not dare go in, but walked sideways along the disused road sniggering and joking, past a lean-to of corrugated iron, until unexpectedly we found a lateral shaft in the mountain which somehow seemed less daunting.

On the left as we went into the tunnel the sheer wall was buffed to a hard sheen like the interior of a cathedral rubbed by the sleeves of pilgrims. The floor was soft with powdered emery and marble dust. Our footsteps were muffled.

We came to the quarry inside the mountain. On our immediate right a strange ladder descended from above. It was irregularly fixed to the wall with a diagonal row of holes drilled into the marble. From time to time a shelf of wood hung free on a web of old wires which curled and bent, feathery with the accumulation of rust.

We were approaching, via the transept, a cathedral cut from the core of the mountain, the cuttings themselves having been reassembled into real cathedrals outside in the air, emulating the void from which they had been taken. A quarry that was in part a cathedral, in part a drowned ship, slanting as the floor followed the imperfect division of some natural layer of sediment.

From the roof down to about a third of its height from the top the quarry had been cut by hand. If the M of Michelangelo were anywhere, it would be up there. Below that the stone was cut by wire right to the ground. The layer cut by hand and the layers below it cut by wire were like relics from two different dynasties.

I took out my glasses. A bad time to discover I had stepped on them the night before. With a bright left eye and a lame right I searched for the initial M somewhere on the roof, but saw only ladders made of cutting wire and old wood suspended from impossible perches. Looking upwards into the air was to look downward under the sea. The decaying ladders on the roof moved like seaweed in a current on the ocean floor.

Caio allowed me to shush the adventurer in him for a moment while we listened to the noises that this place might make. First there was nothing but the roar of the tide in the inner ear. Then I could hear the gentle noise of droplets falling from a great height on to sand or stone, fragile and faint but with a rhythm that was regular. Now and again there was a louder clap, as some wayward element struck a rock or abandoned drum of oil, a flailing ladder or dislodged stone. A remote rivulet pattered.

The colours of the walls were beautiful, with a patina laid down by time and air. There were streaks of oxides of red and green, of iron and copper, where minerals had bled through a thin fissure. As in a cathedral, the light took on a quality different from any source which could be observed, as if light itself carried the colour. Pale green dominated the empty space.

Caio pointed out a huge natural fault on the farther wall, running vertically through the stone. We traced it to our side: we were sitting within it. Some lateral crack caused by the upturned landmass, it flickered like an artery in the striated substance of the marble.

We thought about the men working there and became restless. To decide which nests halfway up a sheer wall had held some foreman directing the machines, to work out how they ran the cutting wires, how they fed the drills from hole to hole, how they set down dry boards across the sumps and trickles in the floor, was to awaken the spirit of those who had abandoned the place.

At the end of the tunnel from which we had come the light of day seemed suddenly bright and fresh. After we came out we stood for a while at the edge of the canyon and looked down on the mountains, the populated plain beyond, and the Ligurian Sea above Viareggio upon whose beach the drowned Shelley had been cremated. Cloud was descending from the right, from Genoa. The setting sun could not dissolve it.

The white torrent shone immediately below us; then I remembered the river bed contained not water but marble. And France with his red car beside it, his tent the size of a plum.

'Zilarating,' said Caio, 'that's the word I've been groping for. Just zilarating.'

Craning over the edge he began to whistle. I had never heard anything like it. He added an extraordinary series of trills, grace notes, baroque ornamentation, enough to turn a nightingale green.

I listened dumbfounded. He stooped, put his head on one side as if listening for a reply and said slyly, 'It gets me credit at the bank.'

From below came the cheerful double toot of the bus taking a corner. It seemed to be time to go.

A moon smudged by thin cloud rose above the lower quarry as we drove down. When we passed France he was carving a boulder, against the background of a whole gulley of boulders.

'I don't quite understand,' said Caio a mile or two from this side of Pietrasanta, 'what this marble business has to do with Michelangelo. If you want to write about Michelangelo, you don't have to even mention Monte Altissimo, do you? I mean you aren't going to suggest that his images depended on the quarry the marble happened to come from, are you?'

Dusk and an approaching storm coincided as we reached the valley floor, and the world became suddenly much darker. On the outskirts of Fabriano we passed parked cars with number-plates in black on white, Rosenheim and Starnberg, Munich and Berlin. Their owners were crammed into a pizzeria a little further on.

'The answer,' I said at length, 'comes from a dream. It's a bit difficult to explain, as it sounds so feeble. Anyway, I dreamed I was looking at a whole exhibition of Michelangelo's sculpture (some of the pieces never made by him, but imagined in the dream), and I suddenly became aware how much their quality depended upon shadow, on holes, empty bits, discarded soft blackness. The dream moved to the quarry he worked in, and it struck me as being the place of ultimate shadow, in my dream, the place where they all came from . . . '

We drove on down through the outskirts of Pietrasanta, groping through to a quiet restaurant on the other side, with the wind bending the trees all about us. Large leaves of sycamores browned by the summer flapped across the road, and water began to pour from the heavens as if from a tap, just as we parked the car.

Summer is the busiest time for restaurants along the coast, and finding a place to eat was a tangled episode, well laundered by the heavens. So it was luck that we ran into a friend called Gianni sitting at an empty table and with an unexpected desire to hear all about the day up the mountainside. It was hard to shout down the babel of languages, but the other customers looked like people who worked with the local masters, rather than tourists.

Gianni was a retired journalist and, as it happened, had spent some time on the subject of Michelangelo and Pietrasanta, just to keep the old brain working, he said. His version went like this:

'Michelangelo was working in Carrara in the Fantiscritti mine. He was happy to be there because Count Alberigo di Malaspina gave him a percentage back from the pope's account for the stone he was buying. Michelangelo *sapeva i fatti suoi*, knew how to take care of himself, so *in parole povere*, to cut it short, he took a bribe.

'The mine at Seravezza had been worked in Roman times,

but was now almost disused. The citizens of Seravezza decided that the best thing they could do to get it re-opened would be to *give* it to the Medici, for free. After all, even if they did not charge for the stone, they would still be employed as quarrymen up there, no?'

Caio leaned over and helped himself to the wine.

'So they met in the piazza of Seravezza and shouted with one voice, *"Palle, palle!"* – which means "Balls, balls!" – the Medici coat of arms being, as you know, a lot of balls on a shield.'

Gianni shouted out *'palle'* quite loudly.

'Pope Leo X was a Medici, no? He immediately ordered Michelangelo to leave Carrara and go to Seravezza and work the new Medici mines. Perhaps he knew that Michelangelo was getting a bribe from Malaspina, and perhaps he didn't. Maybe they earned their money like Arabs in those days, taking from buyer and seller – not that we've changed all that much. Anyway, Michelangelo did everything he could not to go. He said the marble of Seravezza was bad, full of veins of quartz, the road did not exist. Anything! His letters are full of complaints which the historians take very seriously, but you don't have to believe him.'

'Yes,' I said, 'but he did have to spend time making a road up there, didn't he? That's a bit of a waste of effort for a genius like Michelangelo, don't you think?'

'That is true,' said Gianni, 'but he didn't exactly make them personally, did he? Any more than Mussolini, who gave Italy all those roads, ever went out there with a pick in his hands.'

We all thought that very funny.

'If you look carefully at Michelangelo's road, you'll see it is really quite a short stretch, right at the end. After which, incidentally, he turned and went straight to the sea – which in a sense was the foundation of Forte dei Marmi. If he could see it now!'

'Right,' said Caio, 'I've always seen the Sistine Chapel as Muscle Beach.'

'The medieval road from Seravezza went along the old Roman Via Valentina, and ended up on the sea at a place called Malamocca, which is just above Viareggio in fact. The new road was much better . . . I would not be surprised if it was not easier to get the rock from Seravezza to the sea, along his Nuova Strada di Marina, than from Carrara. Mind you, the place was a swamp full of mosquitoes and malaria in Michelangelo's day, as they only drained it in the seventeenth century . . .'

Gianni was evidently prepared to give a rapid run-down on every inch of the countryside.

'And which sculptures were carved from Seravezza marble?'

'They say that the *Moses* . . . I personally don't think that matters so much, do you? What is for certain is that he worked hard here getting down the columns for San Lorenzo, columns which are all lost, or almost all.'

By now we had drunk all Gianni's wine, and Caio shouted for more. Something you can only do if you know the owner. Down he came, a man with black-rimmed glasses and a stoop, who asked Caio to whistle before he gave him the menu.

'A fine man,' said Caio playing for time, 'he is also my bank manager . . . I told you, didn't I?'

Each had the other by the arm, pushing and pulling for the wine list. I got up and went to the open door, and as I walked, Caio relented and performed. He warbled and trilled under the clatter of the rain, while people stopped eating and turned towards him.

I could hear the storm come in from the sea in waves, crossing the building from one side to the other, drum-rolling the corrugated roof of the kitchen. The passing headlights flickered on asphalt and chrome amid a general staccato of wetness. The cars moved slowly, like animals fighting through undergrowth. Laughter, clapping for Caio behind me. The parallel lines of sycamore, pollarded three or four years back, whipped their thin branches rapidly all down the road. The gutter was already full, though the deeper channel for a stream the other side was empty.

The rest of the street turned black.

6 · MICHELANGELO

Around midnight Gianni told me that at the bridge just before Seravezza there was a convent with a column in the garden from the group which Michelangelo had intended for San Lorenzo.

I drove back up there the next morning to have a look. It was not early when I got there, but I found them all still asleep.

'They sleep during the day,' said the keeper of a little antique shop opposite in a deadpan voice, 'and work at night.'

'Are you suggesting they are some sort of nest of vampires?' I asked. He gave me a neutral smile.

'They pray,' he said patiently, 'and it is very tiring for them.'

Irritated, I drove on up the hill and collected some boulders from the base of the stream. Romano had told me that they were good for sculpting, having had the bad bits knocked off them.

As I drove back, I noticed the door to the nuns' garden was open. Chuckling to myself I parked, took out my camera and slipped through. I found the column, a sad thing, blackened by age, with here and there a recent chip taken out of it by incredulous experts to check if it was, indeed, statuary white.

Half an hour later I was through the short cut on the autostrada linking Massa to Lucca, the weather still unpredictable but for the moment drying out. It is the Gulf of the Lion, west of Marseille, which produces these flash storms, I am not sure why. The beauty of them is that the rain is often warm as blood.

Gianni's version of events took it for granted that Michelangelo was crafty about money. Indeed, historians fail to explain how it was that Michelangelo, apparently the victim of himself and all the world in money matters, managed to die a very rich man. Being a Tuscan like Michelangelo, Gianni knew better.

For some reason the many letters of Michelangelo tend to be segregated by scholars into the incompatible categories of 'creative' and 'business'. The volume of his letters dealing with his business affairs up at the quarries makes the whole rivalry between Carrara and Seravezza remarkably tangible.

In May 1517, at a time when Michelangelo was urging the pope to make some sort of an aesthetic decision about the facade of San Lorenzo, he was in Carrara and had already 'collected many blocks, given out money here and there, and sent out to quarries in various places'.[3]

By March the following year he was in Pietrasanta, and was having difficulties with the Carraresi: 'I have been to Genoa to look for ships to load the marble [which] I have at Carrara and at the channel of the Avenza, and the Carraresi have bribed the owners of the boats and hampered me so much that I have had to go to Pisa for others.'[4]

This would suggest that the move from Carrara to Seravezza took place some time between May 1517 and the following March, and that the Carraresi were angry about it.

Later that month he became involved in the road down from Monte Altissimo: 'I ought not to go to Carrara because I would not get the marble that I need there, not in twenty years. I have made a lot of enemies because of this business, and I would have to be made of bronze to return [there].'[5]

'This business'? Meaning the tensions between Seravezza and Carrara concerning the sale of marble to Michelangelo? And to make matters worse, in the same letter it seems that the workers back in Florence were angry that Michelangelo had collected his own marble, and were trying to raise the price of other equipment to recoup.

It was difficult to get good workmen at Pietrasanta, as he was 'a foreigner' (*un forestiero*). The road down from Seravezza 'would have been made in fifteen days if the stonecutters had been worth anything', and he describes a particular rock at a curve which remained to be chiselled away – perhaps at one of those short cuts which Romano said had once existed.[6]

The same letter makes quite clear just how closely Michelangelo directed the works:

> I have brought the quarried column down to the canal safely, fifty *braccia* from the road. It was more difficult than I had expected to bring it down. One person was hurt in letting it down, and another was in the wrong place and was killed instantly, and I risked my life . . . The face of the quarry is very difficult and the workmen inexperienced. So there is need of great patience for a few months until the mountains are tamed and the men trained.

A letter of April the following year describes, it seems to me, the face of the mountain where Caio was frightened of falling:

> Things went badly, and today, Saturday morning, I set out to let down a column with great care. Nothing was lacking, and after it had gone down fifty *braccia*, a ring at the binding around the column broke, and it fell into the river and broke into a hundred pieces. This ring had been made by a friend of Donato called Lazzero, a blacksmith,

and [as to] being sound enough, it appeared strong enough to hold four columns, and to look at it from the outside there could be no doubt whatsoever. But after it had broken, we saw the deception, that it wasn't at all sound inside, having no more thickness of metal than the binding of a knife handle, so that I was amazed that it had held as long as it did.[7]

The assured voice he uses when describing work in progress gives the impression that Michelangelo kept extremely tight control over those who worked for him. But it is also clear that he stood at the centre of a bubbling mass of intrigues welling up from Carrara, Seravezza, Florence, and presumably Rome as well. Whether he fought for his own *tangenti*, money on the side, or merely tried to stop others from taking it, is not easy to establish.

Perhaps fees or stipends in fifteenth-century Italy formed a smaller part of a specialist's income than what he received from sweeteners. Or perhaps Michelangelo felt that 'honesty was the best policy'. At any rate, his behaviour in money matters must have been considered acceptable, seeing that he ended up in sole charge of the rebuilding of St Peter's, the largest building project of the century in Europe.

You don't have to know all the details of Michelangelo's life to be able to grasp intuitively the intention behind his sculpture. What is essential in approaching this extraordinary mind is some awareness of his feeling about stone. Florence offers a unique chance to study this.

Michelangelo was the first sculptor to put into writing the idea that forms can be intrinsic to the stone, and not imposed upon it by the artist. This – together with Leonardo's remark

about seeking inspiration in the casual marks on old masonry –
is one of the most famous dicta of the Renaissance, but here it
is again:

> *Non ha l'ottima artista alcun concetto*
> *Ch'un marmo solo in sé non circonscriva*
> *Col suo soverchio, e solo a quello arriva*
> *La man che ubbidisce all'intelletto.*[8]

Even the finest artist has no idea that the block
Does not itself constrain beneath its surface;
To release that form is all the hand can achieve,
The hand that is obedient to the intellect.

Michelangelo's technique with marble was surprisingly simple.
The single large point, the chisel with two teeth, and occasionally the chisel with three, were all he used. Seldom the flat
chisel, very rarely the toothed hammer, or *bocciardo*, which is
used to create a flat surface by pulverization. His technique with
stone was as simple as his draughtsmanship: he made clear lines
using a single implement, with no smudges sacrificing clarity
for atmosphere.

The first step in making a sculpture consisted of attacking the
block with a fairly large point, and the kind of rage with which
Michelangelo used this instrument is clearly visible in the *Slaves*
in the Accademia and in the *Deposition* in the Opera del Duomo.
The lines of this large chisel run parallel, a little less then an inch
apart, and are identical to the marks left by stonecutters upon the
rough *pietra serena* of the paving-stones of towns in Tuscany
today.

He removes a series of almost flat planes, using parallel lines
within small areas that overlap each other, each little group of
parallel lines going in a slightly different direction. This evokes

a vivid image of Michelangelo pacing around the block, attacking the stone from different angles.

The next step requires the use of a smaller point. In the case of the *Slaves* it is clear that he instinctively knew there must be a limb within the stone and dug straight down to it. A number of limbs were discovered, and each was taken to quite a high degree of finish, but always with the point or toothed chisel. They were not yet smoothed and polished – though the grease or sheen of ages sometimes makes them appear so. Clearly, Michelangelo remained fiercely concentrated on the comparatively limited area about which he was entirely sure. At this point the work consisted of finished limbs coexisting in an otherwise almost amorphous stone, the outer edges of which retained traces of his original passionate attack.

It was with great difficulty that Michelangelo brought together the islands of assured surface into one sole figure. Would the proportions be correct? Would he find himself obliged to sacrifice one especially loved area for the sake of the eventual figure? The risk of incomprehension or crudeness on the part of his assistants was enormous. I suspect that this was the first great inhibition to completion: to decide which part should go would be a traumatic choice.

Even when he had surmounted this hurdle and produced a work which at last functioned in all its proportions, from all angles, the work went slowly. The sculpture which reveals most clearly the thought process of Michelangelo at this juncture is the small *Apollo* in the Bargello, a work so close to completion that its final aura of reticence is quite mystifying. The entire figure is complete, but wrapping the lower limbs are minute traces of former limbs – like an onion which has been ripped open and reveals itself as a series of encasing layers.

If one examines the surface of a more highly finished piece, another problem to do with the finishing emerges. The initial work with the large point occasionally led to bruises or dents in the uneven surface, blemishes which could become more apparent as the work proceeded. Carrara marble is translucent, and the light can penetrate almost a centimetre. This has two effects. First, interior bruises become more visible as the surface becomes smoothed, and second, the surface of the marble acquires a shimmering effect as it is polished, and this tends to blur perception of where the real surface of the form lies.

Michelangelo's sense of form grew from the inside of the marble outwards, and he always felt the risk of damaging its fragile shell. His work communicates an extraordinary feeling for the *skin* of a carving, meaning the surface of the imagined form that is represented, and also sensitivity to the marble itself by which this image is portrayed.

Michelangelo is the first artist who makes us aware that there is as much to be said by not completing a work as by completing it. But to understand how he does this means abandoning our memories of the quantities of unfinished work which have conditioned our taste since his time. Taste is one thing, meaning is another. In Michelangelo's work the meaning is bound up in this thing called flesh, skin. Skin of marble, skin of the observer who identifies with the marble, each acquire a mirror quality as they face each other, fragile, transient.

In many senses Michelangelo is a less complete artist and a less fine sculptor than Giovanni Pisano, his great predecessor. The stone does not do exactly what is expected of it, is never forced to follow a preconceived design. For all Michelangelo's writings stressing the need for clear outlines when drawing, his own carvings are in my view less effective in silhouette than those of Pisano. Pisano, by exploiting extraordinarily bold undercutting and ruthlessly dramatic distortion of the figure, made sure that his *Prophets* (made for Siena Cathedral, now in the Opera del Duomo in that city) would be clear in pose at whatever distance, from whatever angle. This is not true of Michelangelo. At a distance, the interior light which the *Slaves* exude tends to erode the dramatic shape which Michelangelo perceived within the untouched rock at the quarry.

Pisano makes an extraordinarily clear and complete declaration of a mature mind at work within a violent world, the parameters of which were evident to everyone. But Michelangelo takes us to the brink of absolute uncertainty, about the world, about the sculptor's position in that world and about ourselves as observers and occupants of that world.

Great works, according to the aesthetic of our own century, are not finished so much as abandoned.[9] But Michelangelo's works are neither abandoned nor left in a non-finished state for aesthetic reasons. They are certainly not merely interrupted by chance, for many of them stayed in Michelangelo's studio for thirty years or more. Nor can one say with certainty that they are finished at each stage of their progress, leaving no essential feature of their selves undefined. It is merely as if the artist has left the room. At any moment he could have resumed, would have resumed, postponed resuming. The flesh of his sculpture threatens to mature and decay, just like ours.

7 · VIAREGGIO

Until a hundred years ago Viareggio was just a small fishing village and posting station on the Via Reggio or Royal Road. It boomed in the 1890s with the fashion for bathing by the sea, for which its wide sandy beaches were perfect.

This was the bay where Shelley was drowned in 1822 in a boating accident. His body was cremated about a mile up the beach from the mole where the fishing-boats were moored, in the presence of his friends Edward Trelawny and Lord Byron.

There is a film festival in Viareggio in late summer, after the weather breaks, when sudden showers come rattling across the bay from France. I was there earlier this year, to see the first screening of a film directed by a friend called Marco.

We met in front of the Festival Cinema. Green bronze ladies fought cheerfully with chrysanthemum cloud on the fine grey sandstone walls, now obscured by bulletin boards for the artistes and the press. Before the crash of 1929, in an earlier phase of the city's popularity, this building had housed the municipal casino.

Marco was wearing a hat of the kind that directors wear, and for some reason this irritated me. He seemed nervous.

'I don't understand,' he whispered. 'It's only a work of art. How can a film inspire such resentment?' He had just given a press conference and was still shaking.

'Maybe it's the hat.'

Viareggio

He took it off briefly and shook it a bit.

'Griffiths wore one,' he said. 'Eisenstein wore one. Even Bertolucci wears one. It is a known fact that most of the talent of film directors lives in this kind of a hat.'

'It makes you look like a critic.'

This puzzled him.

'Next time you give an interview, check if the nastiest questions come from critics with hats. They'll be the frustrated directors.'

He looked about, and sure enough there was one right by us, with leathery features obscured by floppy felt. He was curled over his fingernails and angling ferociously for the last word. Just behind him someone who looked like Bruno Ganz, a woman on either side dressed in black and looking bored.

I took Marco by the elbow out of the flock of grandees, into the holiday crowds walking slowly up and down the promenade in summer plumage: blue and white striped pyjamas, denim jackets with ducktails and pantaloons of cotton gauze, worn over a slight bikini. And hair − what hair! In nests mounted upwards and bleached towards the ends, or in braids and bows, or curled and brushed out again into tense shavings from which each hair made its own individual watch-spring. How could these hairdos ever be nourished in the dank sea air? It was a pleasure to walk behind them, talking of films and the private habits of friends.

On our right were the shops of the promenade, on our left the reptilian traffic, smelling sour and protected from the crowds by a tongue of municipally watered green. Here and there a patch beyond the sprinklers made an arid zoo for cacti and palms, held to each other by wire or twisted into shapes suggesting stuffed animals. I could not keep my eyes off them, but the crowd looked only to the right, into the shop windows, for everything that could nurture their comfort. Brand-new saddles with silver stirrups and scarves with printed horseshoes, leather overcoats, furs. They especially liked Armani trousers mounted upon phantom waists, with ankles shackled thrice by a hand-tooled belt to show the hang of the material.

I left Marco briefly and went into a bookshop to ask for something about Shelley. For some reason Byron and Shelley were on my mind.

But the tall balding young man behind the counter had never heard of Shelley. Shelley who? A poet? Ah! We have Piazzetta Lorenzo Viano, a street for Enrica Peia, another for Sadun.

'A town of fatal charm for poets,' I murmured.

'We have even asked the *Comune* for a *vicolo cieco* Sandro Penna,' he said, then hesitated, turned to the rear of the shop and came back with a book. 'There does seem to be a Piazzetta Shelley, and it is not far off.'

Marco had some four hours to go before his film was to be shown, plenty of time to walk up there as the crowds thinned, talking of anything that would distract him.

In the Piazzetta Shelley we found the poet supported on a marble pillar in an empty garden well supplied with benches. Courting couples sat intertwined, attentively grooming each others' ears. I could recognize nothing about the bronze bust, which might just as well have been a girl amusing herself at the casino in the good old days. The worn letters of bronze had been picked out here and there by plundering boys, but the brief text was still legible stencilled on the marble in stained green: ANNEGATO IN QUESTO MARE, ARSO IN QUESTO LIDO; 'Drowned in this sea, burned on the promenade.' Sweeping thus briefly into a monument Shelley's mortal remains.

Byron arrived in Tuscany a political refugee, following the exile of Count Gamba whose daughter Teresa Guiccioli was his last mistress. It is assumed that the Gamba family was exiled as a means of getting rid of Byron, but the fact is that they were all deeply implicated in the aborted insurrection of the Romagna in 1820.[10]

In the family of Count Gamba, Byron found not only his 'last attachment' but a whole group of people who shared with him a large number of social and political values. The old Count had once danced round the Pole of Liberty, in the first phase of the French Revolution; Pietro Gamba, Teresa's brother, became a close friend and followed Byron to Greece, where he died. Theirs perhaps was the peculiar syndrome of aristocratic republicanism which went back to the early days of the French Revolution, when the more liberal of the aristocrats voluntarily joined the *tiers état*.

Teresa Guiccioli showed remarkable skill in cutting through Lord Byron's black moods. Perhaps she had come across that sort of thing before. The relationship turned out to be a lasting one for Byron, yet it is difficult to escape the impression that during the two or three years they were together, Byron experienced a growing sense of remoteness. As an exile, Byron grew gloomy. Either that, or his capacity for any human contact (as he hinted in his work) gradually atrophied.

What makes the lives of Byron and Shelley so accessible and fascinating to us is their sexuality. They resemble the turbulent lives of pop stars between the sixties and the age of Aids. They lack only the flash of the paparazzi to make the scene permanent. Like pop stars, they were followed around by groupies – Claire Clairmont, or Trelawny, or Byron's secretary Polidori, who kept tell-all diaries for future publication: 'As soon as he reached his room, Lord Byron fell like a thunderbolt upon the chambermaid.'[11] The appetite, the misdirected urge, the confusion of the lives of these early Romantics – above all the sense that sex is an essential act of communication and yet something intrinsically lonely – are instantly recognizable to us.

Such freedom led gradually but inevitably to the opposite of freedom – a losing battle with the prison of convention. Anything Byron did during the last phase of his life in Pisa tended to add to his rotten reputation back home. The various scandals in Italy were written up: one can imagine them being read out gleefully at London breakfast tables. The literary respect for which he affected not to care seemed to him to be dwindling, and it worried him. Money was involved. The later cantos of *Don Juan* brought nothing like the income of the first ones. There was no real question of going back – and yet his face was always turned towards England, to its gossip, its capacity to provide an audience and a background, even to its landscape. 'I wished to have nothing to do with Tuscany beyond its climate – and as it is, I find myself not allowed even that in quiet.'¹²

In his last two years Byron's obsession with England could be read as a strange rearguard action against the impossible stuffiness of English society. Cant and humbug were his enemies. Like a disease, they overcame his friends: Hobhouse, so worthily turning to good causes, Murray momentarily timorous about publishing his more acrimonious pieces.

An advance guard, like a fifth column, appears at Byron's back door with the Hunt family. Byron inherited, as it were, Leigh Hunt from Shelley, whose idea it was to create an English magazine in exile, to be called *The Liberal*, and who invited Hunt out to edit it. Leigh Hunt tried to become Byron's literary adviser, touched him for cash and was graceless and offensive about it. Mrs Leigh Hunt was always willing to take a position of moral disapproval of her benefactor. Reading Byron's biography and letters it is easy to take sides against the whole messy lot of them, with their children 'dirtier and more mischievous than Yahoos'.¹³

It requires an effort to treat the Hunts fairly. Byron disliked them, not so much for their hypocrisy – in publishing matters Leigh Hunt and his brother John possessed more courage than Murray[14] (they, too, were fighting the fight for the great English republic) – but, unfortunately, Leigh Hunt in Byron's eyes was not quite a gentleman. He was a middle-class liberal, and though Byron had a certain sympathy about the liberal side of it, to be middle class was to be impossible.

In spite of his quarrels, Byron could write to his old publisher John Murray in a way he never could to the Hunts. And there is a very interesting passage in a letter of October 1822 to John Murray which shows Byron's feelings not only about Leigh Hunt, but also about Shelley:

> As to any community of feeling – thought – or opinion between L[eigh] H[unt] & me – there is little or none – we meet rarely – hardly ever – but I think him a good principled & able man – & must do as I would be done by. – I do not know what world he has lived in – but I have lived in three or four – and none of them like his Keats and Kangaroo *terra incognita* – Alas! Poor Shelley! – how he would have laughed – had he lived, and how we used to laugh now & then – at various things – which are grave in the Suburbs. – You are all mistaken about Shelley – you do not know – how mild – how tolerant – how good he was in Society – and as perfect a Gentleman as ever crossed a drawing room.[15]

For those who are fascinated by the relationship between Byron and Shelley at Viareggio in this, the endgame of their lives, it is perhaps unfortunate that the above letter to Murray was not Byron's last word on Shelley. Byron later wrote a really terrible letter to Mary Shelley, all the worse for being carefully written:

As to friendship, it is a propensity in which my genius is very limited. I do not know the male human being, except Lord Clare, the friend of my infancy, for whom I feel anything that deserves the name. All my others are men-of-the-world friendships. I did not even feel it for Shelley, however much I admired and esteemed him: so that you see not even vanity could bribe me into it, for, of all men, Shelley thought highest of my talents, – and, perhaps of my disposition.[16]

A sad text for those who imagine that these self-made exiles were able to form some bond of mutual allegiance against the cruelty, real and imagined, of England, or were able to create among themselves some ideals of liberty and fraternity as a counterweight to their growing sense of isolation.

A remote possibility exists that Shelley was murdered. It does not meet with serious attention from modern biographers, but to me the question remains open.

The story is best told in a letter from Trelawny to *The Times* of 28 December 1875:

At midday on the 8th of July, 1822, Shelley came from his banker's at Leghorn with a canvas bag full of Tuscan crown pieces. Byron, Shelley, Williams, and myself could not be distinguished by the sailors at the harbour, and Byron's and Shelley's boats had their sails loose ready for sea. It was a light land breeze when we weighed our anchors and started at 2 p.m. I was on board Byron's boat, and was hailed at the entrance of the harbour by the captain of the port, asking if I had my port clearances and bill of health. On my answering I had not, that I was going to return that night, he replied that I should be put in quarantine. I was therefore obliged to re-anchor, and Shelley's boat proceeded alone. Two feluccas went out of port at the same time, in the same direction as Shelley's boat. I remained on board. Some hour after the squall came on; the wind and sea mist veiled everything from sight at any distance, and the first thing we saw was several feluccas returning for refuge into the harbour.

When the first vessel anchored I sent a mate on board of her, a Genoese, to see what tidings he could get of Shelley's boat. The Genoese said, 'Why, there are some of her spars on board you,' pointing to an English oar, 'that belongs to her.' This they all denied. On his reporting the circumstances to me, he expressed his suspicions that they knew more than they would acknowledge. I thought we should know more the next day. If I had reported to the captain of the port what the Genoese said, their vessel would have been put into quarantine for fourteen days. That restrained me. I had no suspicion at that time of the disaster that had happened, and the light spars of Shelley's boat might have been thrown overboard.

When they eventually found the wreck and brought her up, 'The cause of her loss was then evident. Her starboard quarter was stove in, evidently by a blow from the sharp bows of a felucca: and, as I have said, being undecked and having three tons and a half of ballast, she would have sunk in two minutes.' [17]

Richard Holmes in his marvellous biography of Shelley will have none of this. He does believe that a boat approached the *Don Juan* and urged her to lower a few sails, at which 'a shrill voice, which is supposed to have been Shelley's, was distinctly heard to say "No" . . .' [18]

79

He also, in a footnote, quotes Mary Shelley's version: 'A fishing boat saw them go down – It was about 4 in the afternoon – they saw the boy at mast head when baffling winds struck the sails they had looked away a moment & looking again the boat was gone.'[19]

Holmes closes his quote here, and in so doing closes also the question of murder. But in fact the letter goes on:

> This was their story but there is little doubt that these men might have saved them, at least Edward [Williams] who could swim. They cd not they said get near her – but 3 quarters of an hour after passed over the spot where they had seen her – they protested no wreck of her was visible, but Roberts going on board their boat found several spars belonging to her – perhaps they let them perish to obtain these. Trelawny thinks he can get her up, since another fisherman thinks he has found the spot where she lies, having drifted near shore. T does this to know perhaps the cause of her wreck – but I care little about it.[20]

The complete letter seems to me to indicate two important things: that Trelawny, even at the time of the accident itself, and not just in a letter to *The Times* written fifty years later, had his doubts about how the wreck occurred; and that Mary Shelley did not want to go into the matter further.

What makes modern biographers dubious about the story is the fact that Trelawny was a very unreliable witness, to put it mildly. He had readjusted his past to fit the image of Byron's *Corsair* – which must have been about as flattering to Byron as if one went to visit Picasso painted blue.[21]

So what other evidence is there?

The question was shelved at the time, probably in deference to Mary Shelley's reluctance to pursue the matter. Then in 1875

Trelawny's daughter wrote to him from Rome indicating that a sailor of La Spezia had confessed to being one of the crew which sank the *Don Juan*, many years before.

This was substantiated by a letter to *The Times* from one V. E., who said the fisherman died in 1863, and had told everything to a friend of V. E.'s, whom he quoted: 'A boatman dying near Sarzana, confessed, about twelve years ago, that he was one of the five who, seeing the English boat in great danger, ran her down, thinking milord Inglese was on board, and that they should find gold.'[22]

Gold? This part of the story is unluckily corroborated by a letter from Byron. 'The day before he was lost he borrowed of me fifty pounds, which were on board in cash when the boat went down.'[23]

The other evidence is unfortunately thin. The damage to the boat, when it was brought to shore, confirmed the reading of those who were willing to believe the murder theory, among them the sailors Trelawny and Captain Roberts, who ought to have known about such things. But modern biographers tend to think that the damage to the *Don Juan*'s prow was caused by the salvage operation rather than by a hypothetical felucca.

There can be no new evidence to add, but one or two observations could be made, taking the Italian point of view into account.

It is very rare, in Italy, for murders to occur without some kind of a background. Italy functions by the interaction of various tightly circumscribed groups, so that an individual has significance and power, not in himself, but as representative or member of a particular circle. In England there are equivalents: the old-boy network, a hypothetical 'Yorkshire Mafia', the Freemasons in some areas of the judiciary, but nothing like the intricate and all-encompassing structures which exist in Italy.

These structures probably derive from the ancient Roman

concept of *gens*, a social group including not only blood relatives but also assimilated friends, dependants, business acquaintances – and even servants: groups of people bound by a sense of mutual recognition, often transcending the other social divisions of class or region – which is what makes them so interesting, and so difficult to assess.

No job, no position of any importance, can be filled in Italy without some kind of *raccomandazione*. This 'presentation' consists of a meeting between representatives of two groups of power, one asking, the other giving, between whom the matter is decided. This creates a complicated web of obligations, reflecting constantly the status of each group in the eyes of the other. All government or administrative posts are distributed in this way, as a matter of course. But also directorships of banks, social services, universities, and a whole series of jobs that in England would be considered apolitical, right down to the sweepers of the street, lowly assistants at the hospitals, teachers in the elementary schools . . . There may be one or two exceptions, but on the whole the rule applies.

An example of how essential it is to belong to one of these tight social groups can be seen in the recent murder of Carlo Alberto Dalla Chiesa.

Dalla Chiesa was a general of the Carabinieri who had had considerable success in fighting the Red Brigades during the sad period from the mid 1970s until the early 1980s. After this, he was sent to Palermo in the hope that what worked against terrorism might work against the Mafia.

In Sicily he started investigating the connection between the big contracts for public works, the Mafia and the political parties. This was intelligent but very foolhardy, since perhaps the most sensitive area in Italy today is the degree to which crime has coopted, or been coopted by, the executive.

In an interview a week before his death, Dalla Chiesa declared that at last he was beginning to understand the social background of the act of murder in Italy. A vacuum had to be created around the victim, he said, detaching him from any group of people who could be offended by his death, and who might revenge it in the future. Once that vacuum had been created, it mattered very little who was the instrument of his death. The victim died alone, severed from all those ties which, in a sense, made him human. With sad premonition, Dalla Chiesa remarked that he had found it very hard, recently, to communicate with any official in Rome.

I would suggest that such a vacuum was in the process of being created around Byron at the time of Shelley's death, and that it is possible that some violent attempt was made on him which stemmed from this process.

English writers on Byron tend to assume that his great literary reputation saved him from persecution at the hands of the police – that Count Gamba and he were protected, as it were, by the cantos of *Don Juan*. I don't believe this. The Tuscan spy Giuseppe Valtancoli said laconically of him, 'He is not unknown as a man of letters, and in his country has a reputation of being a fine poet.'[24] But literature was not the most interesting thing about his lordship. What the spies wanted to know was whether or not Byron was a secret emissary of his majesty's government.

From the point of view of the Papal Curia and the Austrian secret services, it was unthinkable that Byron should be messing about with muskets for the Carbonari, with whom he had been involved for some years, without some sort of political backing. For that reason, they would have acted cautiously towards him. But there must have come a point when they realized that this secret backing did not exist. If and when they came to this conclusion, Byron's position in Italy would have become precarious.

As to Shelley, he was nothing but an eccentric English loner of whom there were and always are dozens, whose movements are often faithfully noted down by the local Carabinieri, even to this day.

Shelley's death was preceded by an incident with which, it seems to me, it should be connected.

Riding back to Pisa after an afternoon spent in the country, the little English party was overtaken by an Italian on horseback who rushed through the group in a way they considered aggressive and insulting. Shelley was thrown from his horse and remained unconscious for some time. There was a chase, a fight, in which a servant of Byron's stabbed the man, who unfortunately turned out to be a sergeant of the Tuscan Light Horse. A servant was arrested – the wrong one, as it happened. The Gamba family were implicated, and were forced into exile yet again, from Pisa to Lucca, which until 1847 was a small independent state.

The English group, including Byron, took the event to be insulting, and I suspect they were right. The incident was a symptom. The message of the Italian sergeant was, 'These people do not count; they are not wanted; they have no protection. They do not belong to any circle that might give them an identity. They are alone.'

The affair of the sergeant took place on 24 March. On 3 April the Gamba family was forced to move to Lucca, and as soon as he could, Byron followed them. On 26 April Shelley and Williams moved to Lerici. The accident in which Shelley died was on 8 July.

It seems to me arguable that after the sergeant was stabbed the mood in Pisa had turned against Lord Byron and his gang. The story Trelawny tells of the mechanics of the boating incident is plausible. The three friends of Milord were seen to go on board, with a bag containing a lot of money. They were followed out. The boat was approached and hailed, in a high sea, in Italian, to reef their sails. There were pieces of equipment belonging to the English boat on a Genoese ship which came into port soon after – Roberts, as well as Trelawny, says so. Given the atmosphere in which this group of foreigners could be seen to be *unprotected*, in the Italian sense, there seems to me no reason to doubt that the sailors of the felucca grasped their chance for plunder when they saw it.

Marco's film was in the end shown at midnight, after some delays. The audience was in a good mood and liked it.

Afterwards we sat in the *piazzetta* down by the mole, near an art nouveau tobacconist, drinking Cartizze and trying not to smoke too much.

Having spent the day reading about Byron and Shelley, I aired my theory about these protective circles in Italian life. Marco thought I was talking about art, as usual, and gave an interesting speech about the subordination of all art to politics in Italy since the Counter-Reformation. The rest of the troupe came over from time to time to shake his hand, before walking off into the spindly forest of tamarisks planted up to the edge of the port.

The Council of Trent. The Sistine Chapel. The baroque churches of southern Germany seen as political propaganda. As usual I found that my brilliant illumination about Italian life had been amply discussed many times before. As everyone joined in, walking to and fro with glasses, I began to feel trapped in an antique pianola.

'And don't forget,' said a young man with a beard, 'if art was one of the first areas to go, medicine was one of the last . . . '

At which point someone told a story about a hospital run by a killer surgeon whom the socialists refused to remove. Last week he cut someone in half, looking for their appendix. We were tired enough to find this very funny.

We rose at last to walk back once more from the mole where the tamarisks grew to the Casino opposite the Excelsior. While we walked I kept check of the distance. Marco said good-night at the door to the hotel. There was a ship incised in the plate-glass door behind his head, and I was glad to see his face less anxious at last, against a background of crystal waves.

I had become gradually convinced that Shelley's body had been cremated right by the Festival Cinema. I crossed over to walk in the dark on the wide sand on the shore. The cool breeze blew in from the sea, and the level sand was puckered with the day's accumulated footprints, the even pattern continuing indefinitely in either direction. By the light of a small moon I saw a forgotten towel, and one open beach umbrella.

Trelawny mentions magnificent pines by the spot where Shelley's body was found, but I saw none. I seemed to remember reading that they had died fifteen or twenty years ago, from phosphates in spume blown in from the sea.

During the night it occurred to me that Trelawny had said 'a mile from Via Reggio,' and not 'a mile from the harbour' as I had hitherto understood it.

The next day I drove slowly towards Carrara, along the coast, past small streams with names I recognized from the official report of 1822, which listed the beaches where flotsam from the wreck of the *Don Juan* had been washed up: Fossa dell'Abate, Motrone, Le Focette. Looking up at the hills on my right I realized we must be quite near the old road from Seravezza, down which they brought the marble from the quarry before Michelangelo made the short cut to Forte dei Marmi.

Viareggio

The beach huts and lidos began to seem poorer: Nuova Italia
– for the Fascist rebirth perhaps; Mar Tirreno – which has a
subliminal hint at Petrarch; Bucintoro – as if we were anywhere
near Venice; Pizzeria Che Guevara (takes you back a bit, that
one); Soggiorno 90 Minuti – for football fans out of season, I suppose.

A weary Lido Fantasia. We reached the periphery where the
columns that marked territorial boundaries of sand and wiry
grasses were no longer of fake marble, but of up-ended cement
drains. The brollies on the sand hesitated and gave up. There
was a large sign in neon with a letter ripped out, like a yelp for
the dentist. A beer hall or two for the migrant Germans or
Dutch.

I stopped for an ice-cream, parking the car by a deserted roller-
skating rink. The pavement was made of marble chips from the
quarries, set in coloured cement, like the cement they use in the
Veneto. I looked at the newspapers at the local kiosk where they
sold postcards of tits of yesteryear next to all Europe's weeklies and
dailies. *Blick!* and *Olà*, the *Telegraph* and the *Neue Zürcher Zeitung*.

I crossed the road which was thick with cautious traffic and
slipped between two wooden sheds to walk upon the beach.
Grannies supervised the very young, who enjoyed screaming
against the wind. The beach was less crowded, but it was still
hard to feel wistful about dead poets. The waves turned like
carved sticks of glass each on a rigid pivot. Far out in the bay a
tanker fled slowly from the arrow of its own smoke. An intense
couple looking at each other made me feel decrepit.

When I found the car again I saw that a child was practising
on the skating rink. She was twelve or so, going round by
herself, sometimes forward, sometimes in reverse, now on one
leg, now the other. She seemed to carry her music in her head,
for there was no sound but a prolonged gasp from the road as
the cars went up and down the coast.

And I thought for a moment about all the dead children who cluttered the lives of Byron and Shelley: little Allegra with her father's bad temper, dead at five years old in the convent where her father had parked her. Wilmouse. And Shelley's secret daughter down in Naples, even younger, hardly started.

Looking up, I saw a child's kite flying from some part of the beach near by. The girl practising her skating was very serious. She had a short tunic on, and her legs were bare.

8 · BEES

It was Vittorio Fosi who gave me my first hive of bees. One night a couple of months after his oxen had been sold, as the fields about his house were being razed and their walls tipped casually into the scraggy edge of the wood, he placed a barrel of bees on a small promontory of living rock some hundred yards from our house. He apologized the next morning, saying they had to leave the house at short notice. All around was chaos, as large squeaking machines churned up the old terraces to prepare the land for planting with big modern vineyards.

This barrel full of bees was in fact a tall wooden bucket called a *bigoncia*, something like an upside-down umbrella stand. These were used in the grape harvests until their recent replacement by bright plastic baskets and the stalk-remover or *deraspatrice*. You would fill the *bigoncia* to the brim with bunches of grapes and then crush them, using a bludgeon called an *ammostatoio*, before tipping the frothy mixture into a huge tub in the cellar called a *tinello*, for the first fermentation of the wine.

My bees-in-a-barrel swarmed every year, and while I felt reluctant to do anything about the actual *bigoncia* itself, because it did not belong to me, I felt I ought to be doing something about the swarms. They would hang in great clumps from a nearby shrub or small tree, sending out scouts to look for future accommodation. One could approach the swarm quite freely.

Replete with honey, the bees were totally engrossed in their euphoric moment of emigration and were as yet free from the protective mode which comes with domesticity – the hive that has at all costs to be defended.

After two or three years spent in useless contemplation of this extraordinary moment in nature, I began to ask around the village for some local expert who could help me dominate these errant bees. It was so beautiful to see them rise up and interweave in the sky their concentrated cloud of tribal madness, before flying in individual ellipses but a collective straight line down over the hills to their new home, but the hole of silence they left in the air after they had gone left me with a sense of waste and incompetence. There must be some way of learning this skill too, I thought.

Giova is your man, they said. So I went up the mountain, to meet a huge peasant with flat calloused hands who lived in a harsh house miles from anyone, overlooking some stony fields which gave way to large neglected forests. Scrub lands, good for honey.

Giova had a wide face and protruding ears. I could see his hives all around his domain, perched on the rims of the dry-stone walls like Japanese tombs. No two seemed to be the same.

Would I like to see his mother, Giova asked me. Puzzled but polite I said yes. He took me into the house, and sure enough there in an upstairs room was his mother, dead. Dressed for travelling, she had her arms crossed in front of her over her black handbag. Her face was the colour of her teeth, which were just visible beneath blackening gums.

People do not look their best when they are dead. It is hard to discern familiar features beneath the greying statues they leave behind. The strange precision of her not human presence, unbreathing, unmoving, filled me with awe. Her bed was neatly made, and on it she lay, complete with shoes. Had she been vertical and alive, she would have been ready for a wedding or a mass. Ribbons tied in a pretty bow kept her hands and feet from straying sideways.

In the half-dark I noticed friends of the dead lady sitting on chairs around the room. I could think of absolutely nothing to say, and they seemed indifferent to seeing me there. After a moment I went down.

I was unused then to the etiquette of sitting up with the dead. There are rules to this social ritual, the principal one being that neither the body nor the family should ever be left alone. You arrive: whoever is there leaves, and you remain until someone else appears who can take over from you. I remember sitting with the old barber from the village together with my two daughters, then aged eight and ten, unrelieved for thirty minutes. It seemed a long time. The little girls were most solemn, with the dead barber, while I found myself telling jokes to his daughter-in-law, inappropriate but absurdly irresistible. From time to time I would sneak a look, trying to recognize some feature of the man I had known, but without success.

'Well,' said Giova calmly, 'tell me about your bees.'

'I am so sorry to have intruded,' I said, feeling deeply embarrassed. 'I am sorry about your mother.'

'Yes,' he said, 'so am I. She was a good woman, and she was still useful to me. She was always active, a hard worker. Only three days ago she was out in the fields, gathering grass for the rabbits.'

I got to know and admire Giova after this unusual introduction. He carved his hives by hand, up on the hillside, each frame slightly different from the next, which worried neither Giova nor the bees, but made nonsense of the concept of the movable-frame hive.

The modern hive was the invention of an American called L. L. Langstroth, who received his inspiration while driving a pony-trap back from his apiary in West Philadelphia to his home in town, on the evening of 30 October 1851.

The bees of his new hives built their combs within wooden frames which had been uniformly cut to exact proportions, allowing combs to be handled in a totally new way. But Giova's hives were carved as the mood took him, and each frame fitted into the slot it was made for, and no other. Thus it was extremely difficult for him to amalgamate swarms, introduce fresh queens, enlarge the brood with frames of new wax, and so on. I never quite got the hang of those techniques but, like all amateurs, I happily imagined I would do so one day. So I went down to the Consorzio Agrario and bought myself a perfect hive, feeling slightly guilty as I did so, as if I was being insufficiently rustic, this being the height of my hayseed-in-the-hair period.

I bought the hive and set it up, but for a season or two it remained unused in the cellar, as there was no way of persuading Giova to come down from his blasted heath to help me catch a swarm in the unspeakable lowlands. 'It's easy,' he would say, at the end of a crackling telephone line. 'Just pop it on top.' If I pleaded insufficient nimbleness, he said he had ten swarms of his own, thank you very much; perhaps later! He was so generous with his time up on the hill, and so bizarre in his attitude to the outside world, that I felt unable to insist.

I longed to give him some money. No particular reason for this decadent whim, merely a feeling of respect for his eccentricity and capacity for blind hard work. But of course, one cannot go around thrusting cash into hands, so with difficulty I arranged that I would buy some of his manure. He was not a man who had a great deal to sell, but he did have this interesting pile of shit, the produce, after many years of effort, of one animal grown for beef. When I was up there, quite a lot of time had to be spent admiring the cow and examining the substance. When

I said how fine I found it he said, 'Yes, I added some buckets from the *pozzo nero*, to give it a better fragrance.' Such passion made me momentarily dizzy. The *pozzo nero*, literally the 'black well', meant the cess pit.

Three years later the writer David Garnett was staying with us, in the month of May, when bees swarm. To my surprise he knew everything there was to know about keeping bees, and had supplied his friends with honey throughout the sugarless First World War. He told me all about Langstroth and von Frisch, one of the most modest winners of the Nobel Prize in terms of research expenses.

Von Frisch earned his Nobel for having discovered the dance of the bees, that language with which a scout bee could tell its companions the direction of a new supply of food and its distance from the hive. In his later years he discovered that they used the polarization of the light of the sun as a means of navigation.

Imagine an eye like a series of mirrors which in some way splits the light. The angle of this split indicates the height and direction of the sun. Add to this a sense of time, and the trigonometrical bee will always be able to retrace the route from flower back to hive by taking a reading from the sun. One wonderful experiment: Von Frisch created a large artificial bee's eye and put it over a source of nectar. The bee would come, sip and take a reading, not realizing that the polarity of this reading was slightly different from that perceptible to its own eye. It would fly off to a different spot, where it would find another hive set by Von Frisch ready to catch it. What genius! A few cheap pieces of glass, logic, patience and exceptional intuition.

Garnett – telling me stories of chasing swarms over neighbours' land and how, once, up a ladder, a half-starved swarm attacked him – called for a waste-paper basket, which he said should be covered with some dark material, as the key instrument to be used in swarm-catching. (I came across this object the other day in the back of the ex-studio, black crêpe turned madeira with age, printed with a design of faded cherries and loosely basted on with blue thread. Inside, traces of crumbled honeycomb, with some of the flakes which are secreted by the bees as they attach their combs to the roof.)

With this devastating weapon we hunted a swarm of bees, which luckily for me had settled low on an olive tree. From there they were gently encouraged into the basket by puffs of smoke. At dusk we took the basket of bees and decanted them with a deft if violent movement on to a running-board set in front of the hive; to my amazement, instead of taking off angrily for somewhere else, they scuttled within the Consorzio hive with all the eagerness of a herd of minute rabbits.

As the years passed and I gained the essential skill of swarm-catching, I extended my hives to three, to six, to twelve. I may have adored my bees, but I found that it is not possible to have a real emotional relationship with them. The emotions they produced in me were obviously unreciprocated. Mankind and insects are developing on different time-scales. When they are wise, we shall be extinct. As for keeping bees, the husbandry has continued for a couple of millennia, perhaps a little more, certainly not enough time for the species to have become aware of our existence. A million years of Langstroth hives will have to pass before the bees might indicate some greeting, as a cow greets her owner when she is led from the stall.

Why then are bees so attractive? What is this powerful emotion the beekeeper feels? Why does one love a bee and feel indifferent about, say, a dung-beetle? Why feel so emotionally satisfied by the hum at dusk of a hive in June as the bees gently fan the nectar into honey with their wings? Why become so distressed when wax moth attacks a weak hive? Why despair on noticing the unpleasant smell of foul brood or observing the parasitical ticks like tiny lobsters which threaten the eventual demise of a hive through intestinal infection?

I suspect that the incapacity of bees to return our love leads to frustration on the part of the beekeeper. You are not noticed. The bees have no gratitude. They purr not, neither do they moo. They wag no tail, nor turn their faces towards you when you enter the ten-acre field. Bees are indifferent to your joy at seeing a healthy row of hives as they are to your despair when they sicken and die.

Some years ago I was one of six beekeepers who attended a meeting at the Consorzio Agrario, called to discuss the promotion of beekeeping. I soon discovered that my five colleagues had between a thousand and fifteen hundred hives each, so I concentrated on keeping my trap shut and staying in the background.

A sleek official from Rome, tie and jacket, etc., harangued us on the need to register our hives so as to become eligible for a government grant, eventually to be supplemented by something creditable from the Common Market. The sum involved would have been considerable to these five professionals, but they turned it down. They turned it down quite violently, and one by one they listed the years of neglect and indifference on the part of the government, complaining about the price of wood for frames, about disinfectant, machines for wax, about the struggle against disease, in which they were abandoned by the health services which could do so much.

I recognized this strong feeling on their part as a side-effect of the insects' lack of response to their loving masters. Knowing nothing of this, the official was stunned. From the Roman point of view, it was like offering a whole pile of money on a plate and seeing these ignorant Tuscans refuse to grab. I have never seen an official look more incredulous.

Disease, robbing and, I must confess, neglect eventually wiped me out as a beekeeper. That and the weight of guilt I felt at the responsibility of twenty or thirty thousand tiny deaths on my soul whenever a hive failed.

A hive keeps going for as long as the queen remains alive, however desperate the fight against moth or foul brood. When a hive loses its queen, and all that is left are two or three hundred orphans, they mourn her. They sing, one after another, a long dying note, like a viola's: *glissando, decrescendo, morendo*. It is one of the strangest and saddest sounds in the world.

In spite of disease, in spite of my infidelity, swarms still float across the valley to enter the one or two abandoned hives which are still out there.

Once I chased a swarm from tree to tree all over the front yard, as the sun grew higher and all of us lost our tempers. I tried everything to make them settle, including shooting water straight into the air to simulate rain. No good. At about three o'clock the bees all rose in the air and flew away over the valley. My attempt to catch them must have coincided with their having discovered a new home. Stumbling over the abrasive clay sods I followed them through the vineyard waving wide my arms and shouting up at them: 'Good luck.'[25]

9 · SIENA

Some time before being evicted from the house he had refused to buy for fear of being in debt for forty years, Vittorio told me a story which transformed the rivalry between Florence and Siena into a slightly sinister folk-tale.

'You know,' he said, 'that the Florentines and Sienese have never got on well together, and were always fighting? Well, one day they decided that enough blood had been shed and the frontiers between the two states should be settled by chance. Two roosters would start out from each city at dawn, walking towards each other, and when they met, that would be the frontier.

'So the Sienese chose a handsome young cock, fed him well, gave him a bed of honour in church, just as they do with the Palio horses, and in general treated him well. But the Florentines took a scraggy old cock of many years' experience, dipped him in cold water and put him out on the roof. He had a sleepless night, and as soon as he saw the vaguest glimmer of dawn on the horizon he said, "I've had enough of Florence. I'm going to Siena."

'At about midday he met the other cock from Siena, looking very well and relaxed. The Sienese cock had woken up late, eaten a good breakfast, prayed a bit, and then started walking, hours after his rival. And that is why the frontier between Siena and Florence is so much closer to us than it is to them.'

Us . . . Them. Vittorio happened to tell me this in the bank, and there was no laughter, but a rustle of dour annoyance on the part of the audience. 'I'm all right up to Poggibonsi,' said one. 'After that, I'd rather not see any of them.'

Idly, on a bank slip I subtracted the date of the Sienese victory over Florence at Montaperti from the date on the calendar on the wall, and it came to more than 730 years. A long time to nourish rancour.

Dante thought very poorly of the Sienese. *Or fu giammai/Gente sì vana come la sanese?/Certo non la francesca sì d'assai.* [26] Meaning 'was there ever such a vain people as the Sienese? For sure, even the French are not as bad.' Vain in the double sense of both 'useless' and 'pleased with themselves', and as far as I can tell Florentines feel exactly the same way about the Sienese (and the French) to this day.

I have always found Siena difficult to penetrate. The obsession of the Sienese for the Palio makes them hermetic, exclusive. Or else the Palio itself is a symptom of some profound emotion that can only exist within the city walls. At any rate, with the Palio, the Sienese need nothing from the rest of the world.

The Palio is a horse-race run in Siena twice or occasionally three times a year around the Piazza del Campo, the principal square, which is beautifully packed with fine sand made of tufa so as to resemble, at least on the horses' trajectory, an open field. Part of the oddness of the spectacle, to the eyes of the non-initiated, lies in this contrast between the dense urban environment and the racing horses which one usually associates with the countryside.

Mattresses and bolsters pad the stone projections of the tighter corners. Horses fall, are ridden over. The race is violent and remarkably brief. A riderless horse can win. Horses get hurt frequently, are occasionally shot. The excitement the race inspires is totally beyond the comprehension of those in the audience who are not Sienese – Italians and foreigners alike.

This is not a race for money. There are no illegal side-bets, no gold cup or cash. It is a race between horses representing the different *contrade* of Siena for the honour of winning the *palio* itself, a long banner made each time by a different artist, the *palio* is then hung in an airless mausoleum of other banners on the ground floor of some *palazzo* belonging to the winning *contrada*. Indeed, winning the Palio is usually crippling for the victorious *contrada*, requiring bribes, costumes, processions, meals in the public streets together with your allies, including representatives of the enemies of the *contrada* which came second, which is apparently the real loser of the race.

'And so did your horse win? You look so happy.'

The girl behind the counter at the Co-op spoke slowly, as if to a congenital idiot.

'Signore,' she said, 'if my horse had won, I would not be here. I am happy because my enemy came second.'

She was very pretty, I thought. Her hair moved slowly in and out of itself, like a swarm of bees. And what is an ignorant unprepared stranger to make of such a remark? And if he sees a grown man walking the streets with a baby's dummy round his neck, how is he to infer that this means 'born again' – after a recent victory in the Palio?

The Palio grew from an attempt on the part of the city council to subdue civic riots, which occurred annually in the middle ages during the Carnival, just as they had done during Roman times. *Carnevale, quando ogni scherzo vale* – during Carnival, anything goes, says the motto. But in 1291 there were competitions or *gare* between rival *contrade* which left several dead in the street. Thereafter the list of what games were permitted shrank.

Not so many sticks and stones, but buffets or fisticuffs were allowed (*il giuoco di Pugna*). And chasing bulls or buffalo, jousts on horseback, gladiatorial combats, wild beasts.

The Palio is the sole survivor of a whole series of contests which in their prime must have been quite terrifying. Though probably the gentlest of these, the Palio today gives a brief but vivid idea of what life may have been like in the late middle ages. It is a privilege to live vicariously, even for a short while, in a period which is otherwise so remote.

The riots of 1291 occurred soon after the Sienese victory over Florence at Montaperti and her subsequent defeat at Colle Val d'Elsa – battles which must have left Siena in a state of high nervous tension. When antiquarians in the eighteenth century began to study the Palio, they stressed its martial background. The original division of the city was into three *terzi*, for defensive reasons, and the seventeen *contrade* which today compete in the Palio are subdivisions of these.

Pecci makes clear that the connection with ancient Roman Saturnalia was consciously cultivated from a very early date. The processions, the extraordinary clothes, even the equipment, stemmed from Roman precedents. He claims that the *macchina*, or chariot, which the *contrade* began to incorporate into their processions in the sixteenth century descended from the ancient litters that under the Empire were placed on the back of elephants.

Describing one of these, of the Contrada dell'Oca, he says, 'In 1650 they brought out a chariot carrying Glauco, the famous singer of Ptolemy of Egypt, who with her sweet song made a goose fall in love with her, and she was accompanied by many singers, players, and nymphs all beautifully dressed, for which they won a rich prize . . . The young men of this *contrada* have always made the best militia ever to serve the Republic.'[27]

The whole mood of these festivities is a mixture of the very serious and the ridiculous: a hundred young men dressed as nymphs, or the rivers of Germany, or shepherds, ancient Trojans, Mermen – but capable of taking up arms in a moment and fighting for real, if threatened by an external enemy.

The battles of Montaperti and Colle were followed by a long period in which Florence curtailed her rival, gradually restricting her access to the outside world. From time to time Siena attempted to break free. A moment of extreme drama occurred in 1555, when Siena was besieged by the Habsburg emperor Charles V.

Ostensibly the stakes were European rather than Tuscan. Siena was one small strategic pimple opposing the attempt of Charles V to unite all Europe into a single, Catholic, empire. But because Cosimo de' Medici was allied with Charles against Siena and the French, the old rivalry between the two Tuscan cities coloured the siege which followed.

The captain of the defenders was a professional French soldier called Blaise de Monluc, who late in life wrote an autobiography so interesting that it was subsequently called 'the soldier's Bible'. The siege of Siena occupies a large section of the book. This is his tribute to the women of Siena:

At the beginning of the fine resolution which this people made to defend their city, all the women of Siena divided themselves into three companies. The first under Signora Forteguerra, who was dressed in violet, as were the well-born ladies among her followers, and she herself wore the short dress of a nymph, which showed her short laced boots. The second was Signora Piccolomini, in red satin, and her peers likewise. The third was Signora Livia Fausti, all in white, as were her followers, with white banners, on which were inscribed many beautiful mottoes. I don't know what I would give to remember them now.

In other words, the ladies of Siena organized themselves just as they might have done in a slightly later period for a Palio. Armed with picks and shovels, their job was to buttress the main gates of the town with earth, against an eventual bombardment. As they marched, they sang songs in praise of the French king. Monluc wrote that he would 'give his best horse' to remember the words of these songs.[28]

During the siege a young tailor of Siena called Bernino made prisoner a handsome young Spaniard who was extremely fit. So he took him down to the Piazza del Campo, without his uniform, to join in a round dance (*ballo tondo*) – perhaps like the one danced by the German cavalry before Montaperti, or that depicted in the Lorenzetti fresco of *Good Government*, which is still today in the Palazzo Pubblico in Siena. And after that, a game of football. Others joined in, and eventually, 'quite naturally', it became a game of buffets.

By and by there were so many buffeting Sienese that they had to sound the call to arms to make them desist. All of which was observed by Monluc, who laughed so much 'at their courage' that the tears fell down his cheeks. As they dispersed, one of them said to him 'just think how we can give it to the enemy, when we give it to each other like this, and in the evening are friends again'.[29]

Much of these natural high spirits has been carried over into the Palio. Today its violence may be muted, but not always.

After a Palio a few years ago, I saw two fully armed Carabinieri walking rapidly towards the hospital. One was young, the other old, and by their accent they came from the south.

'So you see,' said the elder, 'we have to go to the hospital to prevent the jockey of the horse which came second from being beaten up by his own *contrada.*'

'But if he fell off at the first curve and has broken an arm and a leg already . . .?'

'Ah! But they are saying he did it on purpose.'

He shook his head incredulously. Such futile reasons for violence up here in the north! In the south, he seemed to imply, violence at least had a background of consequential logic.

I once met a Sienese gentleman who told me very cheerfully that his father had been killed by a punch in the liver received after the Palio.

'And he knew who did it,' said the gentleman, smiling. 'But of course he would never tell anyone, even as he lay on his deathbed. Not even me.'

Monluc and the French lost, and Siena fell to Charles V, from whom within a few years it devolved into the orbit of the Medici in Florence. But Cosimo I had the intelligence to allow Siena to keep all its institutions, limiting his control to foreign affairs, and perhaps to a discouragement of Sienese economic expansion. Within their walls, the Sienese could go on living more or less as before.

When Archduke Pietro Leopoldo wrote his account of the town two hundred years later, he made it clear that the lives of the aristocrats and upper merchant class were totally absorbed by acquiring and keeping various key positions in the magistrature and civic council, with frequently overlapping areas of jurisdiction, producing enough intrigues, bribes, rivalries, insults, family feuds, etc., to keep them all amused for decades on end. Just as under the Republic. And just like Florence.

In Florence the nobility is extremely ignorant, not studying or working at all, cultivating ease without culture or education and generally with little or no sense of honour. It tends to be arrogant towards the people and other classes, and towards segments of the lower classes, treating all with condescension, expecting not to pay manufacturers, treating servants badly . . . [These aristocrats] are proud and untrustworthy and believe that all Tuscany should be devoted solely to their own advantage and pleasure, as in the days of the Republic. And it is essential to abolish this tendency and to promote the development of the countryside, given that for a thousand reasons money flows from the country into the capital.[30]

There is a painting in the Pitti showing Maria Theresa of Austria surrounded by her numerous children, including Marie-Antoinette, the unfortunate future Queen of France, and Pietro Leopoldo, who for a long period ruled Tuscany. The silks are attractive, but otherwise the painting is dull. It inspires, however, a peculiar fantasy. Did she really instruct her infants, the kindly buxom mother, on all the mysteries of Absolute Monarchy? The need to centralize, to delegate to intelligent servants, preferably of a non-aristrocratic background? Love of law, the cultivation of industry, the need for an effective police? All while dangling her young upon her silken knee?

Pietro Leopoldo describes both his servants and his subjects with a cold and severe eye. Wherever he went, and he travelled all over Tuscany, he cut the social strata into clear divisions, usually finding fault with each. His writings are repetitious and contradictory, occasionally to the point of paranoia. After a while the two adjectives *ignorante* and *quiete* begin to stand out: 'ignorant', in the sense of rude and uneducated, and 'quiet', obedient, without fuss; good subjects.

The ideal he had in mind was a hardworking owner-farmer, perhaps like the yeomen–farmers or small landed gentry of England at that time. With persistent thoroughness he nourished this imagined future populace, using methods more familiar to our own century than his. He liberalized the buying and selling of land, sustained the wheat market, and encouraged the building of new farmsteads. Loans were available at the bank, if you wished to cultivate the land and build a model farm.

But loans, then as now, are more easily claimed by those who are already rich than by those who have nothing. And if, as he himself would have preferred, peasants obtained the investments, over ten years or so their credit would often be wiped out by a run of bad harvests, and the properties would revert to the big landowners who were able to sit out the bad times and buy them up for a song.

Tuscany in the eighteenth century provides an encapsulated model of the difficulties of the age. Intelligent and persistent attempts were made to bridge the gulf between an absolute ruler and the lowest level of society, but the result was that the small affluent castes in the centre became annually better off, and apparently more selfish.

The *Relazioni sul governo della Toscana* is without doubt one of the most extraordinary documents dealing with government in Europe in the eighteenth century. Pietro Leopoldo wrote it before he left to become emperor in Vienna, after ruling Tuscany for twenty-four years. One of its most absorbing qualities is the tone of voice, half as if thinking out loud for himself alone, half imparting advice to his imagined successor. It was never intended for publication, and is filed in Prague and Vienna under the laconic reference of *Familienarchiv* ('family matters'), as if all Tuscany had been his private estate.

Soon after he was called back to Vienna, to take charge of an over-extended empire threatened by the revolution in France, he died. In his writings, the image he leaves behind is in the end more personal and private than political. The second and third volumes of the *Relazioni* summarize every journey he made through the neglected countryside, every *pro memoria* he wrote to himself to arrange eventual improvements. Thin sections are cut through every aspect of local government, from the minister in lace and three-cornered hat to the farmer's oily and corrupt bailiff skulking in the hall, holding his cap in his fist.[31]

And the landscape we look out on can in many ways be said to be his. A landscape carved by hand.

South of Florence the eighteenth-century terraces begin as soon as the stone pierces the topsoil. Though some have been abandoned and others destroyed to make way for modern cultivation by machine, many are in remarkably good condition given the fact that they are supported by dry-stone walls two hundred years old.

The peasant families would build a terrace a year as one of the conditions for leasing a house. The terraces would be made parallel to the horizon, following the contours of the hills, starting at the bottom of a hillside, removing the forest and scrub oaks and pulling the earth down to the side of the new wall, which was made from the stones found right there in the ground. Vertical gullies at regular intervals ensured that the run-off would not cause erosion of the precious earth. It could take a decade to rebuild a hillside from the bottom to the top.

One can think of these fields as sculptures, carved by anonymous masters from the flank of the old woodlands, using the mattock and the pick. Sculptures or gardens, for gardening in the English sense has no tradition in Italy, depending as it does upon criteria which consciously blends agricultural and aesthetic priorities on a large scale. This occurred only in England with the emergence, in the eighteenth century, of a large class of 'gentlemen–farmers'. Such a class may have been the ideal of Pietro Leopoldo, but in Tuscany it never materialized.

And so the houses were built by largely absentee landlords

using the labour of the *contadini* who were later to occupy them. Behind this immense manual labour on the land and in construction lies a desperate rural population which, even as late as the eighteenth century, was still living in miserable lean-tos hidden in the woods. Pietro Leopoldo speaks indirectly of this force of casual labour, the poor, a caste of country people below the level of the *contadini*, and of whom we know very little.

The indistinct demarcation between builders and *contadini* makes it difficult to form a complete picture of how the farms were made. For example, I paint in a studio built within living memory, in about 1890, by a travelling mason whose hallmark was a round central column, which he alone used. He would live in the house of the *contadino* for whom he worked, and together they would collect stones and build the walls. To judge from the look of the building they built about a metre in height at a time, before going back to the little quarry in the wood for more stone. My barn apparently took a year. But the point is that this barn is stylistically dateless. Could be 1750, 1830, whenever. If I had not had access to an oral witness, how would I ever have established its background, or that of other barns dotted about the near hills, all made by this gifted, anonymous builder?

Contracts of *mezzadria* began soon after the Black Death of 1348, and were intended to provide guarantees to the peasants so that they would have some rights over the land they cultivated and the farm in which they lived. The word comes from '*mezzo*', meaning half, and the fluctuations in the relative sizes of these 'halves' provide a clue over the centuries as to who was in the stronger position, peasant or landowner. A century ago, the landowner received more than half; recently, much less. Either way, the system had grave limitations in a modern society. Each year the central *fattoria* of the landowner would be filled with a variety of produce from each little farm, creating difficulties in amalgamating a unified product for the market. The owners were always short of money for improvements, and of course if they lived away from the farm, they were often robbed by the bailiff or *fattore*.

Impossible to say if this civilization was economically viable. It survived, however, until the late 1960s, when a series of laws made sharecropping illegal. Our friendship with Vittorio Fosi allowed us to witness one of the very last phases in a relationship which was effectively more social than economic, and which may have gone back to Roman times.

I could not resist turning to the passage in the *Relazioni* where, in 1773, Pietro Leopoldo passed through my own neighbourhood. To my surprise the entry was very interesting.

At Ama, a little hamlet three miles away as the crow flies, he singled out three families as being

> the strongest in all Chianti. One of them having more than
> 30 *poderi* [small farms] with many storage buildings. These
> [families] are very rich, selling and sending all their wine to
> England. They give much work to the poor, they cultivate
> the land well, they are situated in the best part of Chianti
> for wine . . . Many [farms] are owned by Florentine gentle-
> men [*cavalieri fiorentini*] and there are many *contadini* who
> own their own land and are well off. [32]

Of the three families he mentions, one seems no longer to be living in the area, one has moved six miles and a branch of the third runs our local village shop, among other things. The big *fattoria* of Ama used to be owned by a retired lawyer. It is now a farm in the modern style, with large areas of terraceless vineyards ripe to be flushed by erosion to the bottom of the hill, and large new cellars full of lovely stainless-steel equipment.

Near by there lives one family which might be said to come under the category of *contadino*-owner, that rarity which was the ideal of Pietro Leopoldo. One of this family, Tullio, has worked with me on my olive trees, and a gentler or more experienced farmer it would be hard to find. But the kind of small-scale agriculture which Pietro Leopoldo thought would support a whole political class seldom pays, either now or then, and Tullio has to work on the land of others for a fee, as well as cultivating his own.

10 · SINALUNGA

I met Vittoria's great friend Chiara Paradiso in the library of an ornate *palazzo* in Siena, where the books were housed behind chicken-wire nailed within baroque screens. She talked of her research. From time to time a waiter passed by, offering small stuffed edibles set upon a silver tray, and occasionally we raised our faces to the other guests

It was not hard to sink back into the eighteenth century in such surroundings. Ceiling by Giulio Romano (school of), Sienese notaries passing through, their faces mild but slightly acidulous, like those of their bewigged ancestors in paintings on the wall.

Chiara told me of a room that she had discovered in her country house: by chance it had been kept sealed until her father had come across it in the 1950s. Manuscripts stacked against the wall, and in the corner a decayed spinet. The room in which a once-famous Sienese castrato called Il Senesino, Handel's favourite singer, had died.

Her shoulders were bare and her nose was sharp, and she was engaged in making lists of objects for a doctoral dissertation. It happens that I am fond of lists. Some of my finest moments, according to my admirers, have been spent in setting lists into chronological order. And she knew about paper, handwriting and the use of watermarks in dating. It was a pleasure to listen to such passion, and after a while I began to be curious about the material she described.

Soon afterwards she invited me out to the castle near Sinalunga. The appointment was at the unusual hour of two-thirty, 'to permit a morning's work in the library', she said.

I forgot lunch. The day was hot and the last five miles climbing out of the valley, where the fields turned to woodland, grated on my soul. The oaks appeared curved over themselves like claws grappling with the surface of the earth, and the scraggy fields shorn of wheat cauterized the eyes. To sooth myself, I imagined them carved in wood, using thin hard shadows to emphasize the shapes.

At the end of a long dirt road, the castle rose, black as a wood-cut against the shrieking sun. Two fingers of stone. Sighing, panting, I pulled up and looked up at the battlements with shaded eyes until I could discern the structure of the walls, in even layers like stacked bread. Underneath, a garden of roasted shrubs.

I was not expecting to bump into Vittoria when I arrived, and I was taken aback. I had somehow assumed she was on the island of Ponza for the summer.

'I was,' she said firmly, 'and now I am not.'

Chiara sniggered.

'We were all very happy and contented. It was very peaceful, everyone was very calm, we swam. We could even work a little. Then one afternoon Elisabetta rode her *motorino* down to the village, and ran into a cow. They were both hurt, the cow not very much, Elisabetta more. But for some reason this accident was very upsetting to all of us . . . Perhaps because it was the only cow on the island.'

Chiara sniggered some more.

'Why didn't you ring me when you got back?'

'But Matteo,' she said, 'I don't have to tell you everything about myself and my friends. With your permission . . .?'

Delighted, evidently. She linked arms with Chiara Paradiso. A small conspiracy against the token male.

We were walking among unpruned lemons in cracked pots set on small stands in a row, by a path of weedy gravel. Stunted box lined the path and rosemary took over the gaps in the garden wall.

'A long way,' I murmured politely to Signora Paradiso, 'to drive to Siena every morning.'

'Oh, but I don't live here. I only come here in order to sell the house,' said Chiara.

Another remark that begged a question. A huge wall reflected the heat back into the garden. They were definitely teasing me, enjoying my tense state. I looked up at twenty small windows, one open and a man's underpants hanging out.

'My father lives here,' said Chiara, 'but he tends to hide from visitors.'

'Are we disturbing him? I could leave . . .'

'No no! It's just that he owes such a lot of money . . . We try to sell it every year, and many people come to look, but no one buys. You can imagine. When you think what it would cost to restore a place like this.'

My head ached. The castle had bulbous turrets at each corner. From the armpits of the wonderfully unrestored roof sprung hairy grasses.

Chiara mentioned some Ghibelline ancestor, still further up the family tree than Il Senesino. I started talking about the thirteenth century, fast and squeakily.

'Of course, the valley between Florence and Arezzo was full of Ghibellines after the big towns had been taken over by the Guelfs. Somewhere near here the young man of "*la brigata Spendereccia*", the Sienese wastrel that Dante mentions, must have died, ambushed by the Aretines. I've always felt that he, with a name like that, was a relative of mine. After all, if you count a castrato among your forebears . . .'

'*Ma quanto sei 'struito,*' said Vittoria ironically – how filled to the brim I was with higher education. Except that the shortened adjective was usually applied to clever little boys on the front bench at school.

I was so willing to give them my historical interpolations, dazzle with my views on Dante, the hook-nosed bard of Florence. But they were immune to the charms of a hot amateur historian, and so I let them walk on a bit, among the sad statues and the withered trees of the garden.

I went to a well in the middle, where all the neglected paths met. Sat on its *pietra serena* rim, dropped a fragment into the hole. Pause. Thunk. The well was dry. Instantly the desiccated property acquired a desperate air.

Through a rusty gate closed with chain and padlock the Val di Chiana was hazily visible, with a few flashing pearls on the autostrada in the middle. Far away, in the direction of Arezzo, the Mountains of the Moon, the most beautiful mountains in the world.

The garden was better smelled than looked at. I closed my eyes to its scruffiness and sniffed deeply for the wild body-smell of cypress, the twiggy smell of rosemary in summer and the cool occasional whiff coming from the wood, smelling of nothing at all. The cicadas took up their themes within my head, and I dozed for a short while in the sun.

Sounds of a quarrel roused me. I got up, walked blinking through the bands of sunlight among the trees, skirted the castle on the right-hand side and found the door of a brick baroque chapel leaning against the buttocks of a tower.

The voices came from inside. One deep, two chirrupy.

The chapel was in bad condition, its stucco reduced to fine rubble around the skirting, the altar casually propped with boards and an old curtain hooked across the door into the sacristy. The door-frame was of carved chestnut, the door itself missing.

On the far side, Chiara and Vittoria were looking at a hole in the ground, rimmed with stone, and talking to a contrite *contadino*. Vittoria suddenly knelt on the ground and put her head inside.

Chiara said to the peasant, 'I thought we had got rid of them all.'

'*O Signora*, the ones which were buried in the garden have all been given back to the bishop, but truly I had forgotten about these.'

'Forgotten! But these were the ones which had at all costs to be removed! The ones in the garden were fine, weren't doing any harm to anyone.'

They were talking about dead monks.

'*Veramente, Signora,*' said the *contadino*, amused, 'these ones are not likely to annoy anybody either, in the state they are in!'

I was beyond human company; I was even unamused by the idea, which strikes me now as very funny, that a sixteenth-century cemetery of dead monastics had to be evicted to make way for drains before a potential buyer would look at the place.

'Who knows,' said Vittoria, her voice booming from beneath the earth, 'there may be some saint down here.'

'There was one in the chapel,' said Chiara, 'but we gave him to Baron Ricasoli.'

'Why?' I asked.

She shrugged. 'He was a Ricasoli as well as a saint.'

I left them and entered the cool lower level of the castle through a small door, stumbling over the threshold.

It took me a while to get used to the darkness. At length I saw a staircase going upwards, behind a horse-drawn carriage which had been parked fifty years ago and left there ever since. The outside walls were so huge that the place felt cramped and claustrophobic.

On the first floor an imperial *salotto*, sitting-room, optimistic-ally promised a series of generations that would sit together over the years, in patriarchal unity. Some of the ornate picture frames now held photographs from the 1950s, babes on the beach smiling at sand, incongruously facing an ugly oil-painting of great-grandmother opposite. The frescos, done with glue, were peeling.

I went on upstairs uninvited. The voices from outside became inaudible. I had the feeling of ascending a fortress in the sky.

Up under the roof was a dark corridor not much used, with doors on either side. On the floor, a glove. I picked it up. It was of faded silk, with lace and seed-pearls at the wrist. The hand was remarkably small.

I listened, but could hear nothing beyond the seething undertow of cicadas in the woods outside. I had no business to be up there. I opened the nearest door.

A thin crack in the shutters illuminated the spinet over by the window. The instrument was as healthy and inspiring as the shell of a lobster that has just been eaten – a rubbishy thing of ivory and red wire and discarded feelers.

I caught sight of a glass cabinet in the corner by the other window. I tried it, but it was locked. The top three shelves were filled with portfolios of old manuscript paper – it was hard to guess the date. The bottom shelf had some glass beads, a wooden crucifix and some broadsheets in English. An eighteenth-century caricature of fat men in wigs was pinned at the back, its water-colour faded to sepia. By it, a photo of a painting of the singer himself, Francesco Bernardi, all spit curls and plumptitude. Handel's great discovery, making a fine career for both of them for a while. A singing piglet, adored by the ladies because untouchable. What safer love-object could a gentlewoman have in London in the 1730s?

Did Il Senesino pine for his native Siena? No, there was no

sentimentality in him. The Tuscans are immune to nostalgia, are born unsqueamish about the past; it is one of the nicest things about them. He quarrelled with Handel about money, and went over the road to work with Niccola Porpora. Retired after ten years in London with fifteen thousand florins, a fortune in those days, and lived thereafter in Sinalunga with his spinet and Paolo Rolli, his friend. Leaving the lamenting ladies to rot in their sodden clime without him.

I left the room softly after closing the shutters. I felt I would just rest a moment, think a bit, avoid Vittoria in her conniving mood. So I sat uncomfortably on the tiles of the landing, neither in nor out, neither up nor down, and allowed the day's accumulated gloom to seep upwards through the fortress.

Thinking of Il Senesino led me to think about exile. Exile by force, exile by choice – *fuoriusciti*, such as the Ghibellines for whom this castle had originally been built.

I remembered that on a railway siding in upstate New York, Maro had once shouted out, 'Where are the Etruscan tombs?'

And when faces turned to her, apprehensively, she added more softly, 'I refuse to live anywhere where there are no Etruscan tombs.'

Madness in America is to be avoided, so the others on the platform turned away. Only I return to this image from time to time with sympathy, as the various layers of exile unfold their petals to me with the passing years.

For her, the Etruscan tombs are tangible symbols for an air that has been thoroughly breathed, passed through many lungs, and dirt that has been leavened in pleasure and in pain by human bones. This is something she can brood about as she scrabbles in earth with bare hands in the spring. Any part of the world that has these qualities for her is liveable. She carries her native land with her as she moves.

For Maro, in this suffering world each individual should

listen for a stronger pulse than that of some group supposedly mapped out by race. The extended family, acquired friends, the haphazard election of blood relationships. But beyond these gifts of luck, to which one must be as loyal as possible, she recognizes no other unit save the sum totality of man. You belong by chance, by love to a group of fifteen, twenty people, or else you are of the world. And so, down with ethnic minorities, with their insufferable demands.

High on the list of this mayhem of turbulent races, the English, all the more an ethnic minority for not being even minimally aware of the fact. And I of the tribe of the English, what voice can I raise in their defence?

Brothers, there have been moments in a foreign land, in a coke-sodden backyard in Szechwan, when I have smelled the Londonish smell of my childhood (prior to the Clean Air Act of 1959) and tears have rolled down my nose. Times when slumped in front of the fire late at night, in the guts of a red settee purchased in the Church Street market in 1966, that I have leafed through the London *A to Z* and pined for London. Unable to focus as I fumble, I have searched in the grounds of the gasworks on the map for the Viking graves which, to me, are honorary Etruscan. With bitten fingernail I have traced the passage of the Grand Union Canal (Paddington Branch), blearily, from page to page.

My wife travels free. I travel with a bleeding piece of earth that is for ever Hampstead.

Without thinking I found that I had been staring at the lost pearl and lace glove on the floor. I rose, returned to the room of the long dead singer, and placed the glove on the keyboard of the spinet, groping for an empty chord.

It occurred to me that there might have been some conspiracy between the two distinguished research assistants, in having me see all this material. One never knows what is coincidence, and what is not, does one? For some reason my good humour returned at this idea, partly brought by a cool wind that blew in at last over the hillside as the day waned.

And so I took the pair of them out to the nearby village for supper, where we drank wine and watched the sun sink below the sea, over above Viareggio as a bird might fly.

11 · MONTAPERTI

An undertow of violence is one of the more disturbing features of the *Inferno* of Dante, and adds to its extraordinary atmosphere of anxiety.

It is not clear exactly how much of this violence stemmed from Dante's own experience. He hints that he took part in the siege of a castle near Pisa, fought in the battle of Campaldino and perhaps also took part in one of the raids mounted by the Florentines and Sienese against the Aretines in the late thirteenth century.

> I have seen horsemen moving camp
> > Start an attack, dress ranks
> > And sometimes ride out on a raid:
> I have seen the skirmishers deep among your fields, Aretines;
> > Seen the movement of the plunderers:
> > Seen jousts and tournaments,
> Now to the sound of the trumpet, now to the deep bell,
> > Clashing cymbals, the signal fires lit,
> > With all the harsh sounds possible, both strange and
> > > familiar. [33]

Every devil or monster in Dante seems to stem from some trace memory of a frightening experience in our own world. Behind the centaurs described in Canto XII, for instance, sent to supervise the violent who are immersed in a lake of blood, there seems to lie an unpleasant memory from Dante's own life, the experience of being jostled by some knight on horseback, the knight unpredictable and hostile, the horse fidgety, liable to step on your toes:

> Around the ditch they rode in their thousands
>> Watching for that soul who might protrude
>> From the blood further than his sin permitted.
> We approached those lithe beasts, and Chiron
>> Took an arrow, and with the notch
>> Combed back his beard behind his jaws.
> When he had freed his great mouth, he said to his
>>> companions,
>> 'Have you seen how the one that stands behind
>> Moves the things he touches?
> That is not usual for the feet of the dead'. [34]

Perhaps Dante himself had participated in the bullying of defenceless people:

> The devils all stepped forward, and I thought
> They would not hold by their assured safe conduct
> I have seen such fear in the soldiers
>> Who surrendered under guarantee at Caprona
>> Seeing themselves surrounded by a fierce foe. [35]

Actual violence in the *Inferno* is neither vindictive nor clearly intended to inspire moral awe, but is simply a fact to do with the place. Perhaps the presence of so much nastiness was an accepted part of the background of early-fourteenth-century Tuscany.

At any given moment between the twelfth century and 1530, when the Medici were restored after the fall of the Florentine Republic, a Tuscan town would be engaged in two simultaneous and interacting struggles. The first was that of retaining its independence and imposing its will on its immediate neighbours; the second, that of settling which of the various distinct oligarchies should rule within its walls.

These two struggles would occasionally be punctuated by a third, when a particular emperor or pope would remind Tuscany that larger political units existed, such as the states north and south of Tuscany, or Italy, or even Christendom. When this occurred, the already complex interaction of various dramas within and without the gates of each city would be compounded, usually with horrible results.

The terms Guelf and Ghibelline – how do they come in? Well, they derive from the German *Welf* and *Wieblingen*, and (to make a gross simplification) they signify opposite sides in a perennial struggle within Germany as to whether that country should look south or east for its foreign ambitions. In Italy, Ghibelline came to mean a supporter of the German emperor and Guelf meant a supporter of the pope. This eventually divided the old feudal aristocrats on the Ghibelline side from the new bankers, who were supporters of the pope and the French commercial interests, on the side of the Guelfs.

Because of this tension between bankers and declining landed aristocrats, some historians explain Florentine politics from Dante onwards in terms of class struggle, involving these two groups plus, now and again, the *popolo minuto*, who would rise up and kick out both. It would be nice if the scenario were so simple – especially the last feature, with the imagined shadow of an early guillotine in the Piazza della Signoria. The big guilds who represented the *popolo minuto*, however, embodied only a fragment of the 'urban poor' (if we are going to use these terms), and in fact it was almost as difficult to obtain and retain membership of a guild as it was to join the other social groups. If there has to be a generalization about the intrigues which resulted, a feud between three rival oligarchies or closed groups would be a better simplification than class war.[36]

Blurring the boundaries between the other two classes was the fact that some aristocrats married into banking families, some bankers bought land outside the towns and therefore effectively became aristocratic in sentiment, and so on. We do not yet know in detail how the families of the time were interrelated. What power groups were formed. And even if we could find out these interesting things, there would remain the likelihood that Tuscany, then as now, functioned through small personal power groups, the *gens*, which transcended the social barriers of class and family, otherwise so claustrophobically restrictive.

A hot wind dries out the shrubs outside my window, sends vine leaves, prematurely shrivelled, into eddies that gather in the corners of the garden walls. I look south over a dry landscape towards the hills that lie between Siena and Monte Amiata, halfway to Rome. I can see for many miles, but a small green wood shields me from the battlefield of Montaperti.

Go into any bank near Siena and there are three subjects it is advisable to avoid. Killing wild pigs, the Palio and the battle of Montaperti. Merely graze these subjects and the teller is liable to down stubs and cover the subject exhaustively, however long the queue accumulating behind you.

The battle of Montaperti in 1260 was a colossal and unexpected victory for the Sienese over the Florentines. It was also a victory of the Ghibellines over the Guelfs, since at that time Siena was Ghibelline. The fact that within ten years this victory was reversed has done nothing, over the years, to quench the Sienese enthusiasm for having once in their history thoroughly thrashed the Florentines.

The core of the dispute was essentially Siena's access to the outside world. Siena was and is a remote town. To the north the route to the Val d'Arno lies along the Elsa and the Era valleys, via Colle Val d'Elsa and Poggibonsi. To the east is the road to Arezzo; the road to the south-east is dominated by Montalcino and Montepulciano. To the south-west, Grosseto is Siena's only viable port on the Tyrrhenian Sea. All these towns were fought over in the sixty years before Montaperti, in some cases two or three times.

In July 1254 the Sienese, feeling that they were unlikely to obtain outside help and having lost a few battles with the Florentines over Montepulciano and Montalcino, made a disadvantageous peace. One of the ambassadors who drew up the document was Provenzano Salvani, a leading Sienese aristocrat. Siena agreed not to take in any political exiles from Florence, but when in 1258 the Guelf party kicked the Ghibellines out of Florence, they were instantly welcomed in Siena.

The following year Manfred, son of the last great Hohenstaufen emperor, Frederick II, was crowned King of Sicily, and at that point the natural rivalries of Siena and Florence were overshadowed by the political struggles of the whole peninsula. Manfred's problem was to create a firm line of communication between his possessions in Sicily and those in south Germany. He therefore accepted a Sienese request for assistance, and sent them some German knights, at that time the most powerful cavalry in Europe.

Florentine chronicles suggest that the prime mover behind this alliance was an exiled Florentine Ghibelline called Farinata degli Uberti, who was given an imperial banner by King Manfred; yet Sienese sources claim that Provenzano Salvani was the leading figure in the embassy to Manfred. The knights were commanded by Giordano d'Anglano, Manfred's cousin. Much of what followed depended on the interaction of these three men, each pursuing a very different policy: the Ghibelline exile Farinata degli Uberti, whom Dante portrays as an arrogant and indomitable old aristocrat, continuing his private feud with Florence; Provenzano Salvani, who gradually rose to rule in Siena, partly as a result of his skill during the Montaperti campaign; and Giordano d'Anglano, the German seneschal sent by Manfred to protect the Hohenstaufen interest in Tuscany.

In mid April a vast force of Florentines, which the chroniclers number at thirty thousand – far greater than anything the Sienese could muster and comprising at least one man for each household – set out for Siena, taking Casole d'Elsa and Mensano on the way. They made their way slowly to Siena and camped outside the Porta Camollia, the gate nearest to Florence.

Ten days later Farinata and the German knights, who had had ample time to return to Siena from their fronts south and east of the city, made a sudden sortie. The Florentine forces rallied and the German knights were forced back to the walls, losing the banner bestowed by King Manfred in the process. In one of the Florentine chronicles there is the interesting suggestion that Farinata lost the flag on purpose, to force Manfred to redeem it with some aggressive military riposte. The Florentine army retreated, proclaiming victory and dragging the famous banner in the dust through the streets of Florence.

Manfred sent eight hundred knights as reinforcements, but leased to the city of Siena for three months only, cash on the nail. This fact of course was instantly known in Florence. The problem now became technical. The Sienese had to fight a victorious engagement within a three-month period, and to achieve this, Villani, the Florentine chronicler, suggests Farinata degli Uberti invented a *ruse de guerre*. Two renegade monks were sent from Siena to Florence, so this story goes, to say that there was great friction between Provenzano Salvani and the other leaders, and that if the Florentine army came to the east gate of Siena, Salvani would open it, as he preferred to be ruled by the Florentines than by any Sienese rival.

The Florentine Council listened to the extremely plausible monks and discussed their next move. One of the few who suggested delaying until the German force returned home was Tegghiaio Aldobrandi, who is mentioned early in the *Inferno* in association with Farinata, implying there was a bond between them. (Which is odd, as one was Ghibelline and the other Guelf.)

In early June the Sienese forces engaged in energetic and successful attacks on Poggibonsi and Montemassi, a castle in the Maremma ably defended by one Aldobrandino il Rosso of Pitigliano. They also attacked Montepulciano. Provoked by all this military initiative on the part of the Sienese, the Florentine army moved out against them once more.

I feel momentarily exhausted at the prospect of so much blood, even if it is only to be shed on paper. Outside my window the air is sweet and clear. The vineyards of stencilled viridian end firmly in the middle distance and above them, much further off, are the hills on the other side of Montaperti. The wheat has already been shorn here and there. Even at ten miles, the edge of each field is discernible. They fit together like a jigsaw laid flat, bleached and twisted by years of exposure, the design obscured. When the wheat is all in, the stubble will be fired, and feathers of smoke will send up dark plumes against the distant clay.

The Florentine army made its usual slow progress and camped at Pieve Asciata, a hamlet which used to be a key post on the old Roman road, perhaps even the Etruscan road before that.

(A mile from where I sit, it is where I take the ploughshare when it buckles, so that Mauro can hammer it out again.) Here would be the first real sight of Siena on this route. There the army rested, early in September 1260, sending out an embassy to Siena merely to reiterate its imminent destruction. 'The walls must be destroyed here and here,' they said, 'so that our army can pass freely through. We shall establish Florentine supervisors for every *terzo* of your city. What answer do you give to that?'

Apprehensive, the Siena Council met in the church of San Cristoforo. One timid councillor suggested giving in to the Florentine demands. Playing for time, Provenzano Salvani sent for Giordano, representative of King Manfred and leader of the German contingent. He arrived with a number of his knights and an interpreter, for this German with an Italian name spoke no Italian.

Giordano said that there was no question of giving in. Of course they would fight. That was what they were paid for. A tactful pause followed this, while the Council realized it had no money. Then a banker called Salimbene Salimbeni rose and offered the loan of the entire sum to the city, whatever it might be. Much calculation followed: last month, this month and, as a gesture, next month twice over. Salimbeni went home, placed 118,000 florins on a cart, covered it with a crimson cloth and wheeled it through the streets. The Florentine ambassadors were called in to see the heap of money, the most effective way of demonstrating that the Sienese were now sure of their cavalry.

In fact the cash quickly returned to the city. The German knights bought all the available shoe-leather in the town to make armour for themselves and their horses. A moment of intense activity followed, all the artisans eager to help the gallant strangers. (The German contingent, incidentally, had had to be segregated from the rest of the town, to ease racial tensions.)

A solemn procession paraded through the city, the new mayor providing an example for all by removing hat, shoes, everything but his shirt. Within the Duomo, before a vast crowd, he prostrated himself in front of the bishop, was raised up by him, kissed. The bishop urged the congregation to reconcile all personal feuds at this dramatic moment of the city's history.

Next day the holy images were removed from the churches – the wooden cross with Christ carved in bas-relief from San Giacomo, the portrait of the Virgin from the Duomo. The mayor pledged the city to the protection of the Madonna. When this ceremony was finished, every man reported to his own *Gonfaloniere*, in the *terzo* of the city from which he came, and the army marched out, cavalry first, then the war cart, or *Carroccio*, swathed in white, then the *Gonfalonieri* and the soldiers – or rather all the men of Siena between the ages of sixteen and sixty.

The Florentines had moved off in the direction of Montalcino, but were still near the east gate of Siena from which the betrayal by Provenzano Salvani was supposed to come. They camped between two streams, the Biena and the Malena, in a plain called Le Cortine, about seven miles from the city. There the Sienese army caught up with them and camped opposite. No attempt seems to have been made to take strategic advantage of the lie of the land, but during the night the Sienese made occasional raids on the Florentines, to keep them from sleeping.

The Sienese army rose before dawn. They were facing east, with the sun about to rise in their eyes; so much the worse for the Florentines in the late afternoon. A group of about two hundred Germans was sent off to the right, along one of the streams for an eventual flanking movement.

The Florentines looking west saw the Sienese army shrouded in a strange white mist – 'the Mantle of the Madonna', as the

Sienese chroniclers later put it. One Florentine captain mentioned that a fortune-teller had told him he would die 'between good and evil', and as the names Biena and Malena could be interpreted as such, could the army move off a bit?

Giordano's seneschal, Arrigo, was authorized to lead the charge with his troops, whereupon his young nephew Gualtiero begged for the privilege of riding out in front. Reluctant to risk the life of his sister's young son, Arrigo only relented when one by one the other knights sank to their knees, pleading in his favour 'with tears on their cheeks'. So Gualtiero rode out 'a crossbow shot ahead', with his new leather armour and his chain-mail, under a red tunic embroidered with green dragons and flames of gold thread.

As the mist lifted both sides became aware of a low hill dominating the scene, and made for it simultaneously. The battle started soon after dawn.

The chronicles give the impression of a heroic or even Homeric fight, with champions seeking each other out to pursue individual duels against a background of mayhem among the ranks. Thus the young Gualtiero slew Niccolò Garzoni, captain of the Lucchesi. Arrigo, his uncle, slew the captain of the contingent from Prato. With his lance, Giordano killed Donatello, captain of the Aretines, 'and the green grass became his bed'. When his lance was broken, Giordano drew his sword, 'and he never missed a stroke, nor gave two strokes for one, and for every stroke a limb fell to the ground'.

Arrigo slew Sinibaldo, captain of the allies of the Florentines from Orvieto. And when his lance broke, he drew his two-handed sword and 'sad was he who met him there'. And Niccolò Bigozzi, seneschal of the Sienese, attacked and wounded Aldobrandino il Rosso, of Pitigliano, the Sienese Guelf aristocrat last seen defending the castle of Montemassi the year before.

And the Florentines?

Sometime towards midday the Count d'Arras launched the long-awaited flanking movement straight at the heart of the Florentine army, killing Uberto Ghibellino, the rather improbably named captain of the Florentine knights. After this, chaos. The Florentines ceased to be able to defend themselves and the Sienese foot soldiers went mad. They 'slaughtered more than butchers do on Good Friday'. Nor were the professionals, the German knights, able to make them grant quarter until towards the end of the day, and then perhaps only because of their exhaustion.

At some point during the flank attack there must have occurred that act of betrayal by which, according to the Florentine chroniclers, the day was lost. The Florentine cavalry were all old aristocrats, as horsemen often are. A Ghibelline exile fighting on the Sienese side suddenly noticed that numerous friends and relatives were opposite him, and 'it was not difficult to make them change sides'.[37] Seeing which, Bocca degli Abati, in the vanguard of the Florentine cavalry, raised his sword and brought it down on the wrist of the standard-bearer, Jacopo Nacca de' Pazzi. Down went the flag, down its bearer and down the morale of the Florentine army, down among the dead men.

'Like dragons the Sienese fell upon the stunned Florentines. And the Malena was so flushed with blood, and it flowed so fast, that it would have sufficed to run four flour-mills, there was so much of it, from the Florentines and their allies . . .'

And down, to the very lowest depths of Hell, eventually went Bocca degli Abati, when Dante came to write about him, to the worst of all punishments — to be embedded up to the neck in the great desert of ice.

The Ghibelline exiles of all Tuscany met at Empoli and discussed what should be done to follow up this extraordinary victory. It went without saying that the Guelfs would be exiled and the Ghibellines would take over the government in every town in Tuscany. It is possible that the suggestion was put forward, perhaps by Provenzano Salvani, that Florence itself should be destroyed. The Florentine chroniclers thought so. The town was saved, according to them – and according to Dante – by Farinata degli Uberti, who gave a noble speech in the city's defence. Bocca degli Abati walked out of the meeting in protest.

Within a few short years the gains of Montaperti were irrevocably lost. In order to counter the threat from King Manfred in the south, who was greatly encouraged by finding Tuscany now entirely Ghibelline, the pope invited Charles of Anjou to take the crown of Sicily, thereby initiating the presence of France in Italy as a counterweight to that of Germany. Manfred was defeated and killed at Benevento. (The Florentine Guelfs sent four hundred knights down to fight against him in the battle.) His young half-brother Conradino came down from Germany to try yet one more expedition to claim the old Hohenstaufen kingdoms in the south, was defeated at Tagliacozzo and beheaded soon after in the market-place of Naples.

With French assistance, the Guelfs were soon reinstated in Tuscany. They also obtained some commercial privileges in the south of France which turned out in the long run to be an important new trade route.

Last but not least, the Sienese were defeated at Colle Val d'Elsa in 1269, in a confused but definitive battle, following which Provenzano Salvani was executed.

After the battle of Colle, Siena and Florence for a while achieved some sort of equilibrium. Looking slightly harder at the map, the Florentines realized that they risked very little if the Sienese sphere of influence extended south and west to the sea down at Grosseto, and east to the Val di Chiana, near

Arezzo. In fact the Sienese succeeded in deflecting Florentine attention away from themselves and towards Arezzo, partly because the Valdarno and Val di Chiana down to Sinalunga remained for years a stronghold of the Ghibelline exiles. The two cities participated in raids into Aretine territory, in one of which Dante may have taken part.

When Virgil and Dante finally penetrate the city of Dis, they find themselves in a large circular plain running just inside the walls, filled with an endless series of partially open tombs, each one a seething furnace. The air is filled with the lamentation of those being burned within. This, the sixth circle, is composed of heretics of various sects, each carefully segregated according to his particular creed, both in number and kind being many more, says Virgil, than Dante could imagine ever having existed. [38]

Making their way with some difficulty among this orderly chaos of sepulchres, they come across the tomb of Farinata degli Uberti, the tenacious old Ghibelline captain. The lid of his tomb is thrown back, and flames fly upwards about his body. He sits bolt upright with an expression of extraordinary arrogance on his face, *'come avesse lo inferno in gran dispitto'* – 'as if he utterly despised Hell'. [39]

Why Farinata should find himself in this place, among the heretics and atheists, is one of the knottiest problems of the *Inferno*. According to the Florentine chroniclers, it was the intrigues of Farinata alone which led directly to the defeat of Montaperti. It was he who was the arch-traitor, whose family was subsequently hunted down and exterminated in revenge, including two infant grandsons. He was far more responsible for the defeat than Bocca degli Abati, for instance, whose fate in Dante's cosmography was much worse.

Vivid though the description of Farinata may be, the reasons why Dante placed him among the heretics are vague. Heresy, in the circumstances, was surely not his worst vice. Arrogance and a disbelief in the immortality of the soul were generically attributed to all the old Ghibelline aristocrats, so that (as it were) 'you stuck-up old atheist' might have been a normal insult yelled in the streets of Florence in Dante's time – meaning no more than 'there goes another Ghibelline'.

One explanation for Dante's clemency towards Farinata lies in the fact that at the Council of Empoli following the battle of Montaperti, Farinata opposed the proposed destruction of Florence – much to the disgust of Bocca degli Abati. To have saved Florence was a strong reason for treating Farinata with comparative sympathy. But there is also the fact that, politically, Dante moved further towards the Ghibelline position while writing the *Commedia*, or at least towards the conviction that only a divine monarchy could save the Tuscan towns from mutual destruction.

But there was also a private, personal bond that linked Dante to Farinata. They shared the brutal experience of exile from Florence, and exile, to Dante, was a terrible thing. This is the subject the two of them discuss in their brief conversation among the flaming tombs, with Farinata prophesying that soon Dante will see for himself 'how heavily lies that condemnation'.[40] Exile, that virulent fuel without which Dante would never have written the *Commedia*, and would have remained just another highly educated acerbic Florentine politician – of which there were and still are dozens.

Bocca degli Abati on the other hand was thrown down to the lowest of the low. Almost alone among the inhabitants of Hell, he provokes an actual physical assault at the hands of Dante:

Montaperti

I saw a thousand faces rendered dog-like by the bitter cold
   I still shiver if they come to mind, and always shall,
   Remembering that vast expanse of frozen river-mouth.
And as we walked towards the centre of the earth
   That must attract all things that fall,
   And I, trembling in the eternal cold,
Either by will, or fate, or chance, I do not know,
   But as we passed among those heads
   Violently I kicked the face of one imprisoned there.
Weeping he cried out, 'Why kick me thus?
   Unless you have come to heap revenge upon
   The field of Montaperti, why hurt me so?'
And I – 'My Master, wait here for me a little while
   So I can settle the doubts this man has raised in me
   And later we shall hurry onward, fast as you may wish.'
My guide paused; I turned to face the man
   Who still lay cursing harshly there.
   'Who are you that thus reproves his neighbour?'
'And who are you, walking the lower depths of Hell,'
   He said, 'kicking the cheeks of others?
   If I were alive, I'd give you blow for blow.'
'I am alive, and could be dear to you,'
   Was my reply; 'if you seek fame
   I could include your name among my other observations.'
He replied, 'I seek the opposite!
   Move off and bother me no more.
   Your flattery cannot hold in this precipitous place.'
So then I took him by the hair
   And said, 'Tell me who you are
   Or not one lock will remain up here.'
He replied, 'Were you to tear out all my hair
   I'd neither tell you who I am, nor show my face
   Even if you heaped a thousand curses on my head.'

Round my fingers I had twisted hanks of hair,
  Pulled out more than a handful
  And he, howling, with his eyes fixed firmly down,
When another shouted, 'What's up with you, Bocca?
  Is it not enough to clatter your jawbones in the cold
  That you must howl also? What devil tortures you?'
'No need,' I said, 'to tell me further lies,
  Horrible traitor, for I'll carry back
  True news of you, and of your shame.'
'Go,' he said, 'and give whatever account you like . . .'[41]

Alone of all the sufferers in Hell, Dante subjects Bocca to his own personal revenge, by kicking him in the face and pulling out his hair. But then the moment when Bocca degli Abati cut off the hand from the Florentine standard-bearer crystallized, in Dante's eyes, into a single image the sum of all the social evils of his age. The whole of the *Inferno* revolves around the fiery political conviction that chaos, disorder, discord, were the worst evils of all. Treacher, betrayal, deceit, are merely component parts of that greatest evil, discord.

Compared with the two great Florentine villains, Provenzano Salvani has a somewhat muted part in the *Divine Comedy*. His restless figure is seen briefly and indirectly, in Purgatory.

In fact the lack of definition in portraying Salvani raises a question about the others: how well did Dante himself know them? Not personally, for sure, as he had been born five years after Montaperti, and by the time he was old enough to register their existence all these heroes were dead.

The tradition nevertheless would still have been a live one, so that Dante might have retained an impression rather like the one which a sensitive European born in 1950 today retains of the Second World War. Moreover Dante possessed a direct family association with the battle of Montaperti. One of the 152 picked guards of the Florentine *Carroccio* – a lumbering and useless vehicle, but its retention or capture symbolized victory or defeat – was one of Dante's uncles, Brunetto.

We know nothing more about the man than this (and even then his name might actually have been Burnetto). But if he survived the battle, he might have been the source of Dante's extraordinarily precise view of Farinata and his passionate rage against Bocca. Dante's view of Farinata may be hieratic, but it is also quite personal, a physical presence being palpably there. His view of Bocca – unless I am being too romantic – contains all the bitterness of a betrayed soldier who actually saw the hand cut off, the flag go down, and the Florentine army turn into a river of human blood.

The day after the July Palio, after a confused night of dreams where heroism was revealed in blurred footnotes of a Latin text I could not read, I went to the battlefield of Montaperti, anxious to settle one final point.

I pass by the actual battlefield every week, to reach the Superstrada that runs through the middle of it, linking Siena to Perugia. But it is some time since I have stopped the car in order to walk about the battlefield, thinking of Farinata and all the others.

Up on the right, there is a flock of neat brick flats for office-workers from Siena, looking like well-scrubbed paintings by Simone Martini. It is rumoured that the flats were built by Aldo Moro, Italy's only honest politician – so cruelly extinguished by madmen of the extreme left – using a friend as a front.

Four miles along the motorway a nice old man told me that Le Cortine, the site of the battle according to the chronicles, is the name of a group of houses and, more generically, of the entire valley which stretched back towards Siena. Observing this brought me one meagre illumination. If the armies stuck to the ground between the two little rivers of the Biena and the Malena, they had chosen the only flat expanse for miles around.

I retraced my journey slowly, to park the car at last near where the Malena seemed to join the river Arbia. A whiff of sulphur came to me as I rested there by the side of the road. It occurred to me that the name Malena might be inspired by the whiffiness of this fetid stream.

A kind of beauty-sodden gloom overcame me, like the depression which once felled me when we were driving along the Danube valley towards the concentration camp of Mauthausen, making me forgo our visit to that pinnacle of twentieth-century civilization. I felt a horror indistinguishable from panic, that such wonderful landscape should have been used by human beings for such vile ends, as if intentionally seeking the absolute calm of green fields as the most appropriate background for corpses.

And as I wilted there in the twilight, the epitome of an intellectual grappling with the problem of violent death, a rat came out of the field of fresh maize and stared at me. Not a nice domestic rat, like the *capofamiglia* of the small family that makes its nest in the cellar among the unsold paintings, but a giant rat, a rat on the scale of a Gothic horror movie, an *Ur*-rat to make you rub both eyes, shake out the scrambled membrane of the Waste Land from the skull and say, God's teeth, this is *the* rat.

Two foot at least off the ground, a face like a Chinese pug and hands like a monkey, this beast did not need to hurry out of range. He gave a sort of nod and looked at me. His twinkling eye, I noticed, was about the size of my own.

He turned on his man-slaughtering thighs and reared up, to give a proprietory look at the maize, as if estimating the size of the crop in terms of hungry rodent mouths. A paradise indeed of future meals. His tail was fat and inelastic, looking like a businessman's furled brolly sewn to his jacket. His coat was as sleek and as shiny as if he had been recently dipped in pitch.

In the spring I read as much of the *Inferno* as I can manage, before the sweet warm air travelling over the light green woods makes it impossible to remain indoors any longer. And so chasing the origin of this rat was in a sense the last small footnote to this year's reading. The garbage department of Siena gave me the answer: this was a South American muskrat, escaped from a fur factory which had gone bankrupt in the 1970s. Immune to poison, wise to the gleam of an approaching twelve-bore, he and his many relations had proved so far ineradicable. The revenge of a rabid ecologist, serving right those who assume that this world is ours to command, as Minos, in Dante, commands in Hell.

Complacent in his usurping possession of a field of ripening corn near Montaperti, the rat turned his back on me and slipped quietly through the brown air, between two imagined graves.

12 · POGGIO A CAIANO

Finding the telephone number of an institution can be difficult. The Villa Reale di Poggio a Caiano was not under its initial letters, nor under I for *Istituto*, nor under M for *Museo*. Finally I spoke to a desk clerk at S for *Sovvrintendenza* (a man of unspeakable slowness) who gave me the number. And when I called, they said yes they were open all day and no they did not go to the seaside in the afternoon like everyone else.

I picked Vittoria up at La Certosa, the motorway exit on the periphery of Florence where much seems always to be happening in the way of parked cars, intrigues or negotiations through half-open windows with the young ladies who stand under the bridge. I found her by the bus stop, looking as aloof as possible, dressed in a loose white T-shirt, short dull skirt and fine sandals of gold-stamped leather which showed off her thinnish but muscular legs. I was late as usual. She carried a large floppy string bag from Mexico, worn grey at the surface of its original soft green.

We turned and went back to the motorway crowded with the August migration, and drove a short way north.

A mood of self-protective femininity hung over her and I sensed an undeclared reproach. Standing twenty yards from the famous bridge, with its torn circus placards of prancing horses and twirling nymphs, had perhaps disturbed her. Mind you, this should hardly have offended such a veteran of the Middle East, with all those knives, shrouds, and the white slave trade she so often spoke about.

She engaged in some hermetic limb-count. She put her feet on the dashboard; I was careful not to object. She pretended to doctor a hypothetical split nail, among toes freshly painted bright mauve. Nice ankles, toes bony and expressive. Bored with that, she took from her bag a small palette of rich colours and began to paint her lips, using a soft camel-hair brush. She chose something to match the toenails, but glistening. She got back her sense of humour only when she caught my glance, which might have been anxious. I saw a sudden third eye in the mirror she held, detached and dispassionate as the eye of a whale in the isolated palm of her left hand.

She gave me a brilliant smile, the smile of a girl who is trying out her lipstick.

'Can I give you some perfume?' she said.

'What sort?'

'Jasmine. It's from Damascus,' and she dabbed something on the inside of my wrist just as I was passing an articulated truck laden with small Peugeots.

The car suddenly smelled of incurable wastes of dryness, a desert wind at dusk, cool after the day of fire. Determined to register these images – the hand-held eye, the essential oil from a land of great heat – I concentrated on my driving, feeling no need for words.

We left the motorway at Scandicci, instantly becoming entangled in confused flyovers that threatened the little valley with some future Moloch of a city. I woke up to the fact that she was telling me interesting things only as we entered the slower herds of suburban buildings. A key word snapped me out from some professorial dream. She was talking about sex. About being given good sex, or giving good sex, with this latest lout of hers (I speak objectively), and what it did for her inner well-being, her sense of balance, to all of which I listened with politeness admirably free from any hint of jealousy.

The shops and small factories were colossally shut for the summer. Certain shutters we saw, driving through the outskirts, certain sliding doors firmly padlocked to the ground, certain fences, barbed wire, turrets, all necessary defences both active and passive, boldly inviting the *malavita* to come and raid their Aladdin's interior if they dared. But the cat burglars and masters of B and E were also off by the seaside, toasting their navels and looking at the girls.

At a certain point Vittoria decided she was hungry. We stopped at a bar, our early start having trickled away into the lunch hour. There she had a mortadella sandwich followed by a Blob, which is a neo-post-baroque ice-cream suitable for licking in front of an audience. Her pink tongue between fresh lips tackled four mammaries of brown milk-and-soya, while she listened to the lament of the lady behind the bar. 'How lonely Scandicci becomes in summer, Signora. They have all gone,' she said; 'you have no idea of the sadness.' I could not grasp this woman's accent. Hungarian? In English, Vittoria told me she came from the south, without taking her eyes off the woman, and with that cold bleached quality she gets when paying great attention.

While we stood there, the little bar was visited by many seekers after ice-cream. Harassed mothers wheeling comatose young, and two birdy secretaries one after another, developing a special relationship with the boss while his wife and kiddies were off at the beach. I could not help contrasting their aura with that of Vittoria. Theirs, backcombed hair, spiked heels, mechanically savaged jeans, freshly ironed. All the topspin of provincial chic. One in a shirt of rampant bananas piercing the labia of some tropical hibiscus, worn without the faintest hint of irony. The other with a scrubbed and bleary Miles Davis on her chest, as if trying to suggest a wide cultural experience. Foolish clothes worn seriously, suggesting what a lot these working girls had to lose, might be losing. Vittoria in contrast was a blank. No self-deprecating joke in Akkadian or Greek wove over her beautiful breasts, no flowers of the jungle. A white T-shirt, worn loose. Summertime academia, brains at ease.

Short drive up the hill, a lazy walk to the front gate, and '*Presto*,' said the guard, 'you have only half an hour.' '*Ma come . . .*' said Vittoria, and the rather more heavy '*senta*', signifying 'What on earth do you mean?'

'I am an eminent professor,' I said with a weary smile, 'and I rang yesterday.' 'Oh? Who did you speak to?' Eyes narrowed, he was haggling. Behind him on the chestnut door a piece of paper had the new hours in smudgy Biro. The guards were off to the beach too, overcome by heat, boredom and the call of the rolling wavelets on sea-drenched inner thighs.

Vittoria was for reporting them all to the *Sovvrintendente*, but I took her by the arm (brown, covered with microscopic blond feathers), and dragged her in. The guard, deadpan, pointed to a door.

We entered a room on the ground floor full of arches to support the ballroom above, frescoed with wild bamboo through which fat babies peeped, grinning. Punts with more babies in them, with young and very attractive mothers, struggled through weeds and green water, the sun shining through sedge in the background. Cranes migrated soundlessly from one arch to another. In the middle of the room an imperial billiard-table painted black showed worm-holes among the crudely carved gargoyles of its legs.

Vittoria, still muttering unkind words about the guard, mentioned a name that sounded like Tiepolini. 'Ah,' I said. 'How interesting. Who dat?'

'It means pupils of pupils who painted very very very bad Tiepolos,' she said.

The room ceased to hold any interest.

The next room had upon the ceiling a freshly peeled Florence, with bare breasts, taking Cosimo I to the cloud on which Jove and his gang were having a party.

'Where are the Pontormos?' I asked the guard. And he who deadpan had pointed his finger left, now deadpan pointed his finger vertically upwards, knowing he'd wasted our time.

In a mood of acidulous semi-historical backchat Vittoria led the way up a fat balustered staircase, imposed when the Emperor took the house over in the last century (she said), as Renaissance staircases were never so pompous, certainly not in the country. *Pietra serena*, a stone I like, though many find it dull. A granular limestone the colour of cement, it is hard to carve flat, so that even simple architectural features have a quality of still water turned to stone.

I knew the frescos we were about to see by heart from books, and from photographs of drawings I had obtained years ago. Pontormo is a god to me; one of those painters of whom I think with the affection due to a distant relative. But I had never managed to see the frescos themselves. This was my fourth attempt, always frustrated by confusion about the hours or by the fact they were under restoration.

Even knowing them well, I was unprepared for the burst of vitality which came over me as, alone, we finally penetrated the upper room. Feeling dizzy, I lay down on the tiles.

My heart leaped up as I beheld the people round the bull's-eye window, far above. Such pretty greens, I thought. The reproductions give no real idea of it. Here were the figures which come so often into Pontormo's work: the woman who turns away from the spectator as if in rejection, the old man who looks so frightened, the boy larking about, the dog whose

142

profile is so harsh it seemed like hammered wire. I had no idea whether or not this material was symbolic. But suddenly to recognize them up there was like meeting a long-lost branch of my interior family.

Still lying down, I asked the guards a few technical questions. They came and looked down at me when they replied, entering my field of vision as heads on stalks. I saw that the round window far above them had a sheet behind it, to keep out the daylight which would otherwise burn the attention from one's eyes. This sheet moved in the slight breeze outside. The sheet moved, and the mouths of the guards moved as they talked, but I had the impression that they were the still works of art, and it was the frescos which were alive.

Vittoria was behind me looking at the frescos by Allori and Andrea del Sarto. Her mood had changed to one of total absorption. She also had things to ask the guards. Like waiters, hands behind their backs, they walked across the ballroom to service the need for information with utmost formality. They were well-informed, knew about fresco technique, could point out the *giornate*, knew dates.

'He's using just one primary and its complementary,' I said from the floor. (The primaries are red, yellow, and blue, and the complementaries are the mixture of their two opposites, meaning green, purple, orange.) 'Red. Two reds in fact, one warm, one cold and earthy. And a whole series of greens. How marvellous!'

'*Non è detto*,' said Vittoria; 'it is not said that what you see is what he painted.'

'Such greens! And they look so fresh, as if they were just put on. Or rather,' I added as I felt her beginning to raise an objection, 'as they *might* have been, as he *might* have put them on, when they were fresh.'

She gave an art-historical snort.

Four tourists were hurried into the room from downstairs, dressed in Bermuda shorts, with a video camera to be passed between them. They looked bored and dazed except when pausing to shoot.

One of the guards came over and told me we should see the Bed. I rose, and Vittoria and I trailed round the corner with the tourists to look at this bed, which turned out to be the silk-engulfed edifice in which the first King of Italy reposed his limbs when weary. It looked a bit short for me.

Vittoria said she liked silk, but not green. Purple would be better. 'Nah,' I said, 'what you want is blue. Blue is you.' The tourists looked puzzled.

'Sandra has had a baby,' said Vittoria, looking at the bed.

'Really? And she such an intellectual! Maybe it will be your turn next. Babies are contagious, you know.'

'Mmm,' she said. 'So is viral hepatitis.'

By now disturbed, the tourists turned to leave.

'I cannot understand,' said Vittoria in a loud whisper, 'why one must look at a painting through a lens in order to see it. What is there to see? First, a small hole, and second, weeks later, a photograph. Where is the work of art?'

Back in the room of frescos, the guards attempted to shoo us out with the others, but Vittoria refused to go. She took me over to see the Andrea del Sarto, which had been finished later by Allori, and we asked the guards various questions about how the two men had been able to work at the same image, twenty or thirty years apart.

A shallow recessed staircase curved back to a balustrade over which three colourful louts leaned, shouting at unseen, unpainted, friends below, their behinds were to us, their coloured backs and bottoms expressing invitation and rejection simultaneously. A great peacock looked beady-eyed from the foreground, by Allori in the manner of Andrea del Sarto. Two figures painted from very careful drawings turned away into the picture, towards their friends at the balustrade, uninterested in us.

The banquet by Allori on the opposite wall was more of our world. Faces among the crowds looked out at us with a flourish, indicating they were having a good time and inviting us in.

The guards disarmed Vittoria's belligerence with courtesy, and when we had run out of questions it was clear that we should leave. We found ourselves in the garden again, even though we walked so slowly back through the cool rooms.

As we crossed to a shady tree, the guards drove past, with remarkable promptness, each in a very small, very clean, very nippy car. The wings of the cars flickered like the wings of devils, the kind which hunt in packs.

In the fat heat of the day I listened as Vittoria smoked and read to herself disjointedly from the guidebook in very fast Italian, her back to the root of a large cedar. Bought by Lorenzo de' Medici from Giovanni Rucellai in the 1480s. Started rebuilding in 1485 or so. Cooperation with Leon Battista Alberti, the leading architect of his time. Stairs by Sangallo. Modifications to a perhaps pre-existing loggia. First example of a classic front on a secular building.

We looked at it for a long while, taking this last fact in. Shoving the frontispiece of the Parthenon on to a private house – what an idea! And what a responsibility! From here to Venice and to Palladio, to the English school so influenced by Palladio and from them to America by the late eighteenth century. To the front of a Rolls-Royce in this century, and various jokey quotes in the post-modern idiom more or less yesterday. Porches and parliaments, the bridges of Newfoundland fishing-boats, the stoops of clapboard houses on the US east coast, and ornate mansions in the deep south.

'I think we should stay here,' said Vittoria after a while, 'until one of us has an idea.'

There followed a long silence, while the cicadas took over the shrubbery and the caked lawn dried out the drooping oleanders. The roots of the cedar were uncomfortable, but as I shifted around, Vittoria lay still, looking at the villa. The guidebook lay open upon blackened needles, beside red cigarettes and a thin green lighter. The hot and sodden air was filled with the noise of raving insects as a pot is filled with the bubbling of water on the boil.

'Surely,' I said at last, 'the twirling ribbon round the balls on the parapet means something?'

I meant the central theme in *pietra serena* in the pediment above the columns; the Medici balls with carved drapery flying in a wind of stone.

Long silence. Eventually I heard Vittoria's sleepy voice.

'Lorenzo liked to have Alberti's book on architecture read to him while he was taking a bath. There is a letter somewhere to prove it. It's one of those things I often think about. It's not exactly a historical fact, a book which is read to a man as he is in his bath . . .'

She paused to light another cigarette.

'Alberti's book on architecture is very important,' she said after a while, 'but unfortunately it is also very boring. It is a book of which students read one chapter, maybe two, and then say to their professors, Alberti says this, Alberti says that, and the professors say yes because they also have not read Alberti. So I think that maybe Lorenzo perhaps did not listen very hard, no? This is possible. If you read a book in the bath, you must be relaxed, not serious. I think that perhaps Lorenzo was not listening to the *words*, which are very boring words, but to the *voice*. And I think this is important. The voice of his friend.'

Pause, while I tried to think.

'Nobody,' I said, 'has ever read to me in my bath.'

'Exactly! You see? It is such a personal thing to do! Today we have hundreds of ways to remember the voice of a friend who is not there. Telephone, tapes. It is not so bad now to have a friend who is far away. Alberti was Lorenzo's friend. It is very important to the history of architecture that Alberti was a friend of Lorenzo. They were both aristocrats. I think that they were related. They were friends at school – *compagni di banco*, which as you know is an important relationship here in Italy. And so Lorenzo listened to this book on architecture, very serious, very boring, because this particular serious boring book was by Alberti, his friend. Did he listen to Sangallo in his bath?

This was so typical of Vittoria. As if I knew whether or not Lorenzo de' Medici listened to Sangallo in his bath.

'No.'

'No! Exactly!'

'Yes, but, Vittoria, you can't make a theory out of – '

'Sangallo, Brunelleschi, certainly knew of Vitruvius and were very interested in all they could find on the architecture of ancient Rome, no? But it was Alberti who was able to invent the profession of architect – not because he was an architect, but because he was an aristocrat. Being an aristocrat he could talk to all the other aristocrats and make them excited about Roman buildings. He was not a *capomastro* or *dirigente dell'opera* like the others. He did not dirty his hands. He was an architect! The first! Brunelleschi was not an architect, even when he was doing the cupola of the Duomo. Even then he was just *capomastro*. How you say in English?'

'Foreman.'

'Ah. Foreman.'

She paused to memorize the word.

'When one of the popes died – ' she went on, 'I forget which one – all the cardinals were in Rome for the election of the new pope, no? And Alberti organized a guided tour of all the Roman monuments, speaking about them. Now, you cannot imagine anyone else organizing this, for a simple reason. Only an aristocrat could tell all the princes of the Church, all those cardinals, to go and see the ruins. Sangallo could never say to a cardinal,"Would you like to come and see the Pantheon with me tomorrow? Cardinal Pinco and Cardinal Pallino are coming too." Could he?'

Silence, filled by the cicadas. A square garden capped by a cube of insect noise.

'So Lorenzo bought Poggio a Caiano in 1485. Rucellai was a banker, and the fact he sold it to Lorenzo shows perhaps it was not a good time for bankers. Apparently the late fifteenth century was difficult. There were new powerful banks in Germany by then. The long war between England and France was finished . No foreign loans. But there were wars in northern Italy which made internal trade difficult. Economic things — you know. So Lorenzo likes this house, but he says he cannot spend a great deal of money here. But he says to Alberti, "At least let us build a loggia. That I can afford." And they sit down together, with Vitruvius open, and all the drawings they have been given by the Gonzagas from Mantova and the Malatestas from Rimini — because they gave each other many drawings at that time, as presents, as they are all building new palaces, ideal cities. And Lorenzo says, it must be this high, and so much wide.'

She paused, thinking. After a while, she said to herself, 'I wonder what happened to all those drawings.' Another long pause, and very softly, 'Or perhaps in the Albertina . . . '

The front of the villa spread out its wide face. She ceased to move. One or two cars passing along the main road merely added another remote buzz to the dreamy atmosphere. It was about three o'clock in the afternoon.

I looked up at the cedar. After a while its lateral branches became wide arms, hands, fingers, the palms flat for divining water under the abrasive earth. The pebbles on the drive flickered in the heat. The cedar smelled of incense. Here and there spheres of clipped box broke the sparse flatness of the dried and yellowed lawn.

It seemed that Vittoria had fallen asleep in mid-discourse. I looked. Her hand was open and relaxed. She was half-turned away, towards the building, as if thinking. She was another statue in the garden, whose pedestal had been absorbed over the years by the roots of the great tree.

I hugged my knees and looked at her, secure in knowing that she was unaware of my attention. For if you devour an awakened model with your eyes, the act must be formal, inhibited by a social smile. Sleep is better. Best of all, the stillness of statues.

Vittoria's breasts are quite unlike the breasts of other women. Cloth hangs from them differently, and if she walks, the crevasses change in their diagonals from left to right, right to left, as if the movement is some peculiar internal flickering of the eye. If she lies still, as now, they are marble.

Now the air within her shirt seemed full of curious energy. Great lines of indented material swung over from the nipple of one breast to the other, creating blue crevasses of shadow in the thin white cotton. They had no size or scale. They were the mountainside. Among these gulleys, the rift valleys of minute concentration, I can imagine working, in the green half-light as the mind closes down at night, a fraction before sleep.

Looking up, looking down, I began to be aware of the passage of shadows across Sangallo's frieze, where a cluster of scaffolding and ladders made shapes that were constantly changing. I was aware also of the ebb and flow of air within Vittoria's lungs. And because some twenty minutes passed engaged in these observations, and because twenty minutes is a long time in which to do a simple thing, I have lost, as I remember the occasion, any sense of the difference between the dead building and the living body. Both seemed to be moving. Both images, when I pass over them again in my head, appear to swell and change so slightly that they have acquired some textural quality in common.

Vittoria woke and characteristically pretended never to have dozed off. After a quick surreptitious stretch while still lying down (nothing but a brief tensing of toes and arms), she got up. She brushed behind her at the cedar needles or pieces of cone with which she was covered. I helped in this, dusting off her backside.

Stepping away from my attentive palm, she reversed her skirt so that her bottom suddenly appeared in front of her, and chased from the surface of her dress any wisps that Nature might have left there, nattering about grass stains – the worst – and the need for soft water to rinse with after washing. This finished, she started to walk off towards the villa.

We crunched a short stretch of gravel and ducked through the tape barrier intended to keep out intruders. Then we climbed the curved steps above the frieze, up to the balustrade that circled the house, both later additions in which Vittoria was uninterested.

At the top, after a moment of thought, she started to tell me what we were looking at, as if she were totting up a bill at the grocer's. Had I noticed, she asked, that the window on the left very slightly cut into the side of the column supporting the architrave? Whereas its twin of the other side was ten or fifteen centimetres away from it?

'Ah. So it does. How clever of you . . .'

She started to grope about, pointing out bits and pieces, feeling at the joins of the walls as if only touch would reveal their secrets. I like my heroines active, so I merely watched her. But by and by she got me interested.

'The point is, did they use for the inside walls of the loggia walls that already existed inside the house? Or did they start a whole new facade?'

I said I didn't know.

A small dog came through a side wall of the garden and began to bark at us.

'It is so annoying,' she muttered, 'that the guards have gone home. We should be on the inside of the house to have a look . . . '

'The guards would not have allowed us up here, would they?'

She ignored this. A short sigh came over her, such as overcome babies during play, brief, innocent, but deeply felt.

'Well,' she said, '*ragioniamo un po*. We must sum up the facts! Lorenzo was not as rich as his grandfather, Giovanni di Bicci, the old man who started it all. The house was made for Rucellai, the loggia was Lorenzo's idea. Still, however poor he may have felt, we are talking about relative poverty, and it cannot have cost very much to take out a section of the wall and put in some columns, no?'

'What about the frescos?'

'Oh, they are not expensive. A fresco cost one third of the price of a painting on wood, which cost one tenth of the price of a nice old Roman jewel . . . There's a book about the prices somewhere, but what it means is that frescos were cheap, very cheap. After all they are only earth colours and water, painted on fresh *intonaco* – the plaster. They had to be painted fast, *alla giornata*, a bit every day. Pontormo could do a figure big like a man in one day . . . '

'You mean, they were salaried like the bricklayers?'

'No, I don't think so. They would make a drawing, and then they would make a contract, with stamps, witnesses, penalty clauses, *carta bollata*.'

She caught sight of the top of some windows set at floor level, with gullies in the tiles to let the light in. It seemed a peculiar arrangement. She bent to look, and as she crouched there, we heard a car come through the front gates.

She got up. All we could do was to duck behind the shade of two columns, trying to be thin.

We were a yard from each other, stiff as two soldiers. Her chin in the air struck me as amusing.

'*Professoressa*,' I began, intending to make a joke.

'*Professore*,' she said quick as a flash, '*you* may be, but I have no title yet. I have no *ruolo*, I am not even the assistant of one who is *di ruolo*. I am a personage on the map of the Italian academy who does not exist! I only exist so that my professor can steal my ideas.'

'Professors do not steal ideas,' I said, startled at her bitterness.

'Professors steal anything. Ideas, bodies, pots, facts. Most of all facts! Professors like facts more than bodies, much more. My professor likes my facts, very much. My professor does not like me, but he is in love with my facts. And I cannot give them to him, or he will steal them for himself. And if I do *not* give them to him, I will not become a *professoressa*!' At this she began to laugh and her face came in and out of the shade of the column as a shutter might burn an image on a slow film.

The car had gone, leaving Vittoria to wipe her lips with the back of her hand, in the shade of a column by Leon Battista Alberti. I was sorry to have touched this grievance.

Before we went down, she made me take a photo of a faded wall by Filippino Lippi. As we walked back to the car, she talked about the Brancacci chapel, where the newly restored Masaccios had totally altered our conception of this artist. It may be, she said, that the hero of the chapel is really Masolino or Filippino Lippi, but what scholar will dare say so? What scholar dares back up Moran when he says that the painting of Guidoriccio da Fogliano in Siena is not by Simone Martini? These things are symbols that nobody will challenge. It would be like telling the French that Napoleon was typically Italian, or the Spanish that Christopher Columbus was Genoese. Nobody wants to know such blinding facts such as these.

Her acrimony about the profession had worked its way out by the time we had crossed the spiky grass to collect her bag. We looked back at the villa briefly before leaving.

'I think it is all a quick joke,' she said, her mood suddenly changing. 'Lorenzo and Alberti designed a loggia, because Lorenzo needed the air from the mountainside. It is very hot here, no? It was not easy to plan, because of the existing house, and when it was drawn on paper it looked too wide and too flat. So, as a joke, they put a hat on it like a Greek temple. On paper it looked amusing, no? They gave it to the builder, and it was made. Later it looked very strange, to have some columns below and a Greek temple on the second floor, so they asked Sangallo to put in the screen down below, in front, to make it better.'

'Are you going to write about it?'

'Me?' She started laughing. 'But if it's by Sangallo?'

'Sangallo?'

'Yes.' She gave me a look of triumph, as if having once again proved me an idiot. 'The historians say that this villa is by Sangallo. It is only me who thinks it is entirely by Alberti, and all I have is that Lorenzo liked listening to Alberti in his bath. That is all my argument!'

As we left, the air seemed to cool slightly. A tobacconist across the road was opening up.

'I hope,' said Vittoria, 'that Alberti in life was more amusing than his book. I find this villa cheerful, not serious, no? I am glad that we saw it . . . But if I say it is a joke, they will *never* make me a *professoressa*.'

In the life of Pontormo, Michelangelo is an off-stage thunderstorm.

A few years ago a team of restorers finally dared to clean the frescos of Michelangelo in the Sistine Chapel. The move was fiercely contested. What was revealed was so extraordinarily colourful that it was considered an aberration, a complete destruction of Michelangelo's 'sculptural' qualities. Eccentric colleagues of mine made a huge effort to obtain the best possible photos of what it looked like *before* cleaning.

The only just comment that can be made on one work of art is another work of art. In this respect there exists in Florence a magnificent series of frescos, by Pontormo, which show what the Sistine Chapel looked like to Michelangelo's contemporaries when it was fresh. These frescos of the *Passion* at La Certosa indicate that to the first generation of Florentine mannerists the Sistine Chapel represented a new use of colour, set free from the need to create surface illusion, light and shade. For the first time colours were chosen neither decoratively, nor to create the illusion of form, but according to an instinctive feeling by which the light seems to come from *within* the painting, and not merely reflect back something taken from the world outside.

Pontormo was born too late to have known at first hand the dramatic effect of Savonarola upon his Florentine contemporaries. If Michelangelo is the artist of the suppressed republic, Pontormo became the Polonius of the restored Medici dukes.

He was a man of transparent timidity. While he was working at San Lorenzo in Florence a few years before his death he kept a diary, which is cult reading for those students of the Italian Renaissance who enjoy contemporary documents.

> Sunday morning I had lunch with Br[onzino] and I felt I was very full, so that in the evening I did not have any supper. [42]

The fascination lies in the text's extraordinary sparseness. It appears to centre on the movements of his insides, and whether or not the current duke or duchess came to pat him on the head as he worked.

From the diary, it is clear that he saw very few people. Bronzino for supper now and again; an unidentified young man called Daniello, who must have been a special friend; a few other painters. This is all the circle which the diary reveals.

Now and again Bronzino or Daniello would knock on his door and he would not go down:

> Sunday. Br[onzin]o, Daniello, and Ataviano came to the house, and I bought sticks and cut willow for the kitchen garden; and Br[onzin]o wanted me to go to supper, and getting angry he told me, 'You behave as if you were going to the house of some enemy.' And I was very upset.

(The business about 'sticks and willows' is still a part of Tuscan life. When tying in vines, you hold the thick end of the willow twig in your left hand, loop the thin end twice around vine and pole, pull tight, then change hands and twist the thick end around the thin a couple of times and tuck it under. Even today, it's quicker than using string or plastic.)

Pontormo was one of those people who thought of his body as a whole other island:

> 31 March. On Sunday morning I had lunch with Daniello, fish and mutton, and had no supper in the evening, and on

Monday morning I found it painful to move my body. I got up, and because of the cold and wind went back to bed and stayed there until six. And I didn't feel well all day. Yet for supper I had a little boiled meat with beetroots and butter, and I lay like that without knowing what was to become of me. I think it was very bad for me to go back to bed; yet now that it is four o'clock I feel very well.

He usually dined by himself on something he calls a *pesce d'uovo*, which means literally a 'fish of egg'. Meaning perhaps an omelette folded in such a way that it looked like a fish. It would probably be fair to say, taking all the evidence into due consideration, that Jacopo da Pontormo was totally egg-bound:

Thursday morning I shat two turds which were not liquid, and from inside them came two things like wicks of cotton wool, that is, white fat; and I supped at San Lorenzo very well, a very good little stew, and I finished the figure.

The San Lorenzo frescos were all destroyed soon after his death – which in a sense is a tribute to his fragile personality. He was born after, and died before, Michelangelo. He provided a kind of paradigm for a certain kind of Florentine artist who still exists: the talented man totally eclipsed. Phlegmatic, dour, a bit depressed, more willing to talk of food than art, he behaves as if life is going on somewhere else, but never mind:

On day 6 did the whole torso. On day 7 added the legs.

The word *figura* comes frequently in the diary, and from time to time at the end of the written entry there is a minute sketch to indicate the day's work, the *giornata* of the fresco. 'Today I made the *figura* which goes like this:' and there would follow a minute sketch like a small tangled worm from his own insides.

Deep in her heart Vittoria feels that architecture had been a decadent pastime since Ur fell, and as I have never met an architect who hasn't seemed to me in someway specious, I seldom bother to disagree with her. She is too tactful to extend her snobbery to painters, and she leaves me my love for Pontormo. Pontormo is another matter. Pontormo is my role model, my father-figure. We inhabit the same Europe, of large apparent decadence mitigated by small private truth.

Occasionally Pontormo felt like doing nothing, so he would stay indoors and draw. The Uffizi has many of these drawings, though as with all Renaissance artists many more must have been thrown away. Once, with the help of Vittoria's influential aunt, Maro and I managed to have them all brought up for us. Five boxes. Unfortunately, after three, we started making comparisons, putting this one next to that, just as we might with portfolios at home. It seemed clear to us that five or six drawings had been made on the same day, from the same model, and we wanted to re-create the mood of Pontormo as he worked: cold at first, then gradually more free. Shocked, the head of the print room came over, wagging a finger. In short, we were thrown out. Keeping to the order in those boxes is as necessary in the print room as prayer.

Florence is an ideal base from which to study Pontormo. There is the *Supper at Emmaus* in the Uffizi, with its strange back view and disturbing eye within a painted triangle. There are the frescos at Poggio a Caiano which Vittoria and I visited, and near by at Carmignano a beautiful *Visitation*. There is the *Passion* series at La Certosa, and the magnificent *Deposition* at Santa Felicità, between the Ponte Vecchio and the Pitti on the left as you are walking up. All these works, though sometimes difficult to get to, are within an hour of the centre of Florence.

A fortnight of bad weather in the early spring of 1555 suddenly broke a long succession of brief entries. The weather, the phases of the moon, and Pontormo's bodily fluids suddenly coalesce in one long undigested block of prose:

> Don't eat too much meat, above all pork; and after the middle of January don't eat any [meat] as it is very feverish and bad; and be temperate with everything, because the sack of the humours and the flux burst in February, as the cold in winter congeals them.

To whom are these scratchings written? To himself, as a *pro memoria* of the day's work in San Lorenzo? To his friend Daniello? To posterity? Are they a New Year's resolution, a dietary vow? Perhaps they are no more than an expression of fear. Fear of ageing, fear of illness, fear of change. Fear of anything that might happen, even a quiet meal with friends. Fear is an essential feature of Pontormo's work: the wide-eyed child who looks straight at the artist, as if transfixed at some point beyond death:

> In the year 1555, beginning with the moon of March that lasted until 21 April, in all that moon were brought forth pestilential infirmities that killed many men of good and regular habits and perhaps ordered lives, and blood came out of them. I think it happened that January was not cold but came instead with the moon of March, for one felt a poisonous hard cold fight with the fiery air from the period of great heat, so that it was like hearing fire frying in water, so that I was in a great fear. It is well to be fit before the moon of March, so that it finds you sober in eating food and exercise, and to be careful about sweating.

After Bruce Chatwin died for the first time, to be brought back to life by the doctors only to die definitively a little later, he told me that to die was finally to penetrate behind that great Renaissance painting which lies at the back of the minds of all of us as a symbol for this world and the next.

He was even able to describe the painting. Huge, he said, perhaps Venetian, he was not sure, but with a great number of people engaged in some banquet or ritual festivity. As he approached its surface, he felt an incredible excitement, as if at last he would pass through the shield of mere appearances of which paintings are made. What textures! The clothes! The velvet, the long sleeves, the pearls like little white planets, each an individual all-engrossing other world!

As I stretched out my hand to touch, he said, the figures began to move, to beckon me to join them. He took the hand of a man standing there and walked with him into the painting. It seemed as if he were leading him towards a parapet or balustrade that so often lies within such works – to what thereafter, Chatwin did not know.

Marvellous! Marvellous, he said, that quality of attention to the surfaces of the things of this world which painting gives you. For Bruce was more passionate about art than any other writer I know. He perceived how it changes the way in which this jumble of Things affects you.

I often think about this description of death by Bruce. I hear the sound of his voice. Idly I wonder about the painting he half imagined, half remembered. Perhaps it was related to the frescos in Poggio a Caiano – not the Pontormo, but one of the Allori. He went to the villa, I know, because he told me about it, but at the time he seemed unimpressed by the paintings he saw there.

I wonder if his was an intuition about death, or about painting. Or perhaps about both? Death usually comes to men before it comes to their objects, but paintings eventually die too. Indeed, they really only live while they are being made by the painter, or remade by the sensibilities of those who enjoy them.

For a while they can act as shields against total annihilation, our death first, their death and the eventual death of the planet as it whirls around an exhausted sun, awaiting its own eventual extinction, each finality fitting in the other like Chinese boxes. For me, the outstretched hand of painted flesh from a painted sleeve will do, stretching to support me as I approach the tunnel, before the blinding light.

13 · CAREGGI

Halfway along the back road from Siena to Florence I came across a pick-up truck on its side in a ditch with a young man standing by it.

'Why, Alessandro,' I said. 'Nothing serious I hope?'

He waved his arms and mumbled. Quite a large youth, but his waving arms gave me an instant vision of an earlier boy. As an adolescent he had been much taken with the theme of Death, and while the others in the village played tag or ran their bikes after the cats, he would scare the young with an imaginary skeleton, shouting balefully '*la morte secca*' – a dry death, a clean skull. What made the image unforgettable was that, child and man, his own skull was oddly shaped.

Vittoria was staying at Bagno a Ripoli with her famous aunt, the great Eminence of the Belle Arti, in a villa I had always been curious to see. To my surprise its pleasant seventeenth-century front had been freshly restored with ochre plastering. The effect was unsentimental, almost ruthless.

Vittoria insisted that she knew a back way to the villa of Lorenzo de' Medici at Careggi, our homework for the day, now the largest hospital in Florence. The son of her aunt's neighbour, she said, had been smashed up in an accident, and she had visited him once or twice there as he lay in his plaster carapace. She said she enjoyed going to Careggi. Hospitals were addictive. There was always plenty to look at. Relatives camped out in the corridors, with little bundles and rugs from home to make them comfy. Support for the sick. And the doctors would thread their way through sighing relatives without complaint.

Driving once more through the outskirts of Florence, we were caught in a 'peripheral engorgement of the traffic' — a sign in red was there to tell us so. Workmen in blue spread liquid pythons on the road to be ironed out into asphalt. By the temporary traffic lights two Moroccan or Algerian youths offered a quick clean of the windscreen with a rubber knife. They wore their trousers rolled, and had blackened feet.

Along the Arno the parked tourist buses were having their flanks wiped by their keepers, removing dust from chrome. A young man wheeled a baby among the shrubs of a small park, beneath leggy cypresses. The crowds were already gathering behind the wire of the public baths by the side of the road. Coloured towels were atop the railings. The day was milky at this early hour, promising great heat towards noon.

Vittoria kept up her cheerfully morbid chatter, of orphans and lost limbs, workmen's accidents at the dig, knife fights among usually peaceable Arabs at the four-thousand-year-old site. The steep dip between Fiesole and Castello contained scrubby gardens begging the world to build on them. Here and there were uneven olive orchards with the dead trees still standing, just as they had been when the frost killed them in 1985, each amid a wiry fan of suckers springing up from the roots.

By a strange barred gate we had to ask a woman in a parked car the way. She told us politely and returned to her weeping. Round the next bend we came across the gravediggers. Vittoria thought it all very funny. Such a lot of equipment in tow, the cheerful sextons! Picks, rope, planks, a portable jack, a saw, and their lunches, each in a neat enamel pail.

Careggi

We re-entered the tangle of the main road and drove slowly through a congested junction, where a policewoman with hennaed curls was supervising the removal of an illegally parked truck. Pine needles in her hair; the avenue was shedding them as last year's growth dried out in the summer's heat.

Near *Traumatologia* I had to slow down for an angry young man on crutches, followed by a pleading relative. The hospital chapel was a little further on – that little chapel that is always working.

We parked in a visitors' car park, under some huge poplars growing from the side of a ditch. An empty field went steeply upwards behind their trunks, with one or two sparse vines growing into pruned field maples in the old style. Above this, the hill of villas going up to Fiesole, shrouded by cypresses.

Once through the ornate baroque gateway we were overcome by an extraordinary sense of quiet. A wide path curled in and out of a large stand of overgrown trees with all the concentrated gloom of a Florentine garden. A box hedge on either side smelled of cats' pee, with dusty dark leaves the size of shirt buttons. The villa itself was visible through the wood as a warm cube in the sky. It was hard to look away from it.

As we approached I saw that the defensive, plain facade had been enlivened by a walled-in balcony running all the way round the top, as one might run whipped cream round a cake. A frivolous touch, deflating the martial impression. On the corner, a large Medici coat-of-arms, stone balls upon a stone shield amid stone foliage, a petrified crane's nest up-ended, from which the eggs refused to fall.

'Ah, why don't I live here?' Vittoria said as we walked in.

A small, fairly tight courtyard with flowers in huge pots and a dais at one end, advertising concerts in which to 'relive once more the sophisticated life of a Medici prince'. The grey-eyed Vittoria flashed me a look of irony, in tune with the unconscious humour of life.

Across the yard there was a steep staircase with a patch of bright sky at the top. In the handsome arch with which this ladder to heaven began, a tin lantern provisionally installed a century ago swung and creaked in a faint breeze from the hillside.

We slowly mounted the *pietra serena* steps and indented balustrade, set into a vault that sloped upwards.

Vittoria started chatting about the Medici.

' . . . not Lorenzo's favourite villa. I think he preferred Poggio a Caiano. He could be alone there better. But it was quicker to ride up here from Florence than out to Poggio a Caiano, so he came here more often. All the Medici came up here in fact, especially to die.'

'Die?'

'They did not want to leave Florence even when they were ill. So they just rode up the hill whenever they could.'

'It is certainly true that it is cooler here,' I said. 'Even this short distance out of the city makes a lot of difference. And so what did they die of?'

For a moment Vittoria looked out on to the view from the top, thinking. Faint green and yellow reflections from the garden underlit her face.

'How do you say "*La gotta*" in English?'

'Dunno. What is it?'

'It is what Piero il Gottoso died of.'

'Ah. Would it have been the gout?'

'Exactly! Piero the Gouty,' said Vittoria, 'died of gout. So did Lorenzo, I think. They did not eat a good diet. They just ate a great deal of meat; no vegetables, nothing that was green.'

'Lots of fortified wine,' I said. 'Lots of port.'

'Not port, *Malvasia*. They must have suffered a great deal from – how do you say *acido urico*?'

'Uric acid.'

We arrived at the top and turned left through a tall arch into a room consisting mostly of ornate doorways. There was a heavy table, some not very old busts, a fireplace and five cadaverous doors of carved chestnut. The lintel of the chimney was one long stone, showing what seemed to be lions, but as I approached they turned into armour with whiskery fringes, the traditional symbols for victory in war.

On the wall were two or three large nineteenth-century paintings, showing Lorenzo listening to Poliziano reading his translation from Homer, to old Giovanni di Bicci, founder of the Medici bank. He was looking thoughtful – or perhaps just gouty.

'I can't believe that these portraits are accurate,' I said, after we had looked at them for a while in silence.

Vittoria was looking at Poliziano and his crowd of furred listeners. 'I do not think it would be a very enjoyable party,' she murmured, then in answer to my question: 'You are right. The famous portrait of Lorenzo il Magnifico from which these copies were made was painted by Vasari almost fifty years after he was dead. We do not know if it looks like him. Perhaps there were drawings made by other artists when he was alive. Or maybe a funeral terracotta. Or perhaps there was *una tradizione orale*. Anyway, we do not know what sources Vasari used . . . '

'I must confess I have a certain problem about Lorenzo the Magnificent,' I said after a while. 'I know that art historians say how good he was, how cultured, what a patron, what a poet, what a key figure for the Renaissance and so on. There's no real reason for me to dislike him. Perhaps I side too much with the republicanism of the artists . . . '

Vittoria listened in silence as I put forward poor logic in poor words. She likes to tidy up arguments, give them their due. And so she said that Lorenzo was a hard-working man, soft-spoken, slightly devious. Should not have spoiled his son Piero so much. Should not have died so young.

'As to the problem of how much the Medici gave to art,' she said, 'the matter is very difficult. Lorenzo very probably did not like painting as much as jewellery. Possibly he did not like painters either, perhaps because as you say they were often republican in spirit. Might be difficult to prove. He certainly sent them away from Florence, to Rome or Bologna or Venice, but that might have been an intelligent policy of his. They were ambassadors for Florentine culture. They went with respect, with his *raccomandazione*. Botticelli to Rome. Verrocchio to do the Corleone statue in Venice. Leonardo, Sangallo . . . ' Vittoria looked at the ceiling of painted beams and went through a list on her fingers.

I examined the lintels of the various doors, and listened at them, to see which would be a promising one to open.

'He took Filippino Lippi away from a church in Florence,' she said, 'to send him to Rome, in the middle of a fresco. He had to finish it seven years later.'

Then she waved her hand, cancelling the list in the air, to get back to an argument left unfinished the month before.

'You asked me recently about the prices of frescos,' she went on. 'I looked them up last week. It seems that Paolo Uccello was paid twenty-five lire for the fresco of Sir John Hawkwood in the Duomo, at a time when there were four lire to the fiorino.'

'Is that little?'

'It is very little. It is about one hundred times less than a good Roman jewel' – she started muttering about dates, devaluations – 'perhaps not quite so little, but all the same. As to Lorenzo preferring jewels to paintings, that also may have been a calculation, don't you think? For if it was necessary, he could go to the family bank with a jewel and ask for money, no?'

'As collateral for a loan?'

When she understood the term, she nodded mischievously.

'What! In 1490?'

'I looked it up,' she said. 'The Medici bank accepted jewels as security many times, and they – or Lorenzo – were not the first. A fresco you cannot take to the bank.'

She seemed pleased with herself, having tidied up another piece of the puzzle. And suddenly she said she was bored with the room we were in, and told me to start knocking on the doors.

After poking my head behind one of the large chestnut doors I discovered to my surprise that the villa was not officially open to the public. The entire building was occupied by offices, the central bureaucracy of the USL (Unità Sanitaria Locale – local health service), and the beautiful walls of the inner office had temporary shelves for files and a circle of desks, with computers and typewriters, and bird-like secretaries at work. The shelves, I noticed, were padded so as not to harm the walls.

'*Con permesso*,' I said, 'please could you direct us to the room in which Lorenzo il Magnifico died?'

Next door, they said.

Next door I found one Franco, with whom I'd spoken on the phone a couple of times, arranging this visit. He seemed less than excited to see us, so I told him solemnly that we were important art historians. He got up, disappeared through another door. He returned to say the room was occupied with a meeting, and could we come back in – say – one and a half hours? We could, I said, while behind me Vittoria tried to intervene with a more meaningful '*Senta . . .*'

Signor Franco caught her impatience and said, 'You could always see the loggia.'

'Ah yes, the loggia,' I said. 'Of course.' A finger pointed back the way we had come.

The secretaries seemed delighted to be interrupted, and took us through to a little loggia at the back. *Pietra serena* columns, tile floor, wooden ceiling with indifferent decoration. Beyond, a garden brimming with the insects of high summer, green leaves flickering up to our slightly dazzled eyes, against a background of black cypress.

'Oh well, very nice,' we said. One of the secretaries said the frescos on the loggia ceiling were by Pontormo, with the possible help of Bronzino. We looked up again, a bit more attentive.

'That's not fresco,' said Vittoria after a quick glance.

'How can you tell,' said the little secretary much impressed, 'just by looking up at it?'

I explained that fresco is essentially water-colour painted directly on to fresh plaster without any binding medium. The paint soaks in as the plaster dries, and becomes indivisible from the surface of the wall. This makes it more durable than any other kind of paint on plaster. However much it fades, something can always be seen in the plaster – 'whereas here,' I said pointing upwards, 'the paint has fallen away, leaving nothing underneath. This shows indicating that it was done with some other paint which has not adhered properly to the surface.'

She was a small woman with heavy glasses, and stood formally with one hand in the other as she listened.

'Ah,' she said, deeply satisfied, 'now I have learned something. There were some experts here a few years ago, but they said there was nothing to be done about them, as they were badly restored in the late seventeenth century.'

Vittoria and I started examining the whole ceiling properly, panel by panel. We craned our heads upwards until our mouths opened, like hungry fledgelings. Much of it was crumbling and distressingly retouched, but here and there we found areas where the paint seemed fresh.

Under the heads of some grotesques, a filigree trellis supported leaves and tendrils, pegged at the sides by a beautiful shell done very quickly with fine colours. Within each decorative panel were incorporated small figures, similar to the figure of a woman seen from the back in Pontormo's frescos at Poggio a Caiano. Most of the figures had been coarsely retouched, but here and there one could still detect the vivid hand of Pontormo, with his quick and intense concentration.

'I would imagine,' I said, 'that it is too fragile to try restoring it now, taking away the later bits.'

'Italy is too rich in works of art.' (I had been addressing Vittoria but it was the secretary who replied.) 'There is such a lot you could do here if you wanted to put it back in some order. They say they don't have any money. It's such a waste to have just offices here.'

'But nice for you, Signora,' I said.

'Ah, but I am quite passionate about this place,' she said. 'I know everything about this building! I have explored it from top to bottom. I even come here at night, in my dreams. Do you know that up there' – she pointed to the battlements behind her – 'in the armoury, I found a little window-sill with a carving round it, saying *Hic itur ad astra*, "from here you look at the stars"? The room was in such a mess! There were dead rats and other horrible things, and an owl lived there. The *Signor Preside* made me shut the window. So the owl went away. Well, the other day, when I went up to have a look at it, they had painted over the carving! Imagine! But how can we expect a contractor to have any feeling for the place.'

She seemed furious at the ebb and flow of workmen trampling over her beautiful villa, responsible to no caring body.

'Excuse my question,' said Vittoria politely, 'but why is it that the USL finds itself here? Is there no other place for them to keep their files?'

'Oh, Signora,' said the secretary. 'When we first came, the place was well taken care of. We took over the Nurses' School and they still had their own cleaning staff. Now we are here, and the USL has subcontracted, and the new people don't care.'

She walked to the edge of the loggia.

'Over there,' she said, 'down behind that tree, the nurses said there was a secret passageway, which led all the way to that other villa on the hill.' She pointed, and we saw about a mile away a faded villa like an over-cleaned painting, among green trees punctuated by darker cypresses.

'Ah,' said Vittoria. 'An escape tunnel . . .'

'And there were lots of frescos in the chapel,' she said triumphantly, 'and they painted over them too. Frescos in the cellar, which is full of old boxes and things. Imagine! The old boxes for our computers, in a beautiful cellar with frescos!'

'Which order of nuns was it? I asked.

'Oh, it was an appendage of the Convent of Santa Maria Nuova, and they were here until seventy-nine or eighty. Ten years ago, I think we came here. We don't deserve this place. The nuns took care of it so well . . .'

We went back into their ante-room, and as we were standing there a wild, indeed desperate, young man with a deflated rucksack passed through, greeted with a very respectful '*Buongiorno, Dottore,*' by the secretaries.

Then the nice lady showed us a peculiar instrument low on the ground, a wooden animal with a grotesque face, whose back opened, to squeeze the juice from citrus fruit or pomegranates. The face which vomited out the liquid was similar to the grotesque faces on the ceiling of the loggia.

'I have seen grotesques like this,' said Vittoria, 'in Rome, in the Golden House of Nero, which they discovered in fourteen ninety-something. Or maybe in the eighties. It started a whole fashion. All the artists went to look at it. I went there years ago, just before it closed, and there were souvenir signatures scratched in the frescos by painters who had visited it. There was Pinturicchio's signature, scratched in the wall.'

'And there were huge tortoises in the garden,' said the secretary, 'right up until 1936. The nuns told us so, when we took over.'

I decided to tell her the real reason for our visit. She had such a passion for the place.

I explained that I hoped to discover whether there was any truth in the story that Poliziano had overheard Savonarola speak to Lorenzo on his deathbed. It was a key moment in the creation of the Florentine republic, but there were those who said that this meeting had never taken place. So the first thing to establish was whether such a thing was physically possible, and this is why I had to see the room in which Lorenzo died.

'*Professore*,' said the secretary, 'have you read Bargellini?'

The Professor (me) in some embarrassment said no.

'Bargellini maintains,' she said, 'that the meeting took place at the head of the staircase, in full view of everyone. And that Lorenzo, even though he was ill, rose from his bed in order to meet Savonarola, saying that it was better for a man to approach the Lord than for the Lord to come to the man . . . I've always worried about this, as the staircase which leads up here is so steep. Can one imagine a very sick man going down it? On the other hand, if it was not that staircase, which one was it? The castle hasn't changed that much since 1494.'

I was embarrassed, though not surprised, to find she knew more about the subject than I did. Smilingly we took leave of

171

each other. She seemed excited, reluctant to return to a glimmering screen of ancient medical bills.

We left the villa through a side door into the garden. As I looked down small elements flickered and skipped from side to side within my skull like tropical fish. When my eyes became used to the bright sunlight I realized I was looking at a pathway of small multi-coloured pebbles set in weathered cement. The design showed the Medici balls, set in decayed rococo lozenges leading down towards the garden.

A balustrade terminated the formal patio, supporting two dwarfs on plinths. They seemed disturbingly real, as if some witty duke had cast two of his servants in stone. One sat on an owl, the other on a tortoise, both familiars of the place. The dwarfs struggled against the ivy with biceps of crumbling stone.

The garden was in the English style, which meant that someone had planted a few exotic trees in an apparently natural way many years ago. Two cedars of Lebanon; a eucalyptus with bright red bark; underneath, lawn.

Bored with the municipal air of it all we soon walked back towards the castle, catching sight of a pretty *limonaia* – a place in which lemon trees are kept in winter – built against the external wall. Here we found a group of workmen in overalls of municipal blue eating their lunch out of bags and baskets. A cheerful building, large and airy, with ramps against the back wall on which to place the lemon trees, and a large winch in the middle like a boat-haul for the heavier ones. The workmen sat on the ramps or on upended terracotta pots. As we stood there, a latecomer came in with his arms full of zucchini, which suggested that he was doubling his pittance from the USL with some private enterprise deep in the shrubbery.

Careggi

'The lemon trees this year grew fast for a fortnight,' I said to the nearest man in blue, 'and then they suddenly stopped dead.' He said '*È!*' as if I weren't the only philosopher to have noticed this interesting phenomenon. So we exchanged views on exactly the right mixture for lemon trees in pots, the perfect proportion of sulphate of iron, crushed lupin seed, rabbit shit and earth.

Vittoria left. I followed after a moment. She looked well, walking ahead with very brown legs in a short khaki skirt.

She stopped to sniff a wisteria still in flower against the castle wall, at which it fell completely to pieces, like a magician's wand. I laughed. It seemed so symbolic. She gave me a glance of thunder from a clear sky, and walked away. She does not enjoy being teased.

She told me later, to make up for her sudden spasm of I-want-to-be-alone, that she had been curious to find the zucchini patch, as that bit of the garden might have had more love invested in it than the rest. It was too well hidden, however. But, under a sad rhododendron, she found what seemed at first to be two large rubbish-bags, tied loosely at the throat. Then one of them blinked a vivid eye and instantly they became a pair of peacocks.

Moving abruptly, with pauses for thought, they left the shade and came softly to a sunny glade. Diffident, they seemed to require a frozen glance at Vittoria with each step, first from one eye, then from the other. But once in the sunlight the male forgot about her human presence and began to display for the female. He unfurled his tail like a large Japanese fan and hoisted it vertically above him. He seemed to wear it in the middle of his back. His wing-tips dragged stiffly on the ground; he stamped. The female took no notice. His fan trembled. He looked straight ahead, his head bright blue against the bark-like pattern of his tail.

173

Vittoria said that he was still very young, with only two or three bright green feathers just beginning to grow, as touching as the first pubic hairs on the body of an adolescent. And when he turned, the peacock had a whole fluffy bouquet of soft feathers behind him, so downy they made his tail look like reinforced bronze. In the middle of this delicate nest, his pink anus, pulsating.

Describing the peacocks in beautiful Italian – her English was good but a bit stilted – Vittoria was at her best. She became what she described. She turned, and I saw a tail leap up momentarily from the middle of her back. An effect of the sunlight, before we went our different ways.

As he lay dying, in an upper room at Careggi, Lorenzo de' Medici sent for Savonarola, who was on the brink of the final phase of his turbulent career and was undoubtedly the most charismatic figure in Florence at the time.

The monk entered the sick man's room, and Lorenzo, before even discussing the question of a deathbed confession, began talking of three events which weighed on his conscience: the sack of Volterra – a murky and sad military mistake for which Lorenzo was not entirely responsible; the theft of money from a fund for orphaned girls; and the severe repression which followed the Pazzi conspiracy, a failed attempt to murder him.

As Lorenzo moved restlessly about the bed, Savonarola repeated soothingly that God was good, God was merciful.

'But for true repentance,' said Savonarola, 'you will require three things: faith in the mercy of God – '

'*Questa l'ho grandissima,*' said the poor man. 'That I have immensely.'

'Then you must restore the various monies you have stolen,'

at which Lorenzo looked more upset than repentant, but nodded all the same.

'Lastly, you must restore Liberty to the people of Florence.' At which Lorenzo turned his face away without replying. Savonarola left without giving him absolution, and he died a few days later. [43]

This was the legend for which Vittoria and I were trying to establish some substance.

Could such a melodramatic confrontation ever have taken place? Was it likely that Lorenzo would send for Savonarola, who hitherto had shown singular ingratitude, in Florentine terms, for the help (the *raccomandazione*) that Lorenzo had given him in his early career? If he had come, was it likely that the two men would have discussed the question of Florentine liberty? Such a subject, at such a time?

Lorenzo de' Medici was a man who ruled Florence very much from behind the scenes, leaving intact the institutional 'Liberties' to which the Florentines were so passionately attached. His son Piero, however, was much disliked. Piero's mother was an Orsini, and unpopular, and the Florentines thought of Piero himself as a vulgar and aggressive Roman.

Lorenzo might have felt that he was leaving Piero a fragile inheritance. Apocryphal though the whole incident might seem, it was just possible that Lorenzo had indeed called for Savonarola, in order to try one last time to consolidate support for his son and bridge the large gap between the ruling oligarchy which Lorenzo dominated, and the *popolo minuto* which hung on every word that Savonarola preached.

Savonarola was for the people – or at least for those who filled his church and cried in agony when stirred by his language. The cry for Liberty ascribed to Savonarola might easily have been some garbled memory, tidied up after the event, of a last and desperate discussion about the future of Florence after Lorenzo's imminent death.

One cannot to take at face value the testimony historians, contemporary or recent, for whom Savonarola was a great religious and political hero. His followers at the time were called Piagnoni, 'Weepers', just as his opponents were called Arrabiati, 'Angry Ones', and a middle ground between these two extremes has yet to be reached, even today.

Two contemporary witnesses describe the incident from within Lorenzo's own circle: the philosopher Pico della Mirandola describes the whole incident in his *Life of Savonarola*, and in a letter to one Iacopo Antiquario, the distinguished classicist Poliziano describes Savonarola's visit, but says the conversation was no more than a pious injunction to repent and make peace with God.

In his letter Poliziano makes clear that this conversation took place before there was any question of a confession – to which after all he could have had no legitimate access. Yet he is equally clear that Savonarola left without blessing Lorenzo, and in stating this he undermines his own contention that the two men discussed neutral topics. Poliziano's letter could be construed 'I can't tell you what they said, but Savonarola went away without blessing Lorenzo,' leaving it to local gossip to clarify to Messer Iacopo what in fact had taken place.

Pico della Mirandola's version is equally circumscribed, but he implies that he and Savonarola arrived together, that he left him alone with Lorenzo, but that Savonarola left the room very soon after. There remains the possibility that Lorenzo sent for Savonarola himself, using Pico as an intermediary. This would make sense, as the two men were quite close at the time.

There at Careggi that afternoon, the question boiled down to this. Poliziano said he was a witness to this non-confessional confession. Right! It's too complicated to substantiate who said what to whom, but can we at least establish that the meeting took place? Where was Poliziano standing when Lorenzo turned his face to the wall?

To my surprise, the adventure of examining the death chamber turned out to be well worth waiting for.

I joined Vittoria in the courtyard at exactly twelve-thirty, at the base of the stone staircase under the rusted lamp. We walked up towards the sky once more, turned left into the room of unlikely portraits, knocked on the farthest gloomy door, and were told that Franco was out. I explained we had an appointment; they said I should come back at two-thirty. I said no, Franco said twelve-thirty, and looked firmly at my watch to prove it.

After some hesitation we were let into the Holy of Holies, where no meeting was going on, just the Director, Dr Rossi, standing by his massive desk, unperturbed by the news that we were important art historians.

I explained the predicament. Was this the room in which Lorenzo died? Dr Rossi said '*Prego*', and made a gesture with his hand. As I remember the scene two days later in writing it down, I see a large bed in the central wall, black, tousled, unoccupied – and as it happens non-existent. The presence of Dr Rossi must be very powerful, to bring a bed into my head just by saying '*prego*'.

'Would you care to see the *guardaroba*?'

We said we would be delighted. '*Prego!*' Behind a small door was a tiny ante-room, where two art historians and a USL baron had difficulty in standing together in suitably formal distribution. Frescos soared above our heads, the room being much taller than it was wide.

'But these frescos,' said Vittoria, 'are sixteenth century . . . '

'*Certo*,' said Dr Rossi, 'but the structure of the room is exactly as it was when Lorenzo died.'

We started to snoop around. A second small door led to a short corridor which became narrower towards the end. A slightly provisional wash-basin was set into some sort of indented cupboard on our right. We were within one flimsy door of Dr Rossi's private toilet; with great politeness he urged us to look further, around, beneath, above.

Hmm – 'above' was the word. Opening a cupboard, Vittoria saw part of a flight of steps near the ceiling. 'And where do those go?' she asked. Puzzled, Dr Rossi said, 'Truly, I cannot explain.' We all looked at the outside of the cupboard, where the steps should have descended. Nothing. Sixteenth-century nothing, at that. Then we noticed that there was just space enough, above the lintel of the door, for the staircase to change direction.

With authority, Dr Rossi took us back to his main office, Lorenzo's death chamber, and rang for a secretary. 'Would you kindly take these *studiosi* upstairs, to the room above, and find out if there is a continuation of this staircase up there? When you have done so, please refer back to me.' The secretary looked thrilled. A treasure-hunt!

'I am so glad,' I told Dr Rossi, 'that I have aroused your curiosity about something which would otherwise have been a great imposition upon your precious time.' A very faint smile appeared on the doctor's face as he said goodbye.

But the secretary ruined my fine exit line by breaking into a tale of how just last week she had been talking with Gigi downstairs about this staircase they had discovered on the ground floor, going upwards, and if she was right, there might be a beginning to it as well as an end, surely? Formal again, Dr Rossi said, 'Take these studious personages *up*stairs, and when you have taken them *up*stairs, take them *down*stairs to speak with Gigi, and then come back and tell me what you all discover.'

Ignoring her boss, the secretary was already telephoning

down to Gigi, before taking us through a rambling warren of corridors to the upper reaches of the palace.

In the attic we found a kind of roost of secretaries, in their lunch hour, in a circle, in a haze of cigarette smoke, including one who was pregnant and dazed-looking. 'These are two art historians,' said the secretary. General titters. Through the lunch room, and we were in – what a business – the upstairs secretaries' toilet. Much too cramped for such a crowd, with buckets, mop and a brimming waste-bin.

I overcame my growing embarrassment with enthusiasm. I was the very image of a galloping art historian on the trail. We measured, stretching out arms. A German art historian would do it better, I said. He would be armed with a useful pocket tape-measure. I leaped out of the window on to the balcony that ran round the old battlements, and proved by nimble-fingered deduction that there was just room between drains and outer wall for there to be . . .

Downstairs was more promising. Gigi sobered me up. The secret passage, he said calmly, begins just above the cupboard in the back room. We walked through small rooms made still smaller by endless files of paperwork tied in harassed bundles. We found the cupboard. Above, there was a little hatch. Open hatch, flourish, crane necks – and hey presto, a fine but very small staircase leading upward. Ten or fifteen steps had been removed to make way for yet another toilet, for gentlemen this time.

I made a greedy examination, perched on a shelf of files. The steps were of *pietra serena* and the whole atmosphere was grander than the usual backstairs servants' entrance.

'Definitely a secret passageway,' I said, 'by which the Prince could escape from assassins.'

'Or send away mistresses,' said Gigi.

I didn't care for that. Like a fire-escape in Pimlico.

Vittoria started on a discourse about the paranoia of the Medici, their many escape routes, and their habit of using chimneys as microphones, a use recommended by Leon Battista Alberti in his book on architecture. I could tell by the sound of her voice that the excitement of the chase had got to her.

I shook Gigi warmly by the hand. He looked momentarily uncertain, feeling himself mocked. I took a step towards the secretary to kiss her on both cheeks, thought better of it, and so we stumbled out. In the garden, Vittoria took me by an elbow to walk back down the hill.

'It is enough to show,' she said, 'that Poliziano could have been present when Lorenzo spoke to Savonarola, using the secret staircase, or just by standing in the *guardaroba*. In fact, Lorenzo might have wanted him to be there. If it was not a real confession . . . '

Hilarity overcame us as we crunched the gravel outside, under the vast trees with small leaves far above.

'*Ach so*,' I said. 'One forgets how public a lot of private life was in the early Renaissance.'

'It is possible,' said Vittoria, 'that you have given to the evidence a real argument. Bravo!'

'A fact,' I said. 'A compliment, and coming from you! Why, I could set it in gold and pin it on your mother's hand-me-down Chanel jacket!'

A manic employee of the USL sprayed us with gravel as he rode up to the castle on a small loud bike.

We came out of the baroque gates into the flow of traffic outside the hospital of Careggi, and the mood instantly changed. Some thin cloud came over the adamant sky, suggesting the passage of a new cold front. About time. We could do with some rain.

We found the row of poplars and the car, turned, and drove round a queue of thoughtful relatives out from town on a visit to smashed patients, waiting for the bus to come back down the hill.

Outside the hospital chapel there was a whole truckload of flowers, the truck battered, the wreaths beautiful, faintly like Della Robbia garlands in their shininess. Two groups of well-dressed people stood either side of the dark entrance to the church, looking as irritated as people can at funerals. I saw a shrouded man, part of the volunteer Misericordia who wear black fourteenth-century hoods, carrying a small tray with implements. The hearse was a little further on.

We drove back towards town. A mile further up the road, two strange shops echoed the subliminal theme of mortality that had underlined the morning: La Casa del Materasso, with a whole window of mummified bolsters, and Salumificcio Migrana. Things to catch the eye, with a headache coming on.

14 · FIRE

The fire which consumed Savonarola and his two companions shines out from the unkempt body of the Florentine Renaissance like the eye of an enraged tiger. The trauma of his death profoundly affected artists of the generation of Michelangelo, even though it remains controversial to try to trace signs of it in their work.

Savonarola made his death into a symbol, an enigma. At some point during the three trials, with torture, which preceded his execution, he became convinced that his capacity to foresee the future had been taken away from him. Pondering deeply his own impending death, Savonarola decided that silence at the portal of this great new world was best. Christ on the Cross had made no protest against his persecutors; the last obsession of Savonarola was that his own life was a parallel to that of Christ.

Death was an important moment in the late middle ages. Any biography would concentrate with great attention on the last few hours, the final words. It is as if at that brief moment some fragile gateway was opened between life and death, and the eager eavesdropper expected some revelation which would justify a man's whole life. Savonarola was parsimonious with his last words and took care that his disciples kept silent as well.

It was some time before the execution took place. At a late

Daughters, mid seventies

The young offspring of an 'alternative nuclear family' that retreated deep into the Sienese countryside in the late sixties to produce beans, cabbages and children. Their clothes were sewn for them by their mother.

Sharecropper, or mezzadro, 1968

Vittorio Fosi was our nearest neighbour when we first came. Here he is removing large stones from a collapsed outhouse using his plough-team of white oxen.

The cows would take turns in carrying a calf, or *vitellino*, in alternate years, to be sold for meat. These beautiful animals used to spend most of their short lives in the stalls that were situated on the ground floor of the farm building, giving warmth to the upper storey in winter.

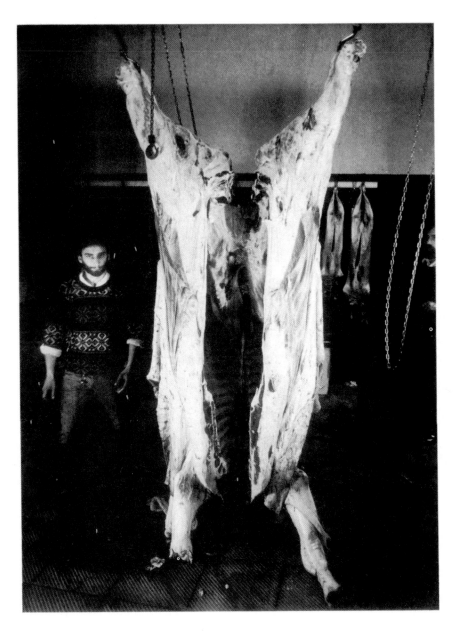

Death of a vitellino

Paolo Burrini of Gaiole hoists up a freshly killed carcass to be skinned.

Local slaughterhouses are becoming a rarity, as the Common Market considers large centralized slaughterhouses to be more efficient. A large slaughterhouse is, however, unlikely to be more humane than a small one towards the animal itself, in this seldom witnessed drama of everyday life.

Factory workers, Pianella

Luciano Fosi (*right*) is the son of Vittorio, our former neighbour.

From about 1970 onwards the sharecropping system was abolished and the former *contadini* became salaried agricultural workers. Their children often preferred to work in the factories in the nearest towns. Luciano here stands among his colleagues in a small plastics factory outside Pianella, between Gaiole and Siena.

Hunters

Luciano Fosi (*right*) with Libero Mugelli, the local carpenter, after a day spent hunting wild boar.

The indigenous Tuscan boar was 'improved' after the war by the introduction of a heavier species from Hungary. The cross is so prolific that in certain parts of Tuscany farmers strap their guns to the flanks of their tractors, like cowboys, to be ready to defend their crops against the wandering hoards of wild pigs.

Village carpenter
Libero at work restoring a chest of drawers, in the little village of San Sano.

Florentine master craftsman

Ettore Fallani, a carver of stone cameos, holding the brass positives from which the pantograph will cut reduced versions in lapis lazuli, Belgian marble or mother-of-pearl. Behind him stands a plaster cast from Michelangelo's David.

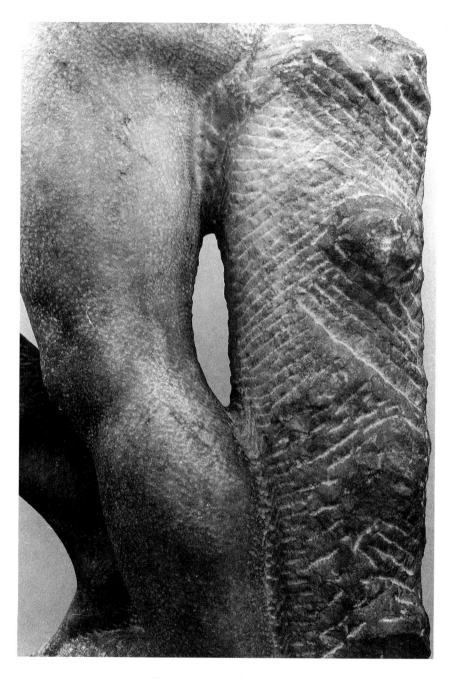

The handwriting of Michelangelo

Chisel marks on the back of an unfinished carving by Michelangelo in the Bargello in Florence ...

Pavement cutter

... and a mason flattening a *pietra serena* pavement in Siena.

These two photographs indicate that the technique used by Michelangelo when he carved stone was very close to that used by an experienced stonecarver today. The same straightforwardness can be seen in Michelangelo's drawings and frescos, indicating that the qualities this extraordinary genius possessed were not so much technical as expressive.

Parish priest

Don Osvaldo Secciani of Monti di San Marcellino, outside the church of San Giusto in Salcio, near Radda.

Bootmaker

Beppe Mugnaini of Gaiole in Chianti, holding a boot he has made, and a small tuba called a *bombardino*, which he plays in the Associazione Filarmonica of Gaiole.

Girls in the band

In June 1991 a concert featuring five bands, from Sinalunga, Torrita, Betolle, Badia San Salvadore and Chianti took place at Sinalunga and lasted all afternoon.

The Banda del Chianti consisted mainly of the Gaiole band, with some elements from Radda. At the back, Massimiliano Frosini, Filippo Nesi, Giacomo Dominati. In the foreground, Angela Nicomedi and Samanta Betti, flutes; Cristina Nesi and Carolina Fabiani, clarinets. Samanta comes from Radda, all the others from Gaiole.

Sinalunga

The bands La Samba of Torrita and La Folkloristica of Betolle are unusual in that they are preceded when they march by majorettes, a practice which is very popular with the public. Traditional rivals, the girls in their different uniforms (one red, one blue) join in a cheerful knees–up at the end of the Sinalunga concert.

Baptism into the contrada

Siena is divided into seventeen constituencies or *contrade*, descended from military associations of the late middle ages.

The allegiance to a *contrada* is as strong a bond as the ties of family. Children are baptized into their *contrada* in a short ceremony outside their church, with a blessing which is also an oath to protect and continue the ancient customs. This child has just become a *Chiocciolina*, or Little Snail, as she belongs to the noble *Contrada* of the Snail.

La mossa

The moment before the Palio starts is always one of great tension.

The horses are required to enter between two ropes before the start is given. The last horse to enter is called '*di rincorso*' and the jockey is allowed to choose his own moment. In the July Palio of 1991, where this photo was taken, the *cavallo di rincorso* refused to enter the ropes because the jockey of the rival *contrada* was in a good position for the start. The race had to be postponed to the following day – much to the annoyance of all the notables who had come to Siena especially to witness the race.

Catharsis

The excitement generated by a victory in the Palio is incomprehensible to anyone who is not Sienese. The race is run purely for honour. There are no side-bets. The winning *contrada* makes no financial gain, but on the contrary often has to spend large sums of money in preparations, bribes, in order to bring the Palio back home. Violent rage, euphoria, grief, triumph, is visible in the streets for some hours after the race is over, giving momentarily an idea of what Tuscan city-states might have been like in a distant age.

stage it was noticed that the gibbet resembled a cross, and a carpenter was sent to cut down the arms to reduce the likeness.

Savonarola and his two companions were then formally removed from the Church. Savonarola made an impassioned speech in its praise, and they were then just as formally reinstated to the Church, with indulgence for their sins, all of which they accepted with bowed heads. It was important that Savonarola died reconciled to the Catholic Church. His was not the revolution of Luther, less than twenty years later.

They were to be hanged, then burned. As they marched along the wooden ramp to the scaffold, small boys thrust nails from below through the gaps in the planks so as to hurt their feet. The three men were undistracted from their intense concentration on the next world.

Savonarola watched his two closest companions die before him, one after the other, and as he himself mounted the ladder a voice from the crowd yelled, 'Now is the time to perform a miracle.' At this point the apologetic biographers of Savonarola break down. Such inhuman cruelty, in the small boys with nails and the ironic voice from the crowd. The wonderful biographies by Villari and by Ridolfi implicitly accept the resemblance to the figure of Christ. But in a sense this voice from the crowd was offering Savonarola one last chance to produce what he himself had always promised, and what his Florentine audience certainly expected – a sign from God that his prophecies and dire predictions had divine inspiration behind them. But he died in silence, shrouding an ambiguous career in a cloak of impenetrable absence.

After he was hanged and the fire ignited, a downward gust of wind for a moment flattened the flames, sending acrid smoke into the crowd. His followers at the back cried out, 'A miracle!' Then the flames rose higher and the bodies, still amid an attentive silence, were gradually devoured by the flames. The fire eventually severed the ropes which bound Savonarola's hands and the heat caused his right arm to rise up. His two forefingers seemed to give the crowd a final benediction and again his followers at the back cried out 'A miracle.' Then those close by threw stones until the arm broke off at the trunk and fell, to be consumed among the hot coals.

His brave death reveals nothing. The real trial by fire had taken place in that same Piazza della Signoria some eight weeks earlier, requiring from Savonarola gifts of leadership and intelligence, not to speak of prior preparation in the political hinterland, which in the end he was unable to produce.

Girolamo Savonarola was born in Ferrara in 1452 and joined the Dominican Order in Bologna as a novice in 1475. After a thorough academic training, which was completed at the University of Ferrara, he was sent to the convent of San Marco in Florence. Chance may have dictated this move; the threat of war in the Romagna might have prompted the removal to safe places of some of the more promising novices. Or perhaps he had been noticed in a debate by Pico della Mirandola, a future friend who later wrote a biography of him.

His early career was not successful. His voice was harsh and grating, and he made none of the sophisticated classical references or quotations from poetry which the more cultured Florentine listeners expected. One scholar has found the accounts of Orsanmichele, where he first preached, and it seems that donations from the flock were slightly higher when Savonarola was preaching, but this beautiful detail seems to me inconclusive as evidence of his supposed early success.

In 1485 he was preaching in San Gimignano, and from 1487 he was in the north of Italy, until in 1490 he was recalled to Florence by Lorenzo de' Medici. First in San Marco, then in the

Duomo, Savonarola embarked on a series of passionate sermons calling for the reform of the Church, predicting the vengeance of Heaven if this did not take place.

He was elected Prior of San Marco in 1491, whereupon he separated the church from its superiors in Lombardy. Thereafter his sermons became directed very specifically at Florence, calling for reform in both religious and political life. For a while he crystallized republican opposition to the secretive rule of Lorenzo de' Medici.

Piero de' Medici, Lorenzo's successor, embarked on a hazardous foreign policy in opposition to French interests. Savonarola predicted that this would end in disaster, but he may simply have been reflecting the anxiety of those numerous Florentine merchants with contacts in France.

Charles VIII of France invaded Italy in August 1494 – a new Charlemagne, as Savonarola put it, coming not in peace but with the sword. Pisa was taken, and in the panic that followed, Piero de' Medici was exiled from Florence. For a moment it looked as if the city might be attacked. Savonarola went to Pisa to negotiate with Charles. In the event, Charles and his army passed through Florence quite peacefully, and continued on south; in the eyes of the Florentines, Savonarola had saved the city single-handed. The other considerations which might have encouraged the French king to be lenient to Florence (the risks to his army, the damage to trade) tended to be forgotten.

Florence underwent a political revolution. Savonarola's popularity was enormous, his sermons devoted to political matters. Many people at the time, and a number of magnificent, highly honourable and extraordinarily thorough scholars since, have taken Savonarola to have been instrumental in establishing the political constitution based on democratic principles which was then drawn up. But the question of Savonarola's precise relationship to the reforming group in the Florentine Council remains to be established. A strict chronology relating his sermons to the minutes of the Council would clarify who in fact had the initiative. Could not Savonarola have been a mere voice of one faction of the reformers, with the job of inspiring support for them among his now vast flock?

What is certain is that reform of the Church, not politics, was Savonarola's prime concern. The two became intertwined in that both seemed to be centred on Florence. By separating San Marco from its immediate superiors Savonarola had seemed to threaten an internal revolt against the authority of the pope. Indeed it seems possible that he came close to challenging the pope directly. When he was excommunicated in June 1497, he wrote letters to all the leaders of Christendom asking for the formation of some sort of council, but whether to appeal against the indictment or to question the authority of the pope we do not know. We have a rough idea of their contents from two other letters written by collaborators to recipients in France and Spain, in which this step is described. These seem to be indirect approaches to the kings of France and Spain, testing the ground for possible support.

The fact that Savonarola's own letters were destroyed is important, and came up in his last trial before the cardinals from Rome. As these letters had not been sent Savonarola could claim that he had not directly challenged the authority of the pope.

The fall of Savonarola was confused in the extreme. The point came when the pope, irritated by Savonarola's extremely powerful denunciations of the corruption of the Church, placed him under an interdict requiring him to refrain from preaching.[44] This task devolved on his close follower, Fra Domenico, who found himself in direct rivalry with a Franciscan preacher,

Francesco di Puglia. (Savonarola was a Dominican, and the Dominicans were rivals of the Franciscans.)

In one of his great sermons in the Piazza della Signoria, Savonarola had raised his eyes to Heaven and said, 'If what I say is not true, may God send down a ball of fire to consume me.' This image must have remained firmly in the minds of those listening. On 25 March 1498 Francesco di Puglia, the Franciscan opponent, challenged Savonarola to 'enter the fire' to prove the validity of his doctrines. This archaic challenge was instantly accepted by Fra Domenico.

Three days later a complicated contract was ratified in the *Comune* which said, among other things, that Fra Domenico would enter the fire to prove that the excommunication of Savonarola was invalid.

Only at this point does it seem to have dawned on Francesco di Puglia that in a duel of this sort, he too would have to enter the fire. He panicked. He was hustled to sign the document by Savonarola's enemies, who apparently said that of course there would be no question of his actually getting into the flames. 'Don't worry. Trust us,' they said. One can imagine the man's feelings. What would they care about me, he might have said, so long as Savonarola burns? Except that it was not Savonarola who had taken up the challenge, but Fra Domenico.

Un vero pasticcio, as they would say today – a real mess.

On 30 March this extraordinary business came before the Council, and luckily the minutes of this meeting have been preserved. [45] A number of councillors seem to indicate that they felt disgust at wasting time on this 'friars' business'. A known enemy of Savonarola said, 'if our founding fathers had known we were discussing such a thing here, they would certainly be ashamed'. A colleague added: 'this is a business of preachers, which ought to be settled in Rome where they canonize saints, rather than in the Signoria, where it is more important to talk about the war and money'.

Indeed, the external position of Florence seemed particularly hazardous at the time, relations with France, Venice, Milan and the Church all being precarious. Girolamo Rucellai said, 'I think we are making too much of a fuss about this fire. The important thing is to get rid of both the Friar [i.e. Savonarola] and his opponents, and then we can think for once of the unity of the citizens. But if you think you can unite the city with this experiment, you can go into the fire, or water, or air, or earth, as long as you apply your attention to the city, and not to monks.' At which an honourable gentleman got up and said that he, personally, found the idea of fire very unpleasant, but if Savonarola wanted to immerse himself in water for a bit without drowning, why then he would be the first to change his mind and start believing. Ministerial laughter.

All this is taken by Villari and Ridolfi as evidence of (*a*) a clever plot against Savonarola and (*b*) the deeply cynical and irreligious sentiment of the members of the Council. Savonarola certainly had his enemies; but it seems more plausible that most of the right honourable members felt horror camouflaged with a kind of sick humour at the idea that time had to be spent in discussing this primitive duel when there were so many more important problems on the agenda.

Fra Domenico's Franciscan opponents – at this point there were two of them – were rumoured to be doing everything possible to get out of the trial. It became the turn of Savonarola and his over-excited supporters to promote it. On 1 April an enormous group came forward after a sermon by Fra Domenico and said that they, too, would walk into the fire for Savonarola.

Because of the interdict Savonarola could not preach, but he could pray, and on the morning of 7 April in front of a large crowd before San Marco, just before leading some two hundred and fifty followers down to the Piazza della Signoria, he prayed: 'You know, O Lord, that I have not assumed this labour through ambition. You know that the call was yours.'

Fire dominates the existence of Savonarola in so many ways. There were the strange Burnings of the Vanities, when his followers piled up symbols of worldly pleasures on an ornate pyre and burned them. This took place during the Carnival, his intention being to create a pentitential festival to supersede a pagan one. Among the ribbons and mirrors, there were even drawings, paintings and statues, put there by the artists themselves. [46]

In the case of the Trial by Fire, however, we are dealing with a fire that was never lit.

They marched down in pairs, ranked in age, singing. Fra Domenico, Savonarola's champion, wore a flame-red cassock, Savonarola carried the Host in a silver case. As they entered the Piazza della Signoria they sang in Latin, calling on the Lord to arise and scatter his enemies.

The crowd was exceptionally divided. The Piagnoni, the supporters of Savonarola, had their own guards. So did their enemies, the Arrabiati, the Scioperati, the Compagnacci – all representing various flavours of political rage which Savonarola had indirectly created. The guards about the Signoria were supposed to be neutral. Within, the Council schemed, or was a prey to scheming. There were supporters of Savonarola who were in favour of the trial, because they believed he would be vindicated, and there were opponents of his who were against it, because they found it disgusting.

If there was a plot, it was to *refrain* from burning anyone on this occasion, for it was not Savonarola who was to enter the fire, but Fra Domenico. By making it look as if Savonarola had refused the challenge, the plotters would destroy his hold on the large segment of the crowd outside who wanted their belief in him confirmed by a miracle.

The unlit pyre ran parallel to the Loggia, from Rivoire's café (as it were) to the Palazzo Vecchio. About two metres high and forty long, it was built of tiles and rubble on which was laid a double line of wood impregnated with oil and gunpowder waiting to be lit. The contestants were to begin walking simultaneously from either end, passing each other as they made their way through to the opposite end.

Fra Domenico prayed in front of an improvised altar in front of the Loggia, after which there was an interminable wait. Repeated embassies throughout the day were seen to come out of the Palazzo della Signoria to beg Savonarola to begin, or so it seemed. In fact the Franciscans were tightly tucked away in the palace, and never appeared to take their places at the far end of the unlit pyre. More messengers came. Would Fra Domenico remove his cloak? His tunic? Sensibly Savonarola said he did not believe in witchcraft, but, well, if they insisted, they would. And each of these exchanges required movement to and fro, from the palace to the Piagnoni huddled expectantly around the Friar, their leader.

The crowd became very restless. At one point a scuffle broke out. It seemed that a captain of one group of guards called Doffo Spini tried to grab Girolamo, and was halted by another captain called Salviati, who was loyal to him. In the middle of the afternoon, it suddenly rained. A sudden drenching downpour of ten minutes which stopped as abruptly as it started. The followers of Savonarola shouted that this was a sign from God that the Trial by Fire should not take place. The supporters of the Franciscans shouted back that it was witchcraft.

Time was needed for the wood to dry, and the day began to wane. Still there was no sign from the Franciscan champions. On the contrary, a new embassy came forward to ask Fra

Domenico to remove his crucifix, which might also have been bewitched. Fra Domenico initially refused, but gave way, on condition that he could at least carry the Host with him into the fire. The Franciscans said this would be sacrilege. A long wrangle followed, in which Savonarola joined, discussing whether or not the Body of Christ could be intrinsically harmed if the Host was burned. This went on until nightfall, when the Council called the contest off.

The crowd put the blame entirely on Savonarola. After all, they had seen repeated embassies come out from the Palazzo to beg him to begin, all to no apparent purpose.

With difficulty Savonarola marched his followers back to San Marco, and by nightfall the place was attacked by a large group of well-armed enemies backed up by a frustrated and angry segment of the crowd from the piazza. San Marco was under siege for two days, and some innocent people were murdered, before Savonarola surrendered. In these two days of anxious prayer, it is possible that already he began to see himself as following the example of Christ, but the various accounts which cover the last actions of Savonarola are tinted by hagiography. Fra Domenico arranged the surrender, after Savonarola had ordered armed resistance to cease. As Savonarola was taken, Fra Domenico joined him, uttering enigmatically: 'I too wish to come to this marriage.'

There is a contemporary text by one Lorenzo Violi which gives confirmation of the substance of the plot behind the Trial by Fire. What makes this all the more fascinating is that the witness Violi summons to substantiate the claim is Simone Filipepe, brother of the painter Sandro Botticelli.

... the man who set it all up said so himself, and he was a leader of the Compagnacci. A courageous and arrogant man who never admitted he had done wrong, but on the contrary was proud of it – Doffo, I tell you. And after the Friar was dead, time and again he'd brag about it and about the schemes and tricks they'd used to get rid of him.

And among the many times he boasted about it, I'll tell you one place he repeated it, often. He was frequently to be found in the workshop of a painter called Sandro Botticelli, a man well known in the city for being one of the best painters of the time. In this studio there was always a group of Scioperati [more enemies of Savonarola], including this Doffo. As they often talked of the Friar's death, Doffo said they never had any intention of putting the Friar of San Francesco [Francesco di Puglia, Fra Domenico's Franciscan opponent] into the fire, and guaranteed this, reassuring him constantly; it was enough that they *pretend* to do so for a while, so that by postponing the business people would eventually turn on the Friar and get rid of him.

It happened that Doffo talked about this so often in the studio of Sandro [Botticelli] that Simone, Sandro's brother, being always present, made a note of it in his diary . . . It seemed to him that this remark of Doffo was worth noting down, to discover the truth in this obscure matter. [47]

That this story centres upon Doffo Spini gives it credibility, for as we have seen he was the captain of one segment of the guard on the day of the Trial by Fire – that same man who tried to grab Savonarola during one of the scuffles.

The fact that Doffo chose Sandro Botticelli's studio in which to boast about it is important for another reason. Simone Filipepe was a noted Piagnone and a passionate supporter of Savonarola. Vasari maintains that Botticelli was a Piagnone himself.

In his *Lives of the Artists*, he suggests that Botticelli turned to Savonarola soon after having undertaken the illustration of Dante's *Inferno*:

> which took up much of his time, and kept him from his work, and was the cause of infinite disorganization in his life. Then he published . . . [a print of] the *Triumph of Faith of Fra Girolamo Savonarola of Ferrara*, and he was very loyal to this sect. This was the cause of his giving up painting so that, without income, his life fell into disorder. Taking passionate sides and giving up work to devote all his time to being a Piagnone, growing old and forgotten, he fell into a bad way. [48]

Simone's own diary has been lost, but now and again fragments from it turn up in quotations in later documents. One of these fragments continues the saga: 'hearing the noise that was taking place in the forward shop, Sandro came to see what was the matter. When we had explained what it was that we had discussed, he said, "I do not see what harm the Friar has done."' [49]

This minute detail is again valuable, for it is one of the only contemporary confirmations of Vasari's allegation that the painter Sandro was a Piagnone.

Nowadays, the story is played down. The list of Botticelli's works does not end in 1498, the year of Savonarola's death. On the contrary the number of works produced per year increases slightly. [50] The latest scholarship indicates that Botticelli did not go into a decline in later life.

Looking at it closely, does the participation of Sandro Botticelli in this studio squabble indicate a passionate taking of sides? Recapitulating briefly, we have on the one side Doffo Spini, ex-leader of the anti-Savonarola faction, an arrogant and fairly violent man with (says Violi) a few mates of similar views who happened to work in Botticelli's studio. And on the other, Simone, Sandro's brother, a known sympathizer of the Piagnoni. A fight starts. Enter Sandro from his inner studio, who asks what the row is about. When it is explained, he says that, in his opinion, he does not think the Friar has done any wrong.

Surely this is the most neutral remark he could possibly make in these disrupted circumstances – tinged, perhaps, with slightly more sympathy for his brother than for Doffo, but on the whole, admirably detached?

Two brief personal considerations, one about Vasari, one about what goes on inside the heads of artists when they work.

Vasari is the founding father of modern art history, and the creator of a certain idea of what artists' lives should look like from outside. For him the figure of the artist is entirely heroic. Vasari took his sense of structure and of moral purpose from Plutarch's *Parallel Lives*, where it is quite evident that the facts are distorted in order to convey a message. Plutarch says as much: his intention is to create moral uplift in the reader by showing the most inspiring sides of his heroes, stressing the aspects of self-sacrifice and patriotism rather than personal ambition. [51]

Because Vasari took Plutarch so literally, we all abide, to this day, by the conviction that art consumes the lives of those who practise it. The blank canvas or the lump of stone have become by association the walls of Corioli or the raging Hellespont. This is a belief not only of art historians, but of artists themselves, who mould their existences according to a preconception that is late classical, topped with Renaissance curlicues placed there by Giorgio Vasari.

And if Napoleon went to bed before a battle with Plutarch's *Lives* to put him in the mood, why not all those who load brushes with paint instead of cannons with lead?

Second point, about the connection of life with art. There is absolutely no doubt (to me) that Savonarola had an enormous influence upon the lives of Botticelli and Michelangelo. Indeed, with Dante and the Holy Scriptures as well, why would they need anything else? But to try to trace the presence of Savonarola in the Sistine ceiling or in the *Calunnia* in the Uffizi is to make a fundamental mistake about what paintings carry over from life into art.

Paintings can never sum up directly the reinterpreted conceptions of others. To do so turns them into illustrations, no different from the advert on TV, the floating hot-air balloon selling soap powder after the evening news. They can be a summary of the painter's own experience, which might incorporate the idea of another man – many other men – but that is something different. It does paintings no good to be unravelled iconographically, pointing out the meaning of the bent tree or the descending dove. Paintings exist as facts, in a world of facts, and facts can be perceived and reacted to, but not explained.

For more than a hundred years after his death, the Florentines placed flowers on the stones of the Piazza della Signoria where Savonarola had been burned. The fact that the great fountain of Neptune stands there now is not a coincidence. The later Medici dukes sought to quench with endless water the fire that, in the imagination of their subjects, had never been extinguished.

Even today, the statue of Neptune itself arouses mixed feelings among Florentines. There are those who call it *Il Piscione* ('The Big Pisser'), as this appears to be the gentlestatue's occupation if you look up at him from underneath, with the fountain on. Every year a wreath appears on the paving stones on 23 May, the anniversary of the fire, when the friars of San Marco come down in procession to commemorate their erring brother. And ever since the last war, a Mass has been held on that date in the Priors' Chapel of the Palazzo della Signoria, by order of the mayor. Savonarola still has his admirers among those interested in reform of the Church or democratic institutions of the state.

.For a while the fountain became an island, while the rest of the piazza was excavated by archaeologists, in what turned out to be one of the most costly holes ever dug by anyone anywhere. Some citizens protested. It was pointed out that the price of this hole would have covered fifteen or twenty kidney machines, the traditional moral counterweights to the frivolous cost of culture. But not a single Florentine remained immune to the fascination of that hole while it was there. It seemed such a magnificent symbol for a city, for a country, for a state of mind.

There were medieval levels, the bases of towers torn down when the *popolo minuto* lost its temper with the aristocrats. There were Roman levels, which were interesting inasmuch as they were Roman, and in Florence, but as Roman ruins go, boring. A small cache of Islamic coins was found somewhere, gold, from the epoch of a rare Fatimid. No statues, no works of art.

But whatever level was reached, there always seemed to be another, deeper, and at the very bottom of the Roman cellar beneath the medieval cellar beneath the . . . at the very bottom, there was always some other hole going still deeper, giving the idea of a city like our own, only going downward, the tiled roofs pointing quietly to the centre of the earth, just as Dante said.

When it rained the deeper holes filled with water. They have paved over the Piazza della Signoria again now, underlining the fact that knowledge is its own reward, deserving to fade almost as soon as it has been so painfully acquired. But while it was there, if you looked hard, craning through the metal fence, in the deeper puddles after the rain one could see the image of a former Florence, a mirror of our own.

15 · OLIVES

Late autumn is often magnificent. The sun shines all day slant-ingly, from low on the horizon, and the light becomes thin and yellow. In the clear air the shadows of the trees create filigree versions of themselves to chase around the earth. Grass patches among the ploughed fields shine bright green. As little mechanical work remains to be done in the vineyards, the clatter of tractors is rare. At weekends the buzz-saws sound like remote animals in the woods, as sharecroppers clear the scrub oaks for heating fuel. The forests turn the colour of dull copper. The air cools quickly after the sun goes down.

It takes about a month to harvest and mill the olives, and much can happen to the landscape and its climate during that time. By the second or third time you drive to the olive press with sacks of olives in the back of the car, the weather can have changed very much for the worse. In January 1985, a snowstorm followed by a deep frost killed most of the olives in Tuscany, save for some up near Lucca and, strangely enough a long swathe of trees along the higher levels of the ridge of the Apennines. The weather until then had been excellent and all the trees except for this strip were still producing vegetation. The temperature sank to −15°C. The sap froze and broke the cell walls in the many trees that were still in active growth, killing them.

The landscape under snow was incredibly beautiful. I drove the girls to school in Siena every day, twenty-six miles, a useless piece of chivalry as the Sienese parents would not send their darlings even down the road in such conditions. My daughters sat in their coats alone and in silence in the classroom facing their teachers. But the voyage was a real adventure for the three of us. Slipping and sliding all over the road, we sang songs of sleigh rides in Siberia, we drove imaginary huskies to the Pole.

Later I noticed that the exhaust of passing cars had been just warm enough to save the trees which flanked the sharp curve of the road at San Giovanni.

The second night of the frost, I went out on the white lawn to watch the full moon rise, all nicotine against the blue, snow-covered hills. A moment of rage and despair overtook me. Fifteen years of cultivation gone in a night, just when my labour was beginning to show results. Snow was on the terraces, snow weighed down the trees, it had half melted and then frozen again, and was breaking branches with the dead weight of ice. As I looked, the cold turned my tears to diamonds.

After the snow had gone, the cleverest *contadino* I knew – in fact Tullio, the owner-*contadino* of Ama mentioned in Chapter 10 – went out into the fields with his chain-saw and cut down all his olive trees. There was not a trace of sentimentality in his cheerful face as he told me this in the village a day or two later. His knowledge of olives was, say, twenty times mine, and the effort he had put into his own and those of everyone else in the neighbourhood was extraordinary, but no tears turned to diamonds on his cheeks.

The rest of us dithered. It is not absolutely certain they will die, we said, though fundamentally we knew they would. The Consorzio Agrario said to spray with this or that tasty brew of poisons, but we refrained. Instead we went out when it was all over and shook the branches, watched the leaves fall like confetti. We picked them up and fingered them, smelled them, stroked the rough trunks of the trees, but nothing sprang eagerly back to life. Then we waited some more, in order to fill out Calamity papers for the Common Market. In the end we found ourselves a year behind Tullio, who had been capable of making an intellectual decision and acting on it just as coldly as the toughest market mogul in the country. When spring came, the olives sent up suckers from the base of the tree, or from whatever part had been unaffected by the frost. The advantage that Tullio had seized was that he avoided disturbing the fragile new growth during that first year. His trees had already been cut and cleared away by the time the sap started to move. The rest of us fought a tiresome battle in June, trying to cut down the dead trunks through a girdle of young shoots that broke off if you but touched them. There followed two seasons in which the olive trees were reduced to bottlebrushes. Only after they had been left alone for two seasons could you begin to think of choosing the new leaders, reforming the tree.

In all this time, of course, there was no question of an olive harvest, and in fact the death of the Tuscan olive trees created a series of problems from which we are only now beginning to emerge. To begin with, all the olive presses closed down and quite a few have not yet reopened. If they did, they found that a new series of hygiene laws had been passed covering the ecological disposal of waste, obliging them to instal cess-tanks or sumps. Many were unwilling or unable to undertake these expenses, which made the mills which did stay open very nervous. It was tiresome taking the olives to an illegal press, with the workers looking about for government inspectors and behaving as bad-temperedly as robber bees.

Then the successful distributors of their own olive oil found themselves without produce just as the market seemed about to blossom. To retain the position they had gained, they bought oil from Umbria or Puglia and marketed this as their own. When this was discovered it threatened to destroy the whole concept of estate-bottled olive oil.

Good olive oil depends on many factors: climate, the particular kind of tree, whether it is healthy, how it is pruned and so forth. Two factors are crucial at the moment of milling: getting the fruit to the press promptly, and having efficient equipment – above all, a clean filter.

Olives tend to oxidize as soon as they are picked, gradually turning acid, and the acid content considerably affects the quality of the oil. The 'virginity' of the oil, so to speak, is relative to this acidity, which has to be below 0.5 to qualify. Do not ask me what this 0.5 means. I can only say that if you leave the olives lying around too long, the acidity goes up. Therefore countries which allow the fruit to fall from the tree by the natural force of gravity are likely to produce oil of dubious virginity. For better or worse, you have to go out there and pick the olives off the trees, and get them to the mill quite rapidly afterwards.

I used to take the night shift at the olive mill. The three to six in the morning shift has a timeless quality, like being in the engine-room of an ocean liner. Late at night, or very early in the morning, one can leave the thrum and chatter of the machines and go out on deck, as it were, to see the huge waves in their petrified state all around the horizon, sniff the empty air, navigate by the stars.

The owner of each batch of olives being pressed looks after his own produce. It is traditional to distrust the miller. Everyone knows that millers are devious creatures, prone to thieving, masters of the frank smile that denotes deceit. Chaucer said so,

Boccaccio said so, even Petronius Arbiter said so, and surely these authors spoke the truth.

The olives are weighed in the night before, and it is legitimate to ask whoever is standing by to help you with your sacks. Apparently last November I commandeered Siena's leading criminal lawyer to help with mine, as he was hanging about and doing his best to look like an indigenous rustic.

Once you have weighed in, you go home to await your turn. And how do you know that the wily miller is not nicking your bags of olives while you sleep? That's a good question. The answer is, first you count them, and write the number on a little slip of paper, which you carefully leave behind on the bags. Then, you will have tied them in a particularly idiosyncratic way that only you can recognize. Bowline-on-a-bight with pink ribbon, perhaps. Or gold thread with a parchment doyley with your name inscribed in sepia. Or string. Something unusual. Finally, all the peasants who are around the place looking lost and aimless are in fact keeping an eye out for anything manifestly dishonest, such as a miller slipping through a side door with a sack, and any direct attempt at misappropriation is likely to be noticed. Aimlessness, at the mill, is a symptom of myopic attention to just such a criminal act. It is a concentrated aimlessness, a purposeful distraction.

When your time has come, your number is up, you take the bags and loose their strings, and tip the olives into a funnel inserted into the floor in one corner of the mill. From this sump a rubber conveyor-belt raises handfuls of olives almost up to the ceiling, from which they fall into a juddering-rattling-jostling machine whose function is to remove, through a series of sieves, any stones or lumps of earth picked up during the harvesting. At the top of the conveyor-belt a powerful fan sucks away the leaves and whirls them through a short tube out into the night, where they fall through the air to form a scrubby carpet in a nearby field.

Jets of water in and out of the sieves cause your olives to re-emerge glistening and healthy-looking from the other end of the machine, where they tip into another sump in the floor in the opposite corner from where they started. From here they are conveyed by an invisible screw into the well of the stone mill in the next room, a process which leaves them munched and mouthed so that they fall beneath the stone wheels already slightly pulped.

The mill itself consists of two granite wheels turned by a powerful electric motor, on a base composed of a third granite slab. The wheels are not cantilevered, so there is slight torsion as they turn, and the olives are not only crushed but slightly ground. If the mill is empty of olives for a moment or two between pressings, the wheels leave on the base a white line like the passage of a snail – powdered granite, indicating the incredible force of these stones.

In fifteen or twenty minutes, two or three hundred kilos of olives are reduced to an oily sludge. Quite a lot depends on the fineness of this sludge. If it is too coarse, the olive stones will resist the press and reduce the amount of oil produced, if too fine, it will clog the mats.

The sludge is mechanically laid on layers of mats with a hole in the middle, and each stack of four mats lies on a steel circle with a similar hole; at which point a pair of mechanical arms takes the quintet and lifts them on to a large steel column set into a heavy cast-iron tray on wheels. This is badly expressed, but to describe the machine properly is beyond me. It is a fairly nasty machine, moving with stiff jerks in a vaguely reptilian manner, and of course it is not a good idea to get in its way. I saw a man have a piece of his head excavated by the empty claw of the mat-carrier, and as I am too tall to be protected by the safety-mesh, I tend to keep away. Managing it is a skilful job, and the agricultural worker who runs it is seen as a craftsman.

The pulp, in its column of seeping mats two metres high, is so heavy that a small manic bicycle is used to manoeuvre the object under the press. The fat wheels of this tiny bike slip on the oily cement, and wrestling with a filled column is a tiresome business. The press itself is simply a heavy steel arch with a hydraulic pump under it, so that the column is pushed up, rather than down. The oil and waste water seeps out from the sides of the mats, down into the cast-iron base, and out into a tank.

At this point the produce consists of a murky mixture of oil-and-waste, which has to be separated by a centrifugal filter. I imagine this beast to be something like the stomach of a shark, only in stainless steel. Its shiny exterior contains a large basin perforated with fine holes, moving round on a pinion at a very high speed. The principle exploits the different viscosity of water and oil. The water goes through the holes, the oil trickles down; or perhaps vice versa. At any rate the black waste water exits left, into a cloaca, while the oil exits right, into a stainless-steel tub. If the mill is obedient to the new sanitary laws, the waste will be tanked and periodically removed to be processed for fertilizer. If not, it is tactful to refrain from asking what happens to it.

Seeing the oil emerge from the filter at last is the moment to gloat, the fine thread of pure oil falling into the basin, yellow-green in colour, with a slight content of minute air bubbles which make curious patterns and whorls in the tub that fills so slowly beneath.

Someone meanwhile is left with the chore of dismantling the column of mats and eliminating the sludge, now caked hard as shortbread. A screw set in the floor digests this substance, whence it is taken out of the building at the back and discarded from a tube into the yard. The pyramid this makes is from time to time removed, so that it can be first distilled for more oil (called *olio di sansa*), and then mixed with nutritious chaff of various kinds to create something yummy for cattle.

The mill I am describing is a dull building, something like a schoolhouse, made lively only by the two tubes of waste which stick out like a pair of ridiculous horns. From one, the leaves flicker up into the air. From the other, the *sansa* falls into the muddy yard.

Cold-pressed olive oil, meaning oil which is produced by stone mills such as I have described, is considered to taste better than oil produced in the belly of a fat metal grinder warmed by a cosy of hot pipes, which is the modern alternative. This is the kind of argument which rages endlessly in the mill as one hangs about, in the same way that Cretan shepherds argue for hours over the relative advantages of rubber over leather soles to their giants' footwear. Heating the oil, the argument runs, increases the production because it becomes finer and easier to extract. But it also 'cooks' the oil, altering the taste, and this should be avoided by all serious producers of virgin oil.

I must confess I feel neutral on this world-shattering alternative. However, I do become fanatical about the state of the filter. A dirty filter leaves a residue which forms a black sludge in the bottom of the earthenware jar in which you conserve the oil, and this can quickly ruin its taste. There are mills which pretend to clean the filter, but in fact merely flush a few litres of water through it. This is irritating, and I protest, but it is difficult to win this kind of argument with the professional who is running the machine. The only answer is to change mills.

Everyone tells lies to get themselves into the mill when the time comes. '*Dottore*,' you say to the miller's foreman, beginning with a piece of abject flattery. 'I have this little *partita* of olives – nothing much, just three hundred kilos or so (i.e. enough for one load under the stones, or thirty minutes in terms of time). Could you squeeze me in?' 'Oh well,' says the *Dottore*, 'if you take the shift at four in the morning I could perhaps manage. Bring them round this afternoon to weigh in − but no more, eh?' 'No, no,' you say, and arrive with about six times the original quantity, close to midnight, when the *Dottore* has gone home, and by feats of remarkable persuasion, bluff your way in.

The olive harvest takes place from November to mid-January, in a good year perhaps even later. The quality of the oil is better early in the season, and if the weather has been seriously cold the olives will have been 'cooked'. Extremes of heat and cold affect the taste in similar ways. If you are in Tuscany over Christmas, ask at the bar of any local village where the *frantoio* (olive-mill) is to be found, buy a small demijohn or plastic container, and purchase some direct. You will be amazed to find that it will cost more than in London, let alone in the Co-op round the corner, but you will certainly be buying the real thing. The substance that never gets to the market, unless by sheer chance.

16 · MACCARI

Beside me at the library the local madman fills in his index cards with fake writing and leaves his left hand permanently upon the pile of faded newspapers whose contents he sums up. He keeps the world in order. I smile at him to show I understand this need, but his work is too serious and important for him ever to smile back.

On the next table but one a young man joined the newspaper-reading section a fortnight ago, and something he called up from the vaults made me drop for a while my researches into Hell and Montaperti. Yellowed, with few pages, it had the desperate air of a revolutionary broadsheet. The contents were bizarre. Short aphorisms like the ones peasants used as guides for planting crops, polemical texts which had it in for anybody in a high place. And wonderful woodcuts done in different coloured inks. Amazing woodcuts.

A fat lady who symbolizes the Fascist Academy feels her limbs dissolve beneath her. Sustained in the air by five stout gentlemen in tails, complete with wing-collars, ties, sashes, fresh white waistcoats, pinstripe trousers, plumes and decorations. She would certainly fall without the help of their small black legs. They carry her onwards in a rush. On her neck rides a Lilliputian general, who waves a tasselled baton in his left hand while his gloved right points forward for the charge.

I leaned over to the young man who was studying this thing, and he most politely allowed me to borrow it. '*Prego,*' he said. What on earth is this? A left-wing broadsheet dated 1936?

The woodcuts were printed along with the rest of the news-paper. It is a brutal medium if printed badly. Over the next week I called up as many as I could from the vaults and became a newspaper addict myself. The artist, I discovered, was called Mino Maccari. I was amazed at the subtlety of the images, given the harshness of the mechanical press. The essential black quality of the design was softened by a burin used like a multiple gouge, of the sort used by commercial illustrators in the last century. The colours were added later, replacing the black elements here and there with dramatic areas of colour.

I was fascinated that this technique could produce objects of such textural delicacy, in such contrast to the political crudeness of its imagery. In the world of Mino Maccari there was no room, it seemed, for the *benpensante*, the man-with-good-thoughts, the nice bourgeois with no desire for violent change, with no ambition, whose skill is in *sistemarsi* – that wonderful Italian word meaning to settle down, to make things nice and cosy. Such a man has no desire for glory or risk. He is a worm.

A sinking ship sends up a desperate spark of hope. A bearded philosopher steers his lifebelt to the rescue. In the bright air a buxom lady in a flowery hat lingers in a black cloud that might be smoke from the ship. Is she real, or a figment of his imagination? The philosopher's smudgy fingers are black, and black the bodice of the smiling lady.

The good vessel is called *Attualismo* and is featureless, like the ship in Fellini's recent film, *E la barca va*, which may indeed be subliminally quoting Maccari's image. The philosopher in the water is Giovanni Gentile, and the woman is the decadent 'Spirit of Hollywood', who is to be saved by this drowning man.

The philosopher Gentile was also founder of the Fascist Institute of Culture, which Maccari in one of his brief poems – can't be briefer – said was a terrible drag: '*Che seccatura/ L'Istituto Fascista di Cultura.*'

As with Goya, the smell of the long-fired gunpowder has drifted from the battlefield, and the image remains. As remarkable art it grips us still, yet Maccari cannot really be appreciated except against the background of the Fascist period in which he worked. This gives him a stature which is unique. It remains heartening that among all the various monstrous regimes which have dominated the first half of this century, this man was able to demonstrate a remarkable sense of humanity, even as he buttoned the black shirt about him. That he was able to do so is one small tribute to Italian Fascism.

Now and again an image appears so crude and direct you cannot believe it was ever published. Here is Hitler crouching down under a blanket covered with swastikas. From his backside appears a helmeted Prussian soldier, complete with spike. Crows fly away from the pair in fright, black flapping crows that seem to echo the twittering swastikas. Elsewhere in the magazine there is a crude warning, '*Dà tempo al tempo/ ma non lo dare ai tedeschi* [Give Time time – but don't give it to the Germans]'.

When Hitler wiped out the Brownshirts in the Night of the Long Knives, Maccari's sardonic comment was, in Munich you'd better wear tin knickers: '*A Monaco di Baviera/ Mutande di lamiera.*'

The favourite butt of Maccari's caricatures were the Fascist leaders themselves. A room of *gerarchi* survey each other, hand on hips, noses high – higher – highest. A pinnacle of a nose, practically scraping the ceiling. What can he see from up there? And here is another in a brothel, so neatly dressed among the flopping tits and bums. The medals are polished, the little moustache brushed – he looks so immensely *serious* in this clatter of precarious high heels.

How did Maccari get away with it?

A sceptical wing of the Fascist party remained anti-militaristic and profoundly anti-German until quite late, and Maccari continued to publish his sardonic comments until 1943. That they were permitted to survive is all the more remarkable if one compares Italy with Germany, which already by the mid-thirties was an acidulous desert. Every town in Germany today has a street or a *platz* dedicated to the Scholl sisters, not because these admirable people were particularly effective in organizing resistance – alas, no one was that – but because resistance in Germany was so rare.

Maccari survived for three reasons. First, because the ideology of Fascism was kept undefined for as long as possible, so as to create the widest possible area of tacit consent. Ideology is perhaps too precise a word for what was essentially an agglomeration of poses centring on different leaders, who in turn were dependent on Mussolini. (One is constantly amazed at the number of essentially non-political technocrats who managed to work for the regime, just as one is surprised today to trace back this or that political or financial institution to the Fascist period.) Second, because Maccari himself was a passionate follower of Mussolini, and the attacks he made on other Fascist high-ups implied a tacit appeal to the leader himself. Third, because the political ideal which Maccari defended was that of the country against the town, the town against the city, the individual against the party, even the idea of the isolation of Italy as opposed to the grandiose temptation of a world policy – in short, in favour of a series of concentric circles stressing the value of the smaller unit against the large. In his own way Maccari practised the politics of the non-political. There could be little threat from one whose battle-cry, effectively speaking, was 'Home Rule for Poggibonsi'.

Mino Maccari was born in Siena, where his father taught

'Cut off the ear with one fine cut/From him who listens to "Quite a lot".'

'Quite a lot'(*parecchio*) would be obtained for Italy, said the politician Giovanni Giolitti in 1915, if she remained neutral during the First World War. This modest phrase epitomized for the Intervenzionisti, and for the Fascist party which came after them, everything that was cautious, bourgeois and provincial in Italian political life – as opposed to courageous, outward-looking, international, which is what the Fascists thought themselves to be.

Maccari's linocut was made long after Giolitti's death, at the time of Mussolini's invasion of north Africa. It underlines the continuity of one 'intervention' and the other, and also shows what violence those who attempted to remain neutral might expect to receive at the hand of the Fascists. It comes from *Il Selvaggio*, 15 December 1935.

This linocut is an attack on a journalist called Telesio Interlandi, who attempted to promulgate the Nazi racial theories that were introduced into Italy in 1938.

Young writers, some of them Jewish, are forced to exhibit their genealogical trees before being permitted to work for newspapers under his control. To all of them he downs his thumb. It comes from *Il Selvaggio*, 15 October 1938.

' These two images by Mino Maccari illustrate how inconsistent Fascist extremism could be. On the one hand he defends the invasion of north Africa, yet on the other he opposes quite openly the introduction into Italy of Hitler's racial laws.

classics at the Liceo Classico. (As if to stress the fact, his Christian name was Latino.) The son Mino fought in the First World War, still very young, before going back to law school in Siena. By the time he was twenty-three he was practising law in Colle Val d'Elsa, a small town between Siena and Florence.

In 1923, in Poggibonsi, with the help of a friend who worked in the wine trade, Mino started an occasional review called *Il Selvaggio*.[52] It was just after the murder of the Socialist leader Giacomo Matteotti, when the Fascist party threatened to split between those who felt that the political struggle should abide by parliamentary rules and those who felt, in Machiavelli's expression, that 'Fortune should be battered and bruised like a woman.'

These yellowed leaves in the public library in Siena gave me the impression that in the early days *Il Selvaggio* conveyed two contradictory messages. The first was that good Fascists should remain within the party, and give Mussolini all the help they could, within and outside Parliament. The second message was to Mussolini himself, saying what an evil and dangerous place Rome was, and how he should take care not to be corrupted.

In this the editors were appealing to a myth about the foundation of the Italian state a mere sixty years previously. According to this theory, all that was mean and conniving, all that was intrigue and backroom dealing, derived from Cavour, while all that was frank and open, all that was spontaneous and free in the Italian spirit, derived from Garibaldi. The political world was divided between the Fox and the Lion, as in Aesop's fable. To *Il Selvaggio*, Garibaldi was 'a man in the highest sense of the word, who acted according to the inspiration of his generous soul without waiting for the approval of the Italian people; an Italian who referred to his own conscience alone concerning every act carried out in the name of Italy'.[53] The message to Mussolini was clear. If he wished to act in a way that was frank and open, and in the best interests of the Italian people, he should go ahead and seize power.

A kind of rage colours the lives of almost all the European artists and writers who matured during or soon after the First World War, as if the violence of that experience festered throughout their subsequent experiences. It even affected the personalities of those who, like Brecht or Breton, had been conscientious objectors or medical orderlies. Breton broke Tristan Tsara's arm with his cane, at the final quarrel between Dada and Surrealism, which some might think was taking an artistic dispute too far.

Maccari fought at the front and, when he returned, painted a self-portrait as a *teppista*, or political hooligan – one who yearns to break heads, to feel bones crunching beneath the flying fist. In fact a large segment of the early Fascist party came straight from the *Arditi*, the special assault troops of the First World War, overflowing with the courage which precedes thought.

Some of the *Arditi* joined D'Annunzio in his extraordinary self-appointed crusade to acquire Fiume for Italy. Up in his villa Il Vittorale on Lake Garda, not far from Salò, where Mussolini was to make his last stand, there is a photo of Mussolini and D'Annunzio striding through a park in the early twenties. D'Annunzio is waving his right hand in the air, while Mussolini scampers behind, his face showing all the adulation of a new boy in the presence of the Captain of Games.

Not all *Arditi*, when they disbanded, became Fascist, and there were some notable battles between Socialist and parliamentarian *Arditi* on one side, and Fascists on the other. But a true Fascist, like an *Ardito*, was so filled with physical courage that it overflowed in every gesture. His chest instinctively strained for the feel of the finishing-tape in Life's Great Race, even when no ribbon was there.

If Fascism was a movement of accumulated and overlapping

poses, then Maccari was its recording angel, or devil, ready to portray its innermost vices. What is now almost impossible for us to perceive is that to him there was a distinction between the true Fascists, the born *Arditi*, and the opportunists who joined after the March on Rome. That faint air of the ridiculous which pervades our perception of all Fascist leaders and their exploits, that absurdity which later turned to tragedy, makes Maccari seem much more courageous and cruel now than he did at the time. He was not caricaturing all Fascists. He was caricaturing the camp followers, the municipal big-shots, the animated occupants of grand uniforms whose high profile strained to hide a double chin. In no way are these stuffed Blackshirts *Arditi*.

Yet the pages of *Il Selvaggio* gradually became crowded, as more and more figures of Italian life failed to live up to Maccari's internal conviction of what a man of culture should be. D'Annunzio was too Frenchified; Benedetto Croce was Teutonic. Maccari considered Pirandello a charlatan whose sense of the Italian was tempered by what he thought intelligent foreigners would want to hear. He absolutely loathed the architect Piacentini, whose buildings today are finally losing their period flavour and manifesting the genuine feeling for Rome and the baroque which makes him one of the greatest architects of this century.[54]

Above all others, Maccari loathed those fellow artists who left Italy for Paris in order to paint like Picasso or Derain, and then came back to make 'mothers suckling babies, unknown soldiers, naked Fascists, on the walls of Milan congress halls'. 'Not when Paris takes them away, but when she gives them back, she offends us,' he commented:

> Non quando li prende
> Ma quando li rende
> Parigi ci offende.[55]

Il Selvaggio survived for twenty years, occasionally running foul of some local chieftain who forced them to move on. From Poggibonsi to Florence, where Maccari helped start an art gallery which showed all the most interesting Tuscan and Italian painters of the time. From Florence back to Siena, then up to Turin and finally to Rome.

At each step Maccari seemed to defend a position previously acquired. In the large urban centres, Maccari extolled the virtues of living in the country. He elevated what was free, innocent and bucolic against what was bound, urban and contrived. The whole concept of modernity, he said, was 'bastard, international, external – a manipulated mixture conjured up by Jewish bankers, homosexuals, the sharks of war, the keepers of brothels – which, if accepted without a murmur, would corrupt and pollute the intrinsic value of our race'. (If this list of phobias sounds sinister, it should be pointed out that the mood was shared by a wide group of intellectuals, not just those who are usually called Fascist.) And, with the sensation of fighting an impossible rearguard action against the inevitability of change, of progress, he wrote: 'We don't reject modern life, but we want to dominate it, direct it, search for ourselves within our own Italian taste – authentic, enriched by centuries of experience, faithful to the blood and to our untamed [*selvaggio*] race.'

With his friend Leo Longanesi, Maccari crystallized a vision of the absolute essence of the country, 'Strapaese', as opposed to the absolute essence of the town, 'Stracittà'. In the magical countryside of Strapaese the peasant could sit next to the aristocrat, the scholar and the illiterate talk together on equal terms. The whole archipelago of worldly temptations would be avoided in the internal landscape of Good Faith. The 'Island of Self-indulgence', the 'Eden of Skittles', would be avoided. In the end Maccari's world view became so limited and extreme that Longanesi took the opposite view: the country was a fine place to go to when you needed to recharge your spiritual batteries, but the real challenge of the future lay in the cities.

The vision of the countryside permitted Maccari's linocuts to become more understated and delicate. Among the smoke-stacks and roads that twist like wires, the formal beauty becomes more important than the message. Even the humble country girl who longs for the state to become more 'interesting' – a pun on getting pregnant – has a formal charm which sets her outside the polemical context.

Fascism began to lose its ideological fluidity towards the end of the 1930s, when Mussolini gravitated to Germany's orbit. The turning-point occurred in 1938, with the introduction of the racial laws. *Il Selvaggio* was one of the few voices raised in public against these laws, and upset a number of the Fascist leaders without actually provoking a revolt. 'Instead of examining talent they examine racial antecedents. We are for the melting-pot; they are for racial purity. We are for arts and reality; they are for ideology. The rest is known. Strapaese has fallen, and racism flourishes.'[56]

This certainly indicates a growth in humanity, if compared with the speech about modernism being a plot of Jews and homosexuals quoted earlier. But there is a thread of consistency in both positions. The core of Maccari's vision is his constant need to defend the position of the individual against the group, the generality. Group activity is what holds us all back:

> La mania di fare il gruppo
> Ci ritarda ogni sviluppo.[57]

When Mussolini established a Ministry of Popular Culture in 1935 (instantly rechristened 'Minculpop'), Maccari protested at its interference 'in every corner of society', stating firmly that 'politics is made from culture, not the other way around'. Fascism was degenerating into 'the culture of the big Hurrah!' In this passionate defence of individual action, Maccari's ideology was always more anarchistic than Fascist.

From 1938 onward *Il Selvaggio* was published with increasing difficulty, although it survived until 1943. After it had closed, Maccari produced what in many ways must have been the most extraordinary exhibition of his life: a series of portraits of Mussolini.

I cannot imagine that the crowds beat a path to his door. The Allied Front was not far off and he held this exhibition in an isolated house near Cinquale on the Ligurian coast. But people did go. One critic describes Maccari walking up and down on the grass outside, overcome by an intolerable restlessness. For what ideal, for which public, an exhibition of portraits of Mussolini in 1943?

Here is the great leader at his desk, posing with his paws on a great heap of papers. His chest is high, his expression superb, but he cannot possibly read in such a position. The heroic caption, 'Must I read?' Mussolini with the King, a wizened puppet. And its corollary, the King as a wily monkey, with Mussolini as a great blind bear on a string.

Strangest of all, Mussolini by the sea, his head bald and pockmarked, seen from the back, his shoulders covered with coarse black hair. There is something touching about that hair. I looked at it for a long time when I came across this drawing. Surely the artist must have loved the man, to observe such an intimate and slightly repulsive detail? Proudly the Duce surveys the sea, stark naked, with puny legs, and we can see, without his being aware of our attention, that there is a simian quality to his physique.

Maccari survived the war, indeed lived long and happily, working well. Many of his paintings continued to depict Fascists and whores, officials and jackboots. Mussolini with Claretta and the King. The Duce lost in a brothel, among gigantic women. The Duce leading Claretta on a string. The Duce practising his goose-step by himself, or all alone among a crowd of *gerarchi* who are gradually growing feathers.

In many ways Mussolini received a kind of humane apotheosis from Maccari. Unlike the other monsters of this century, Mussolini retained some quality akin to those of the heroes of the ancient world. Does that seem a terrible thing to say? On the other hand, does one actually *like* Oedipus, or Achilles, or Agamemnon? One can feel for Hector, or Priam, or for the ones who lost beautifully, because to lose seems more human to us today than to win by the sword. But the heroes are bound in some hermetic circle of violence which rejects intimacy.

Mussolini's life expressed the classical arc of hubris and nemesis: arrogance, fate overtaking it and the inevitable fall. Towards the end of his life, even Mussolini seemed aware of this. When he was rescued from the Gran Sasso and taken to Germany, Adolf slapped him on the back (as it were), said he should cheer up, put a microphone in his hand and told him to give a speech to the Italian nation – it would do him good. Mussolini replied, 'What has a dead man to say to a nation of corpses?' Impossible not to feel a shiver of horror and awe at such a remark! This is the voice of Achilles at the burning ships, of Richard II as he sinks to the ground in a liquid ecstasy of self-pity. Is this how an *Ardito* behaves when he realizes the game is lost? Stare in the mirror and ask, does nobody love me? The agonized cry of the fallen Superman turns out to be the whine of the spoiled baby, the snarl of an animal ego that cannot distinguish between its own extinction and that of the entire world.

★

Apart from his talent, Maccari had many qualities which make him attractive: friendliness to waitresses in bars and to telegraph boys at the newspaper office, affection and courtesy towards his colleagues. He was generous at his own exhibitions, freely giving out quick sketches right and left. Of his great productivity he would say, 'It's a kind of chronic illness. But not catching.' He loathed critics, whose only job, he said, was to add ulterior definitions to the words they superfluously picked to describe paintings.

He was still drawing occasional vignettes for the newspapers long after the war, and they were still devastating. His loathing for the reconstituted Fascist party and its 'moral rearmament' programme in the early 1960s was typical: he drew them all in the sleek modern car which was his private symbol for moral turpitude. And when the Argentinian colonels took over their country in the late 1960s, he had them slithering and sliding all over each other around the Chair of State like snakes.

Anyone seeing these vignettes would conclude that they had been drawn by a man of the political left, but there was no essential change in Maccari's position, which was that of an extreme individualist somewhere to the right of the far right. Perhaps this position is too idiosyncratic to be called a political one at all.

Much of the world of Maccari still exists, if you know where to look for it.

The *Arditi* survive in an obscene version of a popular song of 1936, called 'The Forty-Four *Arditi*' – brave patriots who went to Africa to bring civilization to the natives but became distracted by a series of extraordinary changes which overcame their sexual organs. To learn the verses of this slightly trying ditty is an essential rite of puberty in every Italian school, and in every one of the school outings which clutter the city centres from March to May someone will certainly be humming it.

Go into any newsagent in Tuscany and ask for an object called a *Sesto Caio Baccelli*, a cheap agricultural almanac dealing with market timetables and phases of the moon. Among the intimate tips on when to plant your onions so that they won't bolt, there are examples of the short rhyming aphorisms which Maccari appropriated for his own use and which are quintessentially Tuscan. As I look through my notes my eye is caught by one of Maccari's, which sums up better than everything else his political views: '*Giovanotto/ Scegli un motto/ E fatti sotto* [Young man/choose a motto/and go for it].' Not such bad advice.

Next, go to the corner news-stand and buy a copy of the newspaper *La Repubblica*. On the front page there is usually a cartoon by Forattini, who is in many ways the unacknowledged heir of Maccari. In Forattini contemporary political parties are forced into ancient roles. His view is that Italian politics are run by means of private arrangements between apparent foes, who in fact enjoy everything in common. This is very close to Maccari. '*Il Palazzo*' – the Palace – is just the one building, although it contains many inhabitants. Forattini often clothes Craxi, the leader of the Socialist party, in jackboots and black shirt. As for the Christian Democrats, they are given knives and forks, for they are always hungry.

The high chair which *Il Selvaggio* once gave to Cavour is, in Forattini's cosmology, occupied by Giulio Andreotti. It may or may not be true that this man is the hidden source of all the wiles and intrigues in Italian politics – from time to time he seems to defend the integrity of some pretty rum friends. But if you ask in the bar or in the bank whether Andreotti had anything to do with this or that scandal, the lads will say, 'No. Oh no. You must be joking. At least, not directly.'

Asked recently if he had any regrets in life, Andreotti said,

'Yes, I wish my mother had told me to sit up straighter when I was a child.' Indeed the minister is somewhat crumpled, physically. 'But then,' he added, 'my looks have been the fortune of caricaturists like Forattini, and who am I to deprive a man of the means with which to learn an honest living?'

If the aim of Mino Maccari was that in Italy the Lions should win out over the Foxes, then there is no doubt that he lost, and the Foxes have won. All in all it is better that way. Besides, there is such attraction in the quiet intelligent remark that turns away wrath, made with modesty. He who won can afford to assume the beautiful air of Christian forgiveness − even though of whom, for what, is never made clear.

17 · THE BAND

For the last twenty years I have played my clarinet in the local village band. When it goes well it is like fingering pearls. When it goes badly it is like fumbled plumbing.

Our bandleader is called Cesare, or 'Caesar', and looks the part. He has many qualities in common with my Latin teacher at school in north London, an old regimental sergeant-major from the First World War who was always ready to explain the Gallic Wars in terms of Maxim guns and Mills bombs. The noise the band made in the old days was restricted to two, loud and louder, and there was something quite touching in the way that the red face of Caesar shone through a forest of indescribably large-sound, visible-sound, black bramble thickets and violent knuckledusters of woodwind and brass, yelling at the top of his voice '*Piano!*', just like my mad old Latin teacher talking about the Tenth Legion fixing bayonets before going over the top.

Even in the early days when there hardly seemed to be time to find one note before we were wrenched over to another, I could at least do it nicely, with *pianos* and *decrescendos* and other sounds unknown to the band. Came the wonderful day when I noticed a syncopation before anyone else, merely because I'd seen it in a classical score – being the only one out of thirty-six to do it right I was asked, was it true I had studied six years in the conservatory?

The Band

After years of practice and self-denial, there was not one piece in our repertoire of twenty half-pages that I could not play at a glance. I began to get restless at the unchanging diet. Could we not play some Haydn or some arrangements from Mozart? No? Well there was an odd piece that Beethoven wrote for a band, round about the time that Napoleon was coming to Vienna; couldn't we do that? No? Oh well, drat it, what about the *'Internazionale'*? NO! But, *Maestro*, it's got a theme taken from the Brahms second clarinet sonata. Caesar made a gruff impatient gesture, and a colleague, sniggering, pulled at the back of my jacket. In a predominantly Communist zone, the band was mostly Christian Democrat, and the few Communists among them were feeling anything but *'Internazionale'*-minded just after the invasion of Afghanistan. In its tortuous way the Associazione Filarmonica di Gaiole in Chianti was part of my political education.

From the mid-seventies we shrank. We amalgamated with Radda, and then again with Castellina. We went on playing the same things and still we shrank. We were subsidized by the richest man in Castellina, a maker of pig feed, a tall figure rendered remote and saintly by many years spent poring over accounts. To thank him for the new uniforms we went to play outside his window. The curtains were undrawn, and he did not look up from his desk as we gathered, gleeful as schoolchildren. Startled by our presence and the usual megalithic noise, he invited us in and took down some fizzy wine from a rack that lined the office. It was vintage champagne, ten years old.

Still we shrank. We called in paid instrumentalists from Panzano, whose band was flourishing, among them Beppe, hunched and energetic, like a Giuseppe Verdi in old age but without the whiskers. His son came as well, called Egisto, like the lover of Clytemnestra who stood behind the door with an axe.

Egisto was the most distinguished-looking man I have ever met.

His job was to collect bits and pieces from the storeroom in a small machine-tool factory. He said the firm was just large enough not to notice if he disappeared to the lavatory to read. He wanted to visit Russia. His only regret in life, he said, was not to have bought a decent clarinet when young, and this already infinitely sad man looked infinitely sadder. So I sold him mine and got another. His old one was one of those knobbly things with slide-bars instead of keys, held together with elastic bands. He had difficulties with the new one, and every time we met would ask me alternative fingerings for a high *mi* or *la* – which I could never tell him until I saw them on the page, as I know nothing about *solfeggio*.

I think about his father Beppe every time we celebrate one of the band's grander feasts. He had the gift of living entirely in the present. One band lunch, one cacophonic annual St Cecilia's rave-up, he told me the secret of his extraordinary cheerfulness. His life, he said, was a miracle. During the First World War he was in a tank that was sent into the great battle of Piave on the very first day. When the tank got to the river, it fell in, and everyone was drowned except for Beppe. He was in the river for eighteen hours. When they pulled him out, his officer said, 'Good lord, Beppe, are you still alive? You'll never die.'' And I haven't yet,' said Beppe, to clinch the story.

The officer compassionately took Beppe out of the line and put him into the band. For the rest of the war he played the troops up to the front, and played the survivors down again from the front, but did not go to the front himself. After the war he played happily through the band-rich Fascist years, so stuffed with public functions, and then through the Second World War, ending up with a couple of American players who would pick him up in a jeep and drive him off for sessions of boogie and big band. As far as I know, he is playing still.

What gave an added twist to the saga of Beppe's life, for me, was that 'Piave' was one of the tunes we had to play, as well as being the biggest battle on the Italian Front during the First World War. Annually we would take wreaths round the war memorials, the band in their best, marching just behind the Carabinieri in full dress, looking serious, the schoolchildren in spring frocks and white shirts tucked away in the back. Our daughters had to learn the text by heart at school: 'The river Piave was quietly murmuring in its bed when the first troops passed, on 24 May'. At which Beppe, blowing like mad, would give me a glance of triumph, indicating his pleasure at not having been murmured away by the waters inside a steel tank.

Every town in Italy has a 'Piazza Ventiquattro Maggio' for the First World War, just as it has a 'Via Otto Settembre' for the end of the Second, so to shake hands on these occasions with the almost toothless Beppe was to feel the leathery paw of a piece of living Italy, a symbol that the triumph of life over death is as valuable in its way as victory or defeat.

After some years of congregating at a central point between four decaying bands, the Gaiole contingent began to pick up again. We went back to practising in the local cinema, Caesar magnificent against the backdrop of a huge purple curtain covering the screen, fringed with faded tassels.

One fine evening I found myself in the front row with five fledgeling clarinettists, all girls, about the age of my daughters, if not younger. Their *solfeggio* was slow and piping, their fingers less than nimble, but they were cheerful and keen. At the next public ceremony I found myself half a metre above them, an easy point of reference, a landmark, a sore thumb. So I eased off for a year or so until puberty stormed through the ranks and they grew taller. Now, aided by high heels from Montevarchi, the contrast is less obvious. Their musicianship has also improved. At practice they are capable of remarkable feats: they can even play and crack sunflower seeds simultaneously.

★

Last year the St Cecilia celebrations were later than usual. The poplars had been stripped bare by a November wind two days previously, the untidy fields sprouted with winter grass, while in the gullies and under hedgerows the shadows were bright blue. Unpruned stalks trailing from the vines rattled against the cement posts in the cold breeze.

For once I was not late. There was no group of jacketed musicians in front of the cinema with its low fountain containing fish, nor under the pines linked by a hedge of straggled box, nor yet in front of the school building that demonstrated the upright beauty of poured cement. There was nobody about but Caesar himself, who seemed pleased that for once I was early, and Massimiliano, who used to be a bit of a lad, but who now acts as general secretary and is remarkably responsible at the job. Our hands felt numb as we greeted each other.

Caesar was in a magnanimous, slightly buttonholing mood, and with the feeling of a schoolboy who assumes he can make an ingratiating remark I complimented him on his tie. It was covered with symmetrical jackboots in black set on dark blue, the angle of the boot being reminiscent of the angle set by Italy herself as she thrusts herself down into the Mediterranean Sea. I made a joke about it, which went instantly wrong. Caesar grabbed my collar.

'What you foreigners don't understand,' he said, 'is that Fascism brought a great deal of good to this country. All that is forgotten now, just because it is fashionable to do so – but one cannot eliminate a period of Italian history which . . .' etc., etc. He let me go, and speechless I observed the blood vessels shrink in his face, to become reabsorbed in the usual pallor. The teeth lost their sharpness, he smiled. We were both surprised and shocked, and I felt the need to shake hands again, as if after some arcane and gruelling ritual.

Still shaking, I retreated to the instrument room above the cinema, next to the projector's cubbyhole. Lord, after all these years – what a gaffe! Some people never learn. Put the old Selmer together and try to forget. Outside, the glass front of the petrol station caught the sun. A sign that said ERG in red on white shone above the municipal palm. From the hidden entrance of the main piazza, across the recently widened bridge that was not a bridge but a road, the instrumentalists from town were coming in groups of two or three. There was Beppe the shoemaker, who keeps a pair of wooden feet called Matteo in the backroom, in the dark, with all the thrushes in cages waiting to be taken out on Sundays. There was the pale boy with the tuba, who looks like an embalmed martyr. There was Beppe's plump son, always cheerful, leader of village pranks, who smokes too much. White belts and hat, and blue jackets with a golden lyre surrounded by bay leaves on the breast pocket.

As I calmed down I was joined by two small boys, one called Sugo ('Sauce') and the other Pizza, heroes thus named for their vast appetites. Pizza seemed to be on the point of imminent expansion, and when he blew his trumpet, it too looked plump and glistening. Then came Mirko, manically garrulous when caught out, who plays a thing called a *flicorno*. Then the pale boy with the tuba, alone among his peers in that he kicked no chair, made no unnecessary noise, and yet still seemed cheerful.

We went outside. All my colleagues, my friends, were there, crunching the gravel in front of the fishpond, cheerful that it was sunny, sad that it was cold. A long wrangle about where we should stand took place, before we moved off in unison to where the sun lay, by the petrol pump across the hidden bridge.

Caesar whispered '*Primi Passi*', and we marched through the almost empty town, the huge noise bouncing off the chemist's and town hall on our left, the bootmaker's and the baker's and the bank on our right. The piece had its minimal challenge, a high something three squiggles above the stave, and getting up there without squeaking at six miles per hour is not bad. We marched too fast for the flag waver in front, who got tangled and stopped. Chaos. We marched round the obstacle as water goes round a fallen tree, spurred by the cold air, still much too fast, while I listened for the sound of my own note in the roaring waterfall, like an ornithologist listening for the song of a particular bird during the dawn chorus.

The wedge-shaped piazza came to its funnelled end in a shadow sharp enough to flinch from. Past the butcher's on the right and over the far bridge opposite the former Communist café. The short way back to the church, past the new post office. High on the hill above the town the parallel lines of the vineyards acquired the sheen of corduroy. We were into our second repeat when we hit the short rise up to the church, and came to a ragged halt in mid-bar.

The band had its authorized place in church, just below the dais on which the military veterans sit, on the right as you face the altar. A passionate intrigue convulsed the smaller brasses as we approached our place, to underline the fact that the band was somehow independent from the rest of the congregation. But when the Mass began, the front row of clarinettists joined in, nasally supporting the military pensioners.

So the Mass unfolded against this background of teenage scuffles, while I gradually became immersed in the effort of coming to terms with every phrase, every word, of the arguments coming from Don Bernabei's eager face. The lion shall lie down with the lamb, and the newborn babe shall place its head in the mouth of the serpent. John the Baptist in camelskin on the banks of the River Jordan. The tree shall be cut at the root and thrown into the fire. I found I could follow neither symbolism nor argument, and merely imagined I was there in Palestine, replacing the Italian words with the more familiar echo of the King James's Bible in my head.

★

The Band

On occasions such as these, I think of Otello.

Where Beppe of Panzano had been the artful private with mischief in his eye and luck in his pocket, Otello had been the born NCO. Otello knew where everything in the *Comune* was, where it had come from and who had done what to get it.

Many years ago his job had been Superintendent of Public Works for the whole of Gaiole, which meant the mender of fallen bridges, the master of blocked drains. It was perfectly clear to him which drains were the responsibility of the *Comune* and which should have been mended quietly without bothering him. A look, a remark, was enough. He extended a sense of civic responsibility by appealing to some shared spirit and by so doing, created it. He always appealed to reason, never force.

Through many boring sessions of music practice over the years, Otello became a source of much interesting detail about an earlier period.

'Fascists?' he said, 'we were all Fascists. If you weren't a Fascist, you didn't eat. We had *la tessera del pane*, and if you didn't have the card, you couldn't buy bread. Oh!'

His 'Oh' was brisk and sharp, like a verbal full stop. He lit a cigarette at some moment where Caesar had to concentrate on the *bombardini*, and added, 'Of course, there were nice ones and nasty ones.'

'Really? How nasty?'

'Nothing much.' Otello seemed embarrassed, with a quick glance around the room. 'You know: a pint of castor oil, that sort of thing.'

'Anyone beaten up,' I asked?

'No, oh no.' He looked shocked. 'Not here in Gaiole. Maybe in the north.'

Then, looking thoughtful, 'Still, some were nastier than others, of course.' He used the word '*cattivi*' for nasty; the nastiness of little boys.

Then he would give me a little nudge with the side of his elbow.

'There was this song,' he would say, 'called *"Giovinezza"* ' (which means 'youth'). 'We all sang it. Well of course there was a whole series of verses,' another nudge, 'which were not too respectful.' He sang under his breath, with a sly, walls-have-ears look: 'Youth – we can't stand up, we're so bloody weak.'

'Once we were standing in the piazza at some meeting,' he said. 'Lots of speeches, long speeches, too many, and we ended by singing *"Giovinezza"*. Well! Someone came right out and sang all these alternative verses, so – oh, yes – of course they came over and beat him up.' Otello turned back to the music in front of us. He looked decided, as if to say 'Well, he asked for it.'

With infinite caution I eventually found out who the ancient bigshots of Gaiole were. To my surprise two of them were people whom I had disliked intensely at first sight, the very first time I had come to Gaiole years before. Perhaps some aura still surrounded them. But in other cases no such trace remained. I remember making a pilgrimage to talk to one old man, and found a passionate hook-nosed personage living high above the town, nourishing three calves in a small dark shed. I talked him into a mode of reminiscence, but what came out was a long story about a horserace run in about 1932, in which all the horse-owners of Gaiole took part. He told me the route of this race, round the town. He indicated the exact path they had followed, taking my hand and pointing my finger and tracing it in the air, looking across at landmarks long obliterated by new housing projects and vineyards. 'And when they got to that corner, so-and-so's piebald stallion was in front . . .'

Otello's boss when I first arrived in Gaiole was still the mayor from the Fascist period, democratically re-elected. This semi-permanent mayor was an impressive figure, and unbeatable in municipal arguments. He was a master of what Robert Louis Stevenson called the 'Scotch answer', meaning the reply which turns your question back at you like a vicious boomerang. (E.g. 'Mr Mayor, what are you doing about the town drains?' 'Why? What makes you so interested – planning to make money out of them?') After the war some patriot took a pot-shot at him as he surveyed the town, Mussolini-like, from his balcony. He never repaired the neat machine-gun holes, and the house wore these souvenirs like a string of medals until long after his death, before being plastered over.

(Don Bernabei now inserted into the sermon the word *'metanoia'*, which woke me up. In Italian this would perfectly indicate the feeling of half-boredom so typical of church, but no, he was quoting an ancient Greek word meaning the capacity to steer a ship from promontory to promontory at sea. Massimiliano, the secretary of the band, was engaged in some complex discussion within a circle of some brasses in the back row. The children seated quietly with grandmothers had nothing to amuse themselves with save the feel of their fine Sunday clothes.)

Otello had had an extremely long war – nine years, if I remember rightly. First Abyssinia, then north Africa and, after he was taken prisoner there, a long period in Scotland before he got back home. All without firing a shot, he sometimes said. (Every ex-soldier I have met in Italy has proudly said the same; a bizarre fact if true and interesting psychologically if not.)

Towards the end of his life he talked a lot about his captivity in 'Peeb-less shire'. I even wrote a letter for him, inquiring about old friends up there amongst the heather. He seemed to want to revisit the bleak farm where he had been stationed, under a huge hill a mile outside the village. He brooded about that remote place, and about his little platoon of Italian POWs up in Scotland, doing semi-volunteer work for cigarettes and small cash.

A story of Otello as prisoner-of-war in Scotland. One day he and his platoon were taken to a remote farm, given a wodge of cabbage seedlings, and told to plant out a large field. They set to work. At midday the Scottish crofters sat down in front of the Italian prisoners and ate their lunch slowly and with relish, giving them none. Otello watched stone-faced. I know that look well, the face a Tuscan presents when you have done something wrong or have been rude in some way, and he pretends out of sheer politeness that you, or he, or both, aren't there.

After the crofters' lunch Otello rose and told his still hungry troops (in Italian of course) to continue working, but to snap the stem of each cabbage as they planted it out, just under the surface of the earth. This they did.

A week later an irate English officer appeared in their camp asking what the devil they meant by it, this sabotage of the war effort, etc., etc. Calmly Otello explained, and to the officer's credit he went off immediately to give his first-class bollocking to the crofters, not to the Italians.

There is something magical to me about this revenge, as neat in its way as a folk-tale. How clever of Otello to have avoided fisticuffs with the Scottish farmers out there on the bleak hillside, with its confused explanations afterwards. I imagine him guiding his platoon for a decade through war and peace, deserts and highlands alike, softening orders from on high, guarding his men from blows.

The sermon arrived at an extremely predictable passage concerning cars, TV and the innate cruelty of the consumer society, and recapitulated the theme of 'conversion' (*metanoia*, it seems) as a basis for the good life, and then we were through.

The band played the prayer from Rossini's *Mosé*. At the trio some big piece of brass failed to notice the key change and stuck to a wrong note for two whole bars, adding flavour.

The Band

Caesar called us to order as the congregation went up for Communion. We played Chopin's Funeral March, so simple, almost transparent, on the printed page. I had played it recently all by myself, in a cemetery on a hill near the Certosa in Florence, for Philip. It had been a bad year for friends. Bruce, Anna's beautiful sister Elena, Philip and, most recently, Otello. Please take no more friends from us, dear Lord, before the year's end. And what with the cold and the long sermon, my fingers could not manage the notes, easy though they were, and so playing was as hard as mending the inside of a fridge in the dark.

Out in the sunlight a few cars moved slowly up the road in tandem, like laden bees. We were to return to the cinema, with no nonsense about playing down as we had played up, even though at last we had a huge captive audience. The musicians dismantled their instruments as they walked, accumulating wives or girlfriends at the periphery. Hunger silenced music as we walked up the short cut beneath the pines. We shoved music into pockets that were just too small to hold it, or jangled car keys, or took five minutes for a quick pee at the public baths (*circa* 1950) on the other side of the post office.

The interior of the cinema seemed suddenly dark. The coat-rack was already full of coats, a furry cloud hovering above a mass of musical instruments, boxes covered with black leatherette and sheaves of scores in their little plastic holdalls.

The 'symbols of authority', as a newspaper would put it – i.e. Caesar, the mayor and Tiziano and Romano, the *Guardie Comunali* – formed a group apart at the head of the table, up by the screen with the plush curtain, behind which the cooks were busy in an improvised kitchen. The young seeded themselves into groups by sex and age, without being aware of what they were doing. Round the walls the wives waited for their uniformed menfolk to sit before stepping forward. Each group formed a hermetic nest of intrigue independent of any other.

I looked round. Otello had usually protected my flank in these things, and lacking him, I hesitated. In the end I chose to sit at the divide between youth and age, between a man I had known for years without learning his name and a small segment of the young.

I learned that the man on my right was a worker from the lignite mines at Cavriglia, on the other side of the mountains, overlooking the Val d'Arno. I've always wanted to know about that strange place, where the bulldozers make huge concentric rings at the base of steep and stony mountains.

Quite soon he was talking of the mines, in fast Italian full of allusions, broken phrases and a clipped wink. It was hard to follow him, but I saw in my head an image of the valley as it gradually filled with houses, the small industries spreading out from Montevarchi and San Giovanni and, in the evening and early morning, commuter trains going up and down to Florence. At night, the whole plain filled with tiny lights.

The volunteer teams of helpers served us *crostini*, spread with paste made of spleen, anchovy, chicken liver, capers, rosemary and other *odori*. The effect is salty, and faintly medieval. There was also an albino version of much more recent invention, made of butter and tuna-fish. 'One calls for another,' as they said, especially with the flock of young people sitting on my immediate left. (Pizza, whose head was hardly above the level of the table, asked for seconds before he had had firsts. The child was a great eater. He acquired a curious surface tension as the meal progressed, as if his external membrane came under pressure from within.)

The meat course was cooked to external mahogany and internal atrophy, with never enough salad with it to absorb the salt. I insisted the children on my left each take a leaf or two of greens, which they politely accepted and abandoned, leaving me eyeing their cool green dollops as I dehydrated.

Still my head was bent to this strange, almost violent man on my right. He was telling me of a lignite millionaire from Cavriglia who, having squeezed millions from the government and Common Market in subsidies, meanly put his parents in the old folk's home to pretend he was still poor. I knew those places, where a sad and sullen murmur accompanies the visitor, like pebbles washed by a restless sea.

At length I halted the unquiet visions he was giving me.

'Do you have any children?'

He had a son working for ENEL, with a degree in electronics.

'They gave him this job doing research into alternative energy resources on Monte Amiata. It's a volcano, you know.'

'Above the hot springs?'

'*Esatto.* The whole mountain is a live volcano deep below the surface. My son spends half his life up a pole stuck straight down into the ground, like a huge thermometer. All the instruments are high off the ground, for some reason. Nobody can understand how they work except him. Gets a lot of free time. Sets up the gear, gets into his car and drives off to see his girlfriend in Viareggio. As long as he delivers the readings, they don't seem to mind. That's how it is, no? Arranging your life for your own convenience . . .'

Cake time. The young stretched forth their many fingers.

'And your children?' he asked politely.

'Oh, in England now . . .' I wanted to add, pursuing HE (higher education) and HIM (love object), but it would hardly come out in Italian.

'And do they like it?'

'They are very Italian about England. They take the view that Julius Caesar made a terrible mistake in getting involved with those people in carts, painted blue, led by a madwoman.'

'Ah,' he said, '*la donna di ferro.*'

In fact I meant woad-stiffened Britons led by Boadicea, not Mrs Thatcher; but she would do.

'You know,' I said, 'how they are up there. Moments of stiff politeness, followed by lots of alcohol, then chaos. Confessions of miserable love. Tears. Saskia and Cosima look at it all and say "*Ma!* Have the centuries done nothing to wash off all that blue?" So my children sympathize most with the Italians who left notes on Hadrian's wall, praising the sun, the Mediterranean.'

'And perhaps they miss their mother, eh?'

Clapped hands and tinkled glasses closed the eating part of the meal. Seeing two Caesars at the other end of the table reminded me that these killer lunches always produce an afternoon hangover, than which nothing is worse. The young seemed either to be over-excited, slightly dusted with meringue or comatose.

Speech. Thanks. Cheers. Medals.

What is this, I thought, *medals*? And then they gave me one, our *forestiero*, our token guest, and I felt confused and touched. Small ping of falling tear on plate smudged with late jam tart.

Exeunt, slapping backs and cheerily shaking hands. The ritual of farewell is as formal as is the ritual of sitting down. You can't just slip off. That is called '*filare all'inglese*', i.e. leaving the room as the barbarian English do, without shaking hands.

The young loudly left for the bar, to watch the match of the day. I aimed for the homestead to clutch my head and get a bit of warmth going. The cinema was cold, even though it was crowded. When I came out the sky had dulled over, threatening snow.

We came back for the concert at five.

The curtain protecting the cinema screen had been withdrawn

to reveal a small raised stage, on which we sat. I kept to the far left, so as not to mask with my height any saxophone player behind me. Beautiful music stands, made a hundred years ago by the local blacksmith. My face assumed an expression of detachment, denoting artistic concentration. We are ready. We play.

We play well. When you play well the sensation of performance can actually fade away, while the sensation of listening grows. Your fingers move neatly and precisely, and if a complex passage comes along you stroke an embroidered cushion of delicate silk. But mostly you hear your voice, and Pizza's, and the tuba's at the back, and the girls to the left of you with their different levels of confidence, and all is simultaneously revealed, the mind of the composer and the sprightliness of the various souls with whom you perform. Two parabolas that momentarily coincide, that of technical ability and collective mood.

As we played, I thought of Verdi.

Verdi, the great bewhiskered master, worked for a time with a village band. I seem to remember that he had to teach a blind viola player some essential part late at night, to be learned by ear. Perhaps his experience with the band explains why his music sounds so well when played by wind instruments. Indeed, dare I say it, his music sounds even better played by a village band, with clarinets replacing the violins. There's something neurotic about a violin. It takes over, craving attention, the anorexic ego craving for a paternal hug. But a bank of clarinets is never bad-tempered or sulky, is always intrinsically full.

Anyway, came the day when Caesar shoved in front of us the chorus of Nabucco, '*Va, Pensiero*', or 'Go O Thought on Golden Wings' – I feel quite dizzy just writing out the words – which is Italy's second national anthem. Great excitement in the ranks, adjusting of the part on the stand, a review of the reed, a glance

left and right, like a flock of turkeys who suddenly and simultaneously start preening.

After the usual trauma caused by Caesar yelling '*Piano*'
fortissimo three or four times, because it really does have to start
piano, we eased the way in for Beppe the shoemaker, who has a
really lovely voice on his *bombardino* even if he is a bit hard on
those caged birds in the back room. And then suddenly the
twenty-two eyes of the clarinettists slitted themselves as one
long collective eye. What's this? After a few bars' rest, Verdi
had written us a chromatic scale of semihemidemiquavers set so
close to each other that one bar covered the entire page, and
even so they were intertwined with smudgy ink here and there
with *La* and *Si* written above them from time to time, for the
clarification of everyone but me.

I looked to my right. The young were smiling brightly up at
me. I looked to my left. Otello was sitting there, smoking so
hard that it weakly came out of his ears, giving it the great stone
face. *Ragazzi*, count me out. I turned back to the right, thinking
that perhaps it was my chance to bridge the generation gap.

I could never get it quite right. A chromatic scale is one
where you play all the intervals including the half tones, either
going up or going down. In theory a good clarinettist gets this
chore done within his or her second year. I am not a good
clarinettist. I always seemed to end up with a few too many
notes towards the top, having to substitute some garrulous
triplets for Verdi's strict fours. Sometimes a five came out,
which you do as a triplet and two quick ones.

Anyway I had quite a lot of fun with the young maidens in
tight jeans, acting the kindly father and straightening out here a
finger, there a triplet, while Otello sat looking at the music,
holding his clarinet, with a lit cigarette somewhere near his
knee.

Came the big day. We were in San Sano, my own home

village, on a raised plinth not far from the ornamental statue of a bronze frog drinking from a Chianti flask, looking down towards the new restaurant Adelina had opened the year before, through a fringe of lime trees growing straight out of the asphalt. Beautiful night of early summer, the small audience looking up at us from collapsible chairs loaned by the *Comune*. Just a faint smell of warm cypress, like a radiator left on, the nights not yet warm enough to take off our jackets and relax.

We were dong well, but a qualm like a faint memory of a channel crossing came over me as we approached the first public performance of '*Va, Pensiero*'. Before we tackled it, I rose from my chair, abandoned Otello and squeezed between two nymphs in order to present a united front, to solve the question of the chromatic riff by pattern bombing. They smiled. We played. When it came to the rough passage they took their instruments from their pretty lips, still smiling, and left me to climb up there all by myself. One felt so lonely. I could hear a breeze blowing through the tall trees down by the village fountain, and the terrible silence, like a hole in space, of the audience as up I went, hand over hand.

Otello died very quickly. In June he was away at the seaside when we had a repeat performance, on the same plinth, in Gaiole. In July he came back, sick in his stomach, and before I even heard of it he was dead.

I much regret not having visited him as he lay ill. His friendship meant a great deal to me, within the formal context of reading music together over the years, side by side. I liked the idea he conveyed, that you could overlook and forgive practically anything, provided that you knew exactly what had happened. That confrontation on the moor in 'Peeb-less shire', in which he was more dour than the dour, was a Tuscan masterpiece. He had a cautious muscular face, expressing cheerfulness over some hidden suffering, a bit like Rembrandt's brother.

All the band turned out for his funeral, which produced a kind of paradigm of Tuscan behaviour. To begin with, the service went on for hours. Don Bernabei was an old friend of Otello, and was deeply upset by his death. He started talking about him, about his courage, and what he had said before dying. After half an hour, on an upswing, he described how at this moment Otello was arriving in Heaven, and what he might be seeing. Then he abandoned the microphone and went round the bier three times, sprinkling it with water first, then incense.

The band watched, perturbed. The after-image of Otello standing among us and sceptically watching his own funeral was very strong. *O ragazzi!*

Grey cloud had covered the little valley by the time we came out. People turned up their collars and looked at the sky. The band walked just behind the hearse, a long Mercedes from Siena, and we had great difficulty keeping pace with it. If we played ('*Ritorno a Dio*'), we accelerated and piled up on the chrome bumper like surf on a rock; if we didn't, we seemed to lag behind.

Soon after we had passed the municipal slaughterhouse on the edge of the town, a few enormous drops fell on the road. A wave of horror passed through the mourners. Old friends of Otello, his very oldest and dearest friends, hesitated, looking upwards, torn between respect for the dead and the appalling prospect of getting wet. They dropped out. The band became bad-tempered.

There was maximum disorganization at the gate of the little cemetery. Prunings from the big mulberry still lay on the ground, reducing the parking space. There was just room for the Mercedes to back up, between two cars. A loud public conference debated who should enter first, the band or Otello.

The Band

It was unresolved and everyone entered at once. Muffled comments by pallbearers, bruised ankles.

Once in, more chaos. Where should the band stand? Near the grave, just behind the mourners, blowing down their necks, or at a little distance? We stood a little way off. And where shall Caesar stand? Up on the next level, where we can all see him, six feet or so above us. Among the gravestones, the movement of his arms will stand out against the sky.

Mutters from the crowd: here we will catch our deaths of cold. Mourners crammed the side of the grave and were asked by the sextons to stand back. Caesar raised his hand: we all looked up. Down came the hand, and down the rain simultaneously, and down went the coffin in a sudden rush. The mourners disappeared from the graveside as if wiped off with a rag.

It was as if the band spoke their individual comments through mouths of brass and ebony. Not their grief, which can be smoothed out over years, but their annoyance with bad weather. 'Ritorno a Dio' became an unstoppable *accelerando*, black and white punctuation upon a grey smudged and scratched negative of musicians playing in the rain. No repeats. Total dissolution of the band the moment the last bar ended, the entire congregation now sheltering under the small roof of the *forni*, or ovens, those particularly unpleasant graves set end on into the surrounding walls of the cemetery, which at night are speckled with small red lanterns.

A great silence overcame us all. Tableau. Empty churchyard, save for three frantically active sextons, who seemed to be cementing Otello in rather than covering him with damp earth. He was to be floored there, it seemed, with honeycomb tiles. One or two women, bored, glanced up and around at the ovens, looking for dead friends. Rain fell on all of us, fell into the grave. The far side of the graveyard was streaked with vertical lines of grey.

I was once the youngest of the band, and remained so for years. Lord, what shall I do now, in the practice sessions once a week? Sniggling girls to my left, sniggling girls now also to my right, their plump short thighs in streaked jeans. There's a new one whose freshly pierced ears are pink about the lobe.

Shall I come over the heavy statesman offering sage advice? Or do I slump down, lose a foot or two, and sniggle with them? Or shall I emulate the dead Otello, blank-faced and calm, unperturbed by a new hairstyle as we finger our ageing instruments and blow?

18 · FILM SET

The starlet had knees as beautiful as those of a Gothic statue and Nefertiti cheeks from which a skilled cosmetic dentist had removed a few back teeth. She stood in front of the little church of San Giusto, looked down the hill at the vines heavy with grapes, looked up the hill at the woods and said, 'Where are we?' I found the question touching, given her profession. She was polite, her voice smooth and soft, with qualities of courtesy to be prized on a film set, where all else is chaos.

A christening party set up on the patch of green between the chestnuts and the house of Isabella, the nun who lived alone. Long table with apparently edible food. Trucks around and about, a gum-chewing Roman to stop trespassers or those who had innocently come to see the church.

I saw Sister Isabella, somewhere in the background, looking very happy. Happy? Who would have thought a recluse would show this reaction? But then perhaps even sanctity needs a moment of jostle now and again, under the pollarded chestnut tree.

Dumb Rape was the title; in Italian, *Stupro Muto*. A heartrending tale of a juvenile lead born deaf and dumb, whom the starlet leads to wider awareness of the world by a thorough introduction to the joys of sex. This was to take place upon a heap of rice bags which were to burst at the moment of orgasm, overwhelming his limbs and hers in a general whoosh of symphonic whiteness.

That such a thing was to take place here was a bit my fault. My friend Marco the film director had telephoned me from Rome to ask about locations. At the time there were vague negotiations for me to play a paternal vampire in a film of his about fanged incest. I was surprised to hear this was all off, and *Dumb Rape* in its place, but always eager to help a friend I told him about the church of San Giusto, and that I'd speak to Don Osvaldo to see if he were interested in renting the place. I privately told Osvaldo to charge a lot but this, of course, he failed to do.

All this came about before I was fully aware what the plot entailed. It was left to me to explain to Osvaldo that one or two of the scenes were, hmm, well, a bit close to the limit. He listened with detachment as I explained about the rice bags. As I talked I became curious to know what kind of answer he would give to this one, and I was not disappointed. Don Osvaldo has acquired over the years a magnificent simplicity when it comes to worldly matters. 'Not in church, I hope,' he said, when I had finished. 'People might be surprised to find a lot of bags of rice in a Romanesque chapel.'

In the spirit of jobs for the boys, I then dragged in some members of the Gaiole band. 'What you need, Marco,' I said, 'is a kind of spontaneous popular festivity, after which he chases her into the rice vault – and off you go.' 'Great,' said Marco. 'They take eighty thousand lire,' I said, 'per head per day, cash every evening before they go.'

So a select group of instrumentalists, including myself, played the christening party into church and out, with the dumb couple in the middle, after waiting for a comatose baby who was a long time coming. Men with hand-held radios talked across the ether as the infant approached, buoyed by both parents in the back seat of a Lancia with Roman number-plates. During the wait the starlet and the juvenile lead talked quietly about Los Angeles, and bike races in upstate California at the wake of Steve McQueen.

The next scene involved a reversing dolly shot set up between the long table in front of Isabella's back door and a trailer opposite, upon which we musicians were supposed to stand. The sequence involved the band striking up and descending one after another from the trailer (artfully garnished with boughs of laurel and ribbons of flaccid paper), to play their way to the long table, and incite the guests to revelry by wiggling their instruments. Shyly, the starlet was to take by the hand the juvenile lead. Smiles, claps from the crowd as he moves his indelicate feet, shackled by interior silence, and begins to dance.

Not easy. The band showed neither interest in the technical problem nor obedience in grasping what was needed of them. The girl in Production kept shouting at them to watch their feet, and the chalk marks which indicated where they should be standing. They forgot their cues, giggled among themselves, eventually ceased to find it amusing. The double-bass could not descend from the trailer quickly enough. He cussed the laurel and seemed to find difficulty looking down. The accordianists refused to move. They did not walk and play, they said. They grew hot, turned away when spoken to, became interested in the landscape where the afternoon caused the tough line of hills to shimmer and turn blue.

Art and illusion had to intervene, so the instrumentalists were parked here and there as if it were customary to strike up a dance playing from different spots in the crowd. The accordion players were perched on stools, one forward by a lemon in a pot, one aft against the grey stone wall of the church.

The day grew hot. The actors at table fiddled with the fake

food, which was patiently put to rights by legionaries from Props. The spectators yawned and walked away one by one towards the church.

I suddenly awoke to the fact that the accordion players loathed each other. In their Tuscan way, they were refusing to cooperate. 'He,' said Achille, 'can do what he likes. That's up to him. To me, it is a matter of indifference. He might think that what we are making is music. I am sure he is a very fine musician. I would not know. I have never played with him before. We do not know each other. But music cannot be improvised. That is not serious. You would not want to call what we are doing music, would you?'

Incompatible repertoires. I wanted '*Speranze Perdute*', a beautiful sour waltz in a minor key. The newcomer was refusing to play this, and the Gaiole musicians were sulking.

Marco turned to me wearily. 'Look, do me a favour.'

To my incredulous pleasure, the cast suddenly rose up and began singing 'Happy Birthday to You' in both languages simultaneously. A huge cake appeared (the accordion players still squabbling), with the figure 100 drawn on it in whipped cream upon chocolate. It approached a beautiful old lady in the cast; the cake was placed in front of her. One hundred what? Not years surely? Films. Good lord, one hundred *films*? A sense of awe overcame me, that a nice old lady could be made to endure so much, live so long.

'Take five minutes,' said Marco. Then yelled, 'Take twenty.'

The court photographer came over to record the moment when the cake was cut. The pretty starlet stole the stills with a dazzling smile, the old lady backing ever so slightly away, as one might from an unpredictable terrier.

A momentary sadness seemed to overcome the troupe. The cameraman was supposed to have worked on films the mere murmur of whose titles made me gasp, and here he was on a reverse dolly shot preparing for a rape, while the chickens on a grill in the background burst into flame, to be whipped by a stage hand with casual strokes so that they went back to smoking acridly, as was their job.

The band retreated behind the chuck wagon, to a nest of packing-cases and filled rubbish bags from lunch. Achille wore an expression like soft stone eroded by water. The other accordion player had been chosen for his fine moustachios which, come to think of it, featured in the very foreground of the aborted shots. He had a large plastic wallet filled with music but '*Speranze Perdute*' ('Lost Hopes') was not among these time-weathered scores. 'Surely you know how it goes?' '*Ho capito,*' he said, 'but I haven't played it for twenty years.' He was unable to look Achille in the eye.

'Do not think, dear colleagues,' I said, 'that what we are to do in front of the camera will last. Is it fame that you want? Do you want our dedication and nimble fingers to survive a century or two, an indication to posterity what high standards of musicianship were current in the late twentieth century? To be immortalized? Comrades, relax. We are not destined to survive encapsulated in celluloid. Feel no shame! As soon as Marco has the rushes in Rome we will be dubbed, castrated, played over by a full string orchestra with echoes wired in. You will magically finger a violin, O Achille, and you, O Newcomer, will with deft strokes make music from your fine moustache. It is your faces, O musicians, that are wanted. No other talent is required.'

Mock Alfieri in style, the hyperbolic English is a translation of sensational Italian. I felt that their mood was too serious. Without a smile they would do nothing. At last a smile appeared, and the new man said to Achille, 'Oh well, play it.' Which Achille did. Elio took it up on his clarinet. The bass strummed something, it mattered little what. The man with moustaches looked at Achille's fingers, and by the third time through he had it fine. He had it remarkably fine.

Panicking, I took Achille behind the church, where the support artiste (whose role was the mother of the freshly christened baby) had tethered a clipped and vicious chow to the graveyard railings, and there on improvised staves I wrote down at Achille's dictation his 'Lost Hopes', which were slightly different from mine.

We shot it again, under the drifting smoke from the carbonizing chickens. The old lady had had a slightly weepy moment: time had passed. The cameraman had smoked some cigarettes. Osvaldo had made some fussy remarks about the mess, and retired for an hour to snooze in his car in the shade. The stoic philosophers of Props had returned the table to a state of apparent edibility. The sun had moved behind the chestnuts.

We did it five times. The sun sank through layers of spreading leaves like a hot light seen through a riffle of banknotes. The tempers of the musicians survived – indeed, the worse they played, the better they acted, as they were overcome by the manic quality of making films. For in films you are paid money for a portion of your skin, the lightest cutaneous reality that can be transposed to a sheet of transparent plastic. Though sometimes highly paid, the operation is traumatic as an amputation, a moral theft, and for the while you have to suppress your sense of physical pride.

'Can we go then?' Marco said yes, he did not see why not. 'Can we be paid?' The band gathered round me in a deceptively casual manner, tapping their instruments here and there like the flanks of animals.

The head of Production was a wench of forty with dark glasses and a Biro behind her ear and she said, 'You'll not leave the set one minute before seven this evening. After that I'll pay you and kick you out on your arses and with luck I'll never see you again. *E buona notte!*'

The harsh voice of Rome.

A thoughtful silence descended on the people behind me. I could feel the accumulation of that air of total stupidity with which Tuscans defend themselves against the constant need of Romans to prove they are more callous than anyone else in the peninsula.

Marco looked at the sky, sucked his foul cigar and turned away. I wanted very much to go over and pat him on the shoulder, but that would have been breaking ranks.

At that fine moment, poised between friendship and detachment, Marco unwittingly farted.

For a moment nothing happened. Then a movement came over the musicians behind me, like a light wind moving through a forest.

'O Marco,' came a voice, '*ci vuole solo un sassolino.*' (All you need is a little stone.) A ritual answer given by little children when this elementary human predicament occurs in class.

He could have smiled, made a vivid answer, but instead he walked away. And in so doing he lost my sympathy, attempting to retain an imagined dignity rather than coming down to the level of the muddy troops.

I left. The woman from Production piled on a few insults to cover her master's retreat, and as usual I became quickly irritated with the 'realism' of the Roman spirit compared with the softness of the Etruscans.

In leaving, I made a great mistake. In fact you might say that I lost the battle. It was a question of holding the thin red line. Everyone got paid, and paid well, after hanging around for another half hour. Even Osvaldo got a bit more than he'd initially asked for. Everyone got paid but me. Now, I can whistle for my wasted day. No one gets a bill settled in Cinecittà after the film is in the can.

★

They never shot the scene on the bags of rice. Sugar-chops turned out to have a clause in her contract forbidding her to be shown in the nude, being a serious actress. She might have been bullied out of this had the juvenile lead not revealed on his manslaughtering pectorals a tattoo of a bald eagle holding a shield and a parachute, and the words '102nd Airborne'. This was considered inconsistent with his role of mute Italian pauper-prince.

Marco told the producers that it would have to be a film of 'atmosphere'. I much regretted not knowing what language a pair of Roman soft-porn producers used to discuss this particular art form.

19 · SATYRIC

Art is often a disease that life acquires by contagion. A month later, while Maro and I were down in Sicily taking part in a group exhibition, the agricultural helpmate beside whom I've worked for years assaulted Georgina, my second daughter's best friend.

He joined us six or seven years ago, replacing a bent old saint no longer able to keep the olive trees trimmed. As large and energetic as the former had been cowed, Furbuffo had the little terraces in order within a year.

He fired once more our torpid agricultural ambitions. Together we reclaimed a hillside gone wild thirty years before, cut the tangled broom to the ground, nourished the self-seeded oaks, planted pine and ilex among the crumbled stones of fallen eighteenth-century walls. Recently he had grown ambitious about the dark wood itself, dragging the plough among the oaks, making harassed paths southwards through the trees.

Stones were his bane. His ambition was to clear the whole farm of them, lifting the jagged fragments of sedimentary limestone, *galestro* and *albarese*, into the cart, and creating a private pyramid in the corner of a remote field. From time to time we would hear him, even in high summer, making a crash in the middle distance like a small building falling down a cliff.

In my studio he would lift heads of stone, and wooden

251

figures six foot high, as if they were dolls. He told me where they would look good, and would take them in his arms to the ideal spot against a background of foliage.

Everything about him was on a Homeric scale, even his voice. Maro would point outside if ever he tried to talk to her in the house. At which he would shout, '*Si, si,*' so that the whole downstairs boomed, then flinch and raise his hand to his mouth as if trying to grab the words in the air, even as they left his throat.

Georgina on the other hand was with us briefly for the first part of her year out. A substitute daughter for us, in a mood of self-absorption, doing nothing during the time of year that used to be term-time. The last sweet flavour of childhood before the ornate gateway of university, and beyond it the real world. A dreamer.

And then she was stumbling over the wet fields, hysterical, the mood of quietness shattered. He looking after her, pale eyes protruding from reddened features, a worried frown, making as if to follow, to explain. Gesturing after her with a hand like a clawless bear. Suddenly glimpsing him through Georgina's eyes, I could see Furbuffo as terrifying.

Maro and I had a day or two in which to run through this imagined movie in our heads, music-less and jittery, with no facts to go on but that she had abandoned the house in a thunderstorm and had been saved by a friend who happened to be passing by, after goodness knows what kind of phone calls for help, conducted publicly in poor Italian at the local bar.

I was furious with him. I cannot even call him by his real name, or choose an innocuous one. Furbuffo let him be, both tragic and crafty, feigning innocence and avoiding the direct confrontation, like the baritone of misfortune in an opera buffa.

I telephoned him late at night from the desk of a third-class hotel in Sciacca, the night the exhibition opened, drunk and inarticulate, staring wildly at the ceiling of stencilled cherubim. 'Shame,' I said. The night porter was used to such scenes and remained aloof. 'Shame on you, shame on our household. What have you done? How dare you?' I let my accusations flash down the wires as imprecisely as possible, having nothing substantial to go on. Alcohol and disgust spurred me. It was two in the morning and far from home, with the bags of surreptitious weekenders hidden under the potted greenery in the hall, waiting for an early start.

I have never felt less English. There are things you do not do if you come from the frigid isle. You do not telephone an employee at two in the morning upon an unconfirmed rumour of rape, yelling your sense of grief and squalor out into the night. Some instinct must have told me that if I kept quiet, Furbuffo would take my silence as acquiescence. Any responsibility he might have felt would evaporate with the passing days. Incoherent chastisement at long distance was what he would have expected if his employer was, as for a moment I felt, Italian.

His voice quavered. Down the crackling telephone line I heard it echo about the concrete corridor of the council house on the outskirts of the little town, by the slaughterhouse, above the main road. 'I never! Who has been telling lies about me? What has she said? Nothing took place – nothing, I tell you. What! I hold you in all possible respect, Signor Matteo. I would never permit myself . . .'

'*What has she said?*' That was enough to make me feel that something had in fact taken place.

Trembling, I smoked a cigarette with the hall porter.

A trace memory came back to me of an incident that occurred some years ago, on the Ponte Vecchio in Florence. As Maro and I were admiring the Christmas jewellery, I noticed that a young man near by had his hand deep in her bag. Now I consider myself a man of peace, so it was with surprise that I noticed that my left hand was around his throat, and that I was raising him slowly from the ground. Is it normal, I yelled, for you to put your hand in the pockets of others? Is it? My thumb was on his artery. A semicircle of curious people instantly made a theatre around us. His face changed from mild concern to incredulous fear, to panic. He realized he was about to be throttled.

At this point a thought went through my head. Am I over-reacting? Is this fascism? I dropped him, and he was gone. The crowd, mildly perturbed, returned to its earlier ebb. My wife and I fluttered at each other like poultry after a quick brush with the weasel. It took us some minutes to subside.

'My man!' said Maro comfortingly. 'Now why can't you do things like that more often?'

I was shocked by my own violence, by the realization that I *enjoyed* the thief's fear. What qualities of reason or detachment in my soul could outweigh this reflex of pure violence?

So again I thought, why, this is fascism, as I turned from the hall and walked upstairs. The unclear accusation, the sense of large disaster, betrayal, *brutta figura*, my voice echoing in the foyer of a large hotel, his in a *casa popolare*, bound by seven years of agricultural cooperation now gone in a whisk, a whimper.

We came back by water, from Palermo to Viareggio across the inland sea. The air was sullen and milky as we docked, the port stacked with slabs of concrete as if the war were not yet over. We entered the long valley between the sea and Florence through a tangle of small industries that were gradually devouring the marshy land, with marine birds feeding among the sedge behind the wire periphery of future factories.

'Let us take the slow way back,' said Maro quietly. 'It is so much prettier.'

Prettier, and ten times as long – that was the point. The slow road to postpone a showdown. O Christ! The late morning shuffled quickly in the pack, and it seemed to grow dark some few minutes after we penetrated the hills. The sky was deep blue over the pines above Poggibonsi. Slit eyes appeared in the windows of the new bank, illuminated by lights switched on automatically at dusk.

'Better step on it,' Maro said after our subdued day's drive, 'he might go home. I'll drive on to collect Georgina' – who was staying with a friend.

I caught him at the door, making for his gutted Fiat.

I sacked him immediately. No excuse, no explanation accepted. Out! There was no other way to discover what had taken place. Boil a small hard fact out of seething grandiloquence.

'I trusted you,' I said, making as if to shoo him away. 'I do not yet know, do not want to know, what you did to the poor girl. For me it is enough that within two days of leaving you in charge, you frighten her so badly that she runs away into the fields at night, runs to the village and telephones England. Phones England! Do you realize how frightened her parents must have been? What am I to say to them? What am I to say to her father? Her father! How can I look him in the eye, ever again?'

'O *Signor Matteo!* I cannot tell why she ran away like that! For me it is a complete mystery. Perhaps she suddenly felt ill!'

His eyes wet and protruding, the whole of him glazed with anxious sweat. He was trying to tell me that Georgina lied to me. I was so furious I could not speak. Seeing this, he changed tactics instantly.

'No, no! That is . . . Nothing happened! Nothing at all!'

'I only hope that this is true. I am sure it is true! You are at heart a good person and I am sure you would never do anyone any harm. I'm certain of it! Even now, I still would be glad to trust you, if I dared. But it is not for me to say. Do you realize how dangerous these things are? If her father asks for an explanation, what do I tell him? They know their daughter well, know that she does not imagine things. She showed no fear when we left her here in the house alone, the day we left.'

And, with heavier overtones, 'These are questions, Furbuffo, which entail inquiries by the authorities. These stories touch upon the jail!'

'Truly,' said Furbuffo, shouting as quietly as he could, 'I showed her only the greatest respect, of that I can assure you. Never in my life have I harmed another. Never. I have never done any wickedness towards anyone. Never!'

His brother came in from the fields. A remarkable pair in their way, working until a time of night when even an owl would find it hard to see, singing among the terraces in the dark.

An hour later Furbuffo sank to his knees.

'Ever since you shouted at me,' he said, 'I have not felt in good health. Ever since you woke me at two in the morning, the day afterwards. Woke the whole house! The whole *palazzo*! The children crying, my wife asking what the matter was – she knows nothing – why I was so upset. They could all see I was upset. That I was suffering. And now what am I to tell them?'

'But Furbuffo,' I said, fairly amazed, 'we are surely not here to talk about your suffering.'

'I have not slept! I come in from work and I sit by the fire, and I start crying because I am so uneasy, and the children ask me, "*Babbo*, why are you crying? Why are you so nervous?"'

Eyes squeezed tight by red cheeks as meaty as biceps, limp hair cut short, curling like weeds in a current. Huge hands one held within another, stout fingers with broken nails; or waving them at me palm forwards, in some attempt to placate, to worship. He was begging me for forgiveness by showing me his wounds.

His brother unfolded his crossed arms and said calmly that at this point he might as well tell me exactly what happened. A look of mingled doubt and calculation came into Furbuffo's eyes: was this the winning strategy? 'All right,' he said at last, getting up and coming close, looking me in the eyes.

'I was changing the wine, right? And we needed a pot from the kitchen, something with a handle so that I could get the dregs in the bottom of the vat, right? So I came into the kitchen and asked the Signorina if I could take one. But she did not answer me. Maybe she did not understand. So I followed her, and I found her standing in the studio upstairs, and I asked her again, if we could take this pot, and she said finally yes. And then I saw her standing there, and she looked so pretty that – just to indicate that I admired her very much – so I asked her if I could give her a kiss. Well! The Signorina perhaps, you know, doesn't understand Italian very well, so she said again to me yes. And so I did. But no more than this . . .'

Stepping forward, he gave me a fairly chaste kiss on the cheek, perhaps a little near the mouth, but all the same a fairly straightforward buss.

Relieved, but also flabbergasted, I said, 'But how on earth could you accept her yes as being sincere, *voluto*, when you yourself say that she could not speak Italian? Good God, she had only been in the country for about three days! What sort of a welcome – what hospitality! Of course she did not understand what you were saying!'

'Ah, but I meant it with all respect,' he said. 'And she did say yes.'

A look of reasonable cunning, as of 'I'm trying to help you', came over his face. Then seeing me getting really angry he mumbled, 'But it was nothing, really nothing.'

So saying he stepped forward and kissed me again.

'Do stop it,' I said, wiping my face with the back of my hand. 'Believe me, I can see your point!'

'Ah! So you see! It was really nothing!'

'Look,' I said, trying to sum up for him, 'the kiss may have been nothing special in itself, and you can thank all the saints that I believe you, and that it went no further than that . . . In fact we can all be incredibly relieved, it seems to me.'

Then I tried to repeat the theme of having taken advantage of Georgina's lack of Italian. But it was hard to concentrate. In the back of my mind it occurred to me that a defence lawyer could make a lot of mileage out of her puzzled *Si*.

Half-heartedly he took another step towards me.

'No, no,' I said, 'please don't kiss me again. I don't think I could stand a third.'

Once again he showed his respect for my inviolable personage by showing me the palms of his hands, and stood there dumbly awaiting the word that all was right again.

'You both tell me that you are fundamentally a good boy, and I believe you,' at which he nodded five times and repeated *Si*.

If it weren't for his size, looking at him standing there so hopeful and self-pitying, I could almost believe him innocuous. But it was not a question of uncontrollable desire, still less of calculation. He was a victim of something much more primitive: the incapacity to think forward, to imagine even a very immediate future. How easily it might have gone further, I thought. From one thing to another, via misunderstanding, smothered panic, in an upstairs room.

'So you see,' said the brother as I stood silent, 'now that you know, it's all over. There! That was simple wasn't it?'

'What do you mean?' I said, aware that in my reverie I had missed some important cue. 'Not at all. I am very happy to hear that nothing serious took place, but this does not affect the betrayal of trust which you made to me, the moment my back was turned.'

It took a moment or two for Furbuffo to realize that forgiveness was not inevitable, would never take place. With a huge shout he collapsed on to the floor again and to my horror started to beat his head against the tiles. The whole room boomed and echoed, his sinal cavity by chance awakening some sympathetic voice in the plumbing under the floor.

'I am finished,' he said. 'You might as well kill me right now, here as I lie at your feet. I am a man who has been utterly destroyed. *Un uomo finito.* How can I go home tonight and face my family? What will they say at work? What will they say in the village?'

'Good Lord,' I said, 'you don't mean to tell me you have been telling everyone all about it?'

'No, no,' he said quickly. 'But, with all due respect, the Signora Maro won't be able to keep it a secret. O! With all respect, you know how she is.'

'The Signora Maro will keep it quiet.'

'But what can I say to the others, to explain that I have lost my job?'

'You say as little as possible, and put all the blame on us. Say we have lost millions on the stock exchange! Have to save our pennies for something else, some other luxury.'

The brother and I exchanged glances. I took comfort from his calmness.

Furbuffo instead seemed unable to face up to it.

'But I enjoy working here!'

'I know you do, and it's great to have you here.'

He brightened.

'But unfortunately it is just not possible . . . I don't know how to choose the words with which to tell you this.'

Hearing himself rejected yet again, he set about banging his head on the floor again, at which I suddenly lost my temper.

'Oh, for the love of heaven stop breaking my handmade tiles with your forehead! Can't you understand? These are things which involve a denouncement, a trial, even prison. I am not going through all this confrontation because I dislike you or reject you or whatever. Surely you can see that there are some objective standards at stake?'

He flailed about on the floor, wailing.

'What about your own daughter,' I screamed.

Face down, he mumbled, 'But she's only thirteen!'

By this time a part of me was engaged with the fantasy of making out a denouncement in front of Tiripepe, the *Brigadiere di Carabinieri* down in the township, in formalese, including my mother's Christian name and the crime all in one long sentence. Identity and act between neat consecutive commas, sworn before the silver grenade in flames.

'Get up,' I shouted. I felt like kicking him. 'Get up off my floor! We've been here for over two hours – I arrived at five-forty and it's now ten to eight – and you still cannot see that you've done something wrong. You are just concerned about your job! There's nothing more I can say to you, save perhaps give you a good beating.'

Instantly he was up. 'Oh yes yes yes,' he said, and went outside, coming back in a moment with what to him was a light wand, and to me was the trunk of one of the larger olive trees that had died in the frost, one of the pile waiting outside the back door for the buzz-saw and the axe.

'Beat me,' he said. 'Beat me hard hard hard, and when you have beaten me we will leave, go home, sleep soundly and in the morning all will be forgotten. This terrible thing that has happened to us,' he said, as if inflicted by fate from outside. 'Beat me as hard as you like, I shan't complain.'

I told him I could not speak to him any further. Could certainly not beat him. That I was speaking ironically. I was joking, I said. An incredulous look came into his eyes, that I could be so heartless at a time like this, at his expense.

'Put it back,' I said. I had to keep it simple. 'Put back the log, please. Nobody here can lift it but you.'

A moment of calm came over us as he came back into the room. He seemed finally to have accepted it.

'If I had known it would end like this,' he said sadly, 'I would have done much more.'

I did not like the sound of this.

'I mean, if I was to lose my job anyway.'

I thought swiftly that I had better not inquire quite what he meant, risking still murkier depths.

'After all,' he mumbled, 'the postman in Montecaio with that English schoolteacher who was here for the summer, the blond one . . .'

(Goddammit! All English girls are longing for it the moment they step off the plane, aren't they just?)

'And to think I took such care, during August, to treat all the young *signorine* with respect. I did not even look at them! Why, when they were sunning themselves by the pool, I would drive all the way around the vineyard with my tractor, a much longer way, so as not to observe them as they were lying there.'

'Perhaps,' I said, 'you should refrain from telling me this.'

'If only you knew how protective I was, when the Signorina Georgina was here alone. Why, the very afternoon you left, I came back at midnight to make sure that everything was in good order. The *signorina* was in the house, I could see her. She had not pulled the curtains, and I could observe her walking around inside, from room to room. And when a car came by with a hunter, I asked who he was, what he

261

wanted, and sent him away, so that she would not be disturbed. I stayed until late, very late, all to make sure she was all right.'

What extraordinary rooms had been opened in the primordial labyrinth of this man's mind by an act committed in my house? Whose person might I be risking in the future, by keeping the incident closed?

'Are you a religious man?' I asked him.

A devious look came into his eyes, down there on the floor below me. He admitted he was. 'Why?'

'Because at this point I feel that the only thing that can be done is for you to confess everything to the priest. In fact I will make a deal with you. If your priest tells me that he thinks I have treated you unfairly, I shall consider taking you back.'

Fair enough, I thought, given the circumstances.

Doubt still overcame him.

'But,' he wailed, 'he's the biggest gossip in town!'

And so I had to give him a lecture about the secrecy of the confessional, and how the priest, if he betrayed it, would most certainly go to Hell, and roast. Him on his knees, and me talking about roasting in Hell . . .

With the help of his brother, he left at last, and I was able to telephone Maro and Georgina to say they could come back.

While waiting for them in the silent house, listening to the creak of the fridge and the birds on the roof settling down for the night, I suddenly became aware that Furbuffo was still out there, sitting in his car, perhaps trying to think of further things to say. This silent brooding touched me. I could imagine him, a huge man in a small dark car, trying to recapitulate the argument.

They missed each other by five minutes. The cars must have passed each other on the road.

★

Don Bernabei telephoned us about four days later. I was delighted that Furbuffo had actually gone to see him, and arranged to talk with Don Bernabei himself a day or two later, taking Georgina with me.

She took great care in dressing for the occasion. Crisp white shirt with a small lace collar, suggesting a girl trained by adamantine nuns. This she starched to the consistency of transparent cardboard. Long black skirt, dark tights, shoes with a 'sensible' bow. Tight black belt, so that the shirt stuck out. Her breasts alone below the hard creased linen were proof of immaculate innocence.

She kept me waiting, as the hour for the showdown with the priest drew near. At the upstairs mirror she removed with small white pads any trace of make-up that lingered from the urban day. Her lips needed no lipstick to improve their pinkness, her eyes required no lining. Then she changed mirrors, and I watched as with silent drama she combed her curly hair, in long persistent strokes.

Strange though this may seem, I had not yet asked for her own account of what had happened. Hesitantly I described to her Furbuffo's version of her recent experience. She looked at herself as I talked, kept combing, and gradually blushed.

I waited for her own account. None emerged. Georgina combed as I waited, and in the end I was left with nothing but the swish of the brush in her long curly hair, hypnotic, recurring, like waves ascending an estuary.

At length she gave herself a chaste centre parting and tied her hair in a tight knot behind, then pulled out one single curl as if it might have escaped from such severity all by itself.

Then to my amazement she removed from a small case an old rosary of mother-of-pearl and silver, with a diminutive crucifix at the end. This she twined around her neck and hid with the closed lace collar, to be perceived under the shirt, rather than seen. It had belonged to her grandmother apparently.

She turned to me and said, 'How's that?'

Indeed, she seemed the very epitome of virginity.

We were late getting to Gaiole, and stood outside the church for a while in silence, listening to the evening Mass. The singing seemed weak and untuneful, the bare walls of the recent construction were unlikely ever to receive their marble facing. The Arizona cypress in the playground of the kindergarten had grown considerably since my children had been pupils there, and was crowding out the diminutive swing. There were new flats going up the hill.

We heard the service end, and the priest move from the sacristy to his private quarters without coming outside. Eventually Don Bernabei came to the door. He had intelligent eyes, and possessed a quality in common with certain saints that lie in glass cases beneath the altar, in that his teeth protruded.

He let us into a small room off the sacristy, with a large desk and some very full cupboards in the background. Faintly formal atmosphere, headmasterish. He seemed very pleased with Georgina, and stooped with an abrupt bow as we sat down, perhaps to see her better.

'This,' Don Bernabei told me, placing his hand upon her knee, 'this child is an innocent, as we can see.'

Georgina nodded, sitting up straight.

'It is quite clear . . .' he said, and hesitated.

I would have thought it was quite clear that any red-blooded man would have had difficulty in keeping his hands off her.

'It is quite clear that this poor man has certain problems,' he said, meaning Furbuffo. At which the conversation became serious, undistracted by the presence of Georgina, who continued to sit bolt upright on the hard-backed chair, eyes demurely down, nodding from time to indicate polite attention.

Sadness came over me as I listened to Don Bernabei. I had no idea that Furbuffo's background was quite so tortuous, or his family so beset by financial and emotional strains. The priest made a plea for Christian forgiveness, and for a moment I hesitated in my determination to be rid of a very valuable hired man.

That the girl herself had suffered, there was no doubt. That Furbuffo was untrustworthy was irrefutable. There was not much that Don Bernabei could say that could move me. What made me hesitate was Georgina herself sitting quietly to my left, the innocent virgin dressed up as an innocent virgin. Her subtle revenge via starch and white linen. Perhaps she should not have made such an effort to dress the part.

When Don Bernabei had ended, I could do nothing but look at her, puzzled. The priest too seemed slightly mesmerized. At length I murmured, 'A temptation.'

He understood immediately what I was talking about.

And so I managed to make a small speech. I said that we were a family of artists, and that artists led lives which were in some ways unusual. In the summer the young lay about the lawn, dressed in very little, *con grande disinvoltura*, and now and again I would draw them, and they did not mind. Draw them, in a word, stark naked. A matter of studying anatomy and composition, of course, as he would surely understand. But that the atmosphere this created might be expected to confuse anyone whose background was more 'traditional', so that a permissiveness might be felt where none existed. For in fact these young people, including this lady on my left, were in their way very serious (thank heavens!), brilliant in their exams, ambitious for their future.

All the time, I was thinking of the man in late autumn, ploughing the terraces in a biting north wind, cheerfully.

So that if we could by chance arrange this transaction between ourselves, as man to man, and little by little, I would be deeply grateful. By Christmas, he would have found something else, I was sure. For there was no question of him coming back before this young person (I gestured surreptitiously towards Georgina's white starched frontage) returned to her native land.

Don Bernabei looked down at the table and sighed.

Afterwards he insisted on giving her a bar of chocolate, from a small pile on a shelf in the kitchen. For me, a massive Vin Santo, causing instant hangover, even as it is drunk.

Georgina tried to refuse the chocolate, and looked so demure and pretty as she bowed to Don Bernabei, curls slightly falling forward around her face, that a viper would have turned sweet-toothed at the sight of her. Only later did it emerge that this was not more of her low-keyed mime, the innocent pretending to be innocent. She did, in fact, dislike milk chocolate. Another case of art and life intermingling.

A quiet six weeks passed by.

Furbuffo stayed away until the olive harvest, when, sur-rounded by peers in a far field, I felt I could not deny his presence without causing comment. It would be quite untrue to say we lived in a state of siege, even though there was something about the whole story which seemed to me never to have been brought into focus.

Getting the olives to the press coincided with a flurry of foul weather, though the days were streaked with low sunlight in fine yellow bands. I slid across the road, crashed the car, remained alive. Rose at two in the morning to sit it out with the olives as they went under the press, while starting an eight-foot terracotta later the same day at the kiln in Castellina. Briefly, we came to one of those difficult moments in life when you are obliged to postpone inessentials, like sleep.

Maro went north, to Milan, and I was left alone with Georgina and the tanks of olive oil.

They were short of plastic tanks at the olive mill, so I tried to sell my oil in a hurry. One of the buyers was Franco, the man who supplied all the isolated houses like ours with gravel for the roads.

As we were bent over the scales together, pouring the green concentration of my fields into a small demijohn, he told me that up at his new job Furbuffo was telling everyone about his tussle with Georgina, in the hopes of gaining sympathy. What! And we'd tried so hard to keep it quiet, for his sake? 'I know,' said Franco. 'He's mad. And of course his mates say he was completely in the wrong, shouldn't brood, should be grateful not to be in jail. But he keeps on about it!' (Franco, sniggering, made the bent column of oil wobble in the side of its plastic funnel.) 'And so they have made a little song about it up there, you know, to tease him. When he comes in, in the morning, they sing it, and he gets angry. It is truly very amusing.'

A song!

Two nights later I arrived back from a hard day at my statue to find the house dark, with no reply to my peremptory knock. Potatoes in one hand, stuffed pig's trotter in the other, the seasonal fare, abandoned at the woodstack as I tried to find a way in.

Brief panicky note on the scrubbed cypress table in the kitchen. The house dark and cold. 'Gone to the neighbours. Come and get me. Furbuffo . . .'

My heart doubled up. Adrenalin, like a hailstorm at sea, crashed around my chest.

Telephone. Weak voice the other end.

'He looked in the window. I'm sure he did. I'm so sorry. Please come and get me.'

Trace memory of Peter Pears in *The Turn of the Screw*, seen when I was twelve, staring in through the window, all fangs and ferocious desire. A sense of the unreasonable demands of life on a tired artist needing sleep. This rape we all fear; this child's anxiety. This menace. By what unfathomable chance had Furbuffo guessed that she was once again alone in the house, for half a day?

Light mist as I drove out again, among oak trees whose leaves had quite suddenly turned brown. Olive trees at the edge of the road, occasionally tatty, shorn of their fruit.

Georgina looked pale when I found her. It was no longer a question of dressing the part. She waited for me to speak, with a kind of tense vacancy, as if prepared to stand up to the most brutal interrogation.

Seeing her in such a state I felt I could not, would not, try to get to the bottom of this new assault. The idea that Furbuffo was genuinely obsessed with her was terrible. I was fairly sure that it could not have been him she saw peering in the window. We talked of other things, and gradually she calmed herself, became more lively, less wan.

The house seemed large and remote at our return. A peasanty smell pervaded the ground floor, a phenomenon which strikes me whenever I feel tired or have been away for a while, as if the walls when left alone immediately revert to the ghosts which at some level must still inhabit them.

Georgina, I am sure, felt homesick for her parents, for home, for England. She went upstairs early, leaving me restless for a while, listening to the noises of the night. The imagined thrashing of a large man in the undergrowth. The night, the house itself, seemed to behave strangely. Observed with such attention, life can seem unfamiliar, your own self an intruder.

Yet when I went to sleep I did not dream of Furbuffo, but of a clump of strange scented cypress trees moving in a high wind, somewhere in the north of Japan.

Nymphs and satyrs have to make their own arrangements. To identify with them is not the business of mere humans. As in so many things, it is we who are on the outside peering in.

20 · PORCUPINES

The Tuscan porcupine is a protected species, looking somewhat like a large Red Indian head-dress with legs.

About a dozen years ago a hungry and empirical porcupine tasted an iris root and found it good. It is not absolutely clear why the beasts took so long to discover that irises were edible. Perhaps the porcupine is not too bright, or perhaps its eating habits are governed by strict dietary laws. Perhaps the taste for iris was initiated centuries, millennia ago, taking time to become a dominant fad, like Nouvelle Cuisine – the luxury of fresh, paw-held root.

It took five or six years for the news to circulate, but eventually there was hardly a wild iris left in Tuscany. Those that remained were themselves protected (protected against the protected), by clumps of neat, vaguely organic-looking barbed wire. The blossoms and the wire expressed themselves at the same height above the ground, because the porcupine, suffering from back problems due to carrying around all those quills, seldom looks upwards, and quite a low fence was enough to discourage him. So flowers and wire in the spring would flourish in unison, above the tangled periphery of the open prison into which the iris was, for its own benefit, herded.

The sight of these floral concentration camps was unattractive to me, so soon our irises, left to take their chances, began to disappear. From time to time one would catch sight of the porcs at night, shuffling about in search of the perfect rhizome, the corm of dreams, grumpily retiring to the middle distance if one approached. In the morning, havoc. Unfortunately the Tuscan porcupine has no respect for the garden. In a word, is a messy eater.

In spite of this porcupines are, or were, attractive animals. On the roads at night in tribes, overcome by an air of private activity, they would turn their backs to the headlights of the car, presenting a row of backsides like flowers made of spillikins. Only once, in revenge for some vast bed of beautiful native iris savaged by guzzlers, I took a side-swipe at one with my Fiat. This was not a good idea. When I took the tyre to the garage the next day, the mechanic pulled with pliers a fat quill from my radial, with the muted reproach of one who finds bloodsports a sacred calling, reserved for the hunter with shotgun by Beretta rather than the driver armed with tyres by Pirelli.

The Tuscan iris these days can only be found in the tamed beds of nurseries such as Degl'Innocenti's, near the Certosa turn-off, which specializes in wild woodland species in danger of being munched or trampled out of existence. In a sense he helps to preserve these embattled plants, yet there is something strange about a wild iris in a pot. This flower was, after all, the symbol of Florentine Liberty, which they bore to the field of battle on their banners, even against each other – the Guelfs with a red iris on a white field, the Ghibellines with a white iris on a red field. Liberty in a pot is merely sad.[58]

Maro the gardener gradually came to terms with the loss of the irises, and replaced them with alliums that arrived from London, in a fat paper bag like weathered suede.

The porcs took four years to discover that allium, too, could be eaten. Maro stared for a while at a rugged hole beneath a wisteria, where the bulbs had been. But gardening, like Zen, produces hidden resources, and she said at last that she'd put in some fertilizer, to perk up the wisteria, and that the porcupine had saved her some trouble in making the hole.

The image of a four-legged digger remained. A little later we came across a porcupine dead in a ditch, killed by a car somewhat larger than mine. Again there was a silent pause as she looked downward. Eventual sigh.

'He has such a withered hand from scrabbling in the dirt,' she said. 'Like mine.'

The porcupines lived in lairs hidden far in the wood, detectable even to humankind by smell. Not merely messy, also stinky, was the porc. Scattered about their front doors (a grubby hole under a rock), would be many discarded quills, like medieval crossbow bolts a foot long, banded in black and white. For a while it became fashionable to substitute these quills for blooms in dried-flower arrangements in the home, perhaps as a low-keyed reproach.

I speak of the porcupine in the past tense, more or less, as the creatures, having undergone a remarkable population explosion following the craze for eating iris, suddenly began to decline in numbers. They ran out of iris. Or perhaps hunters, anxious about the side-effects they might have on more legitimate prey, poisoned them. (The strychnine-loaded iris root lobbed into the lair by the light of the full moon.) Or merely consumed them roasted. Local hunters would tell great tales of the porcupine, how 'good' he was, in the sense of a pot-roast. How he could cut a steel trap with his jaws. How he could chew his way out of a glass cage. All excellent reasons to promote the beast to the status of prey, albeit furtively.

I miss the porcupines. I like walking feather dusters. I miss the irises. It's annoying to find the native flower more or less extinct, all because of the greed of spine-pigs. Most of all, I do not feel that chance has acted fairly in depriving us both of the flower and the animal. If not one, then the other, but not both.

Porcupines declined to a point where they were no more than a subject for mildly distracting conversation in the bank, where they had to compete with the far more engrossing subject of wild boar. *Il cinghiale*, or rather, *lo cinniale*, as they tend to pronounce it in the neighbourhood, is a serious beast. Go for it if you discover it on the menu, for this will be a pig that has lived.

Scattered in lairs throughout the woods, but especially in those where they are protected against hunters, the boar breed large families of frisky, ravenous boarlets, one of whose chief amusements is mud-sliding. I have not seen this sport practised, but the slides are easy to find – long swathes of smooth mud, with the occasional imprint of hair, and surrounded by a syncopated notation of eager little hoofs.

The indigenous wild boar is apparently extinct. The present incumbent was introduced from Hungary after the war, and as it was larger and more fertile than the species formerly hunted by the Etruscans, the newcomers soon chased the old Tuscan wild boar out of existence, or swamped it genetically. And the ethnic purity of the new cross is still under some pressure, as occasionally a tame porker runs off to join the free and the brave, bringing a touch of smooth Dutch pinkness to mitigate the hairy Hungarian.

The way in which the hunting lobby defeated the referendum against hunting early in 1990 was in its way a classic example of Italian tactical duplicity in politics. It was clear from the opinion polls that about half the electorate was indifferent to the subject. It was also clear that of the remainder, i.e. of those likely to vote, more than half were against hunting. Now for a referendum to succeed, more than half the electorate has to place its vote, either for or against. The hunters' strategy was therefore not to vote at all, so that their absence plus the absence of those indifferent to the referendum would result in a turn-out insufficient to attain the quorum.

Democracy at work, in its way. But the hunters never said, 'We will defeat this bill by not voting, rather than by voting against it.' They started a whole campaign saying, 'We believe these appeals to the mass electorate are irrelevant and fundamentally illegitimate in a democracy which votes for representatives who ought to legislate responsibly for them, blah blah blah.' A lot of the undecided said, 'Yes they've got a point there'; whereas if the non-vote had been clearly identified as being a vote-against, many of the undecided might have joined the ecological lobby which wanted hunting to be curtailed. The bill was lost, the hunters won, with only about 40 per cent of the electorate voting.

Speaking for myself, I loathe boar hunts and the whole lore of shooting things with guns, right down to the special clothes painted in camouflage patterns, and clinking fetishes dangling from them – all those trinkets used for scaling fish, or currying horses, or skinning recently deceased fauna. Signor Trapassi at the bank knows this. He knows that when I ask some question about boar, I do it to tease. Can a boar eat through a telephone pole, I might ask innocently. He looks back, doubtful; but the urge to reply is too strong and 'Yes,' he will say, 'in certain circumstances a boar will . . .'

Incredulously I listen to him recount the most marvellous things, straight from a medieval bestiary, wondering if he can possibly believe what he is saying. I keep a straight face while he elaborates the circumstances of the wild pig's godlike feats, and the queue of those with things to do grows silently behind me.

An uneasy feeling comes over me as I find these elements of Tuscan life coming out on the page so facetiously. A semi-ecological jeer – is that all I can manage? To dwell in my mind for a while upon the image of Signor Trapassi, in his innocence, disarms me. My private and utterly English game of teasing him is undone by the fact that I make him fall for it every time. He pauses as he services a cheque; the *cinghiale* can, indeed, cross the Via Aurelia and discover new rooting-grounds on the other side. 'It is not an impassable barrier to the wily *cinghiale* – you may smile, but I assure you, Mr Spender, it is not. The wild boar is a match for a truck, at any moment of the day or night. He awaits his moment, and passes from the Parco dell'Uccellina on the one side to the great field of maize on the other, stern in the air, looking neither left nor right.' Whereupon Mr Trapassi takes from an inner drawer smudgy photos of *cinghialini* taken at dusk, without flash, in the wild, and everyone in the bank has to go 'Ah', and not lose their tempers at the delay.

Last month I sent him a postcard showing a man on a horse in a swamp in the Camargue, holding a large spear and wearing a black boater. Man and horse richly backlit, dark and poised for action. Sunset squidging behind the reeds in the background. The whole scene was an absolute classic of sentimental kitsch, featuring the loneliness of Man the Hunter as he waits astride his trusty steed to stick a porker in the back with his long pointed instrument. The ultimate Male, alone and intrepid, battling against the elements, biding his time. Abiding the click of Mamiya or Hasselblad.

In the leafy square of a small village in Provence I stared at this thing for five or ten minutes, wondering if I dared . . . '*Egregio Signor Trapassi,*' I wrote at last, 'This is how you should do it. This is the real thing. This is definitely You.'

And when I came back, I found he was touched. He thanked me. He leant over the counter to give me his hand, and he stuck the postcard somewhere in the background, along with the daily price of the D–Mark and the dollar. And as he thanked me, I felt ashamed.

21 · POOL

South-east from Grosseto the hills all seem to have been cast in the same pudding-bowl before having been tipped out, one against the other, on the undulating surface of the raised sea floor. The fields are fringed with hedges containing oaks that have been allowed to grow to unusual size. After the cold withdraws, the wheat turns emerald and for a short while the combed lines of drill-sowing stand out against the earth. The colours in spring mingle fresh green against the russet of the oaks' still unshed leaves.

Thirty miles from the sea, in the floor of a small valley, a sulphur spring froths from a rock of its own making. The precipitated lime of millennia shines out from the surrounding greenery like dripped candlewax. The water from this spring tastes of metal; of heat; of summer; of blood. A place to visit in winter when the body begins to creak as if held together internally by over-taut wires. A day or two under the pulsing water relaxes. It tans the body with a sulphurous patination indistinguishable from skin burned brown by the summer sun.

Up the valley from the limestone mountain gushing with water, a strange hotel surrounds a tamed volcanic pool. Its atmosphere is as neutral as limbo. Slabs of travertine from the tile factories face its concrete core. Mexican grasses line the lawn. It could be anywhere. There, Maro spends a week or so when

276

the winter verges on spring, but before the plants are moving. She paints the surrounding hills in egg tempera, from within a circle of quiet womanhood, childless, manless, immune to time.

On my way up to spend one day in this retreat, I saw a rainbow above a curved field, one colourful and precise semicircle above another of smudgy red and green. Here and there an almond had put out a speck or two of white among its bare branches.

I lay by the pool after the long drive, waiting for a while before immersing myself in its mysterious waters. The steam had the smell of an extinct animal. The taste on my lips was powdery, peppery, from the fetid air. The swimmers on the far side had their heads in the sky and their feet in cloud. Their knees, their chests, their heads were devoured by steam as they slowly stepped into the water.

Those about me seemed to dress and undress in slow motion. Their clothes sat on the ground like couched animals, guarding the identities of their owners. There was no body-teasing, as on the beach. The pretty and the ugly seemed alike, as if fleshliness were discarded with their clothes.

I entered the pool, and the water was warm and yielding.

Prehuman fantasies took over, of reptiles and volcanoes, of time in units of a million years. An old lady with her hair pinned up behind swam carefully, like a tortoise. Her face assumed an inquiring blankness as I swam towards her, as if all expression had been scraped off. We looked at each other fully, surprised, unsmiling. It seemed that I had never looked at another person with such intimacy. No lies, no pretensions, could survive immersion in this sacred pool.

I lay on the surface and breathed out. To my surprise the water did not sustain me. Motionless, I sank. Prickly bubbles traced thin lines about me, seeking the upper air, and I took part in a rushing process of oxidization. The thunder in my ears was mine, was his. I touched the bottom and to my horror it was made of slime. I pushed upwards, panicking, and my foot sank into the stuff. I surfaced at an angle, heart hyperactive.

In front of me was someone whose plastic hood was pulled down over her eyes. A nose and a mouth behind transparent silver, and her soul somewhere within flashing remote signals of recognition. A second later and I recognized Carla, a friend of Maro's, who asked me smiling what I thought of the '*brodaglia primordiale*' – the primordial broth. She is my mother, I said incoherently. We swam to the side. Carla told me my joke was instinctively accurate. In this kind of liquid, lightning started the chain of amino acids with which all living things began. She was a chemist, and should know.

I was unable to make sense of the polite words I was saying and Carla left me in a blue deck-chair, telling me not to overdo it.

Weariness came out of the pool and slipped through my feet, which seemed so infinitely remote, so dead. Everything seemed to await an event, an arrival, a decision. The rows of fake baroque chairs in the dining-room, just visible through plate glass. In the room of green baize card-tables I could see the silhouette of grotesque aspidistras and elephant-ears, thriving in the sulphurous air. The table of stacked newspapers. The motionless row of pines in the garden. The gymnast who coiled a rope; the waiter bringing out a single glass upon a tray.

Lines of words, lines of charcoal on paper, appeared and evaporated in the steam. I felt a sense of grief as my brittle implements of self-defence abandoned me.

I woke in the cold. The umbrellas were furled upon the lawn, and as I looked the pines were suddenly lit from beneath, like fireworks. Carla and Maro were calling from the other side of the pool. The visors of their plastic caps were down, and they were beckoning in unison.

★

Pool

Returning from Pitigliano the next day I drove through gullies which the archaeologists say are Etruscan, the marks of their crude picks still visible in the tufa on each side. There seemed to be more curves driving back, more houses with cars just beginning to light up in the gathering dusk. The landscape had the peculiar feel of having been made on a slightly smaller scale than that which modern men are used to.

In a small village a row of freshly pollarded lime trees waited to put forth wild growth from every wound. I stopped briefly at the so-called Tomb of Hildebrand – one more ornate than the rest, with carved columns and differentiated terraces like a house with split levels. As I stood sniffing the spring smells of the earth, and the rotting stone and the urine of many tourists, I suddenly realized I had been there before. I heard Maro's voice in my head saying 'the perfect bed-sitter for a very small, very unambitious writer'. Tight smile, this second time round. Nowadays writers too are my colleagues.

Driving on, the red houses of the roadworkers, marked ANAS in black letters on a white band, struck me as being more Etruscan than the remaining tombs. Their position at corners and their vivacity seemed right, and above all their temporary feel, for the Etruscans were not particular about building to last for ever. I thought for a while of the transience of certain cultures, and how admirable not to want to leave behind the ten-part fugue, the pyramids.

Last swim in the dark, before an early night and departure the next morning. The hotel seemed one of those places that will always be there, has always been, for it is not of this world. Maro and Carla came down in their robes as I entered with all the whirl of the outside world, clutching my notes on Pitigliano. I felt reproved.

At the pool the exhalations from the surface rose in great whirling sheets twelve or fifteen feet into the air as the night grew colder. I returned once more into the black primeval blood, the reward that Minos holds for those who die in violence. From the edge a man with folded arms observed us.

Our three heads met towards the middle, and again I observed a look of extraordinary surprise upon their faces. An owl hooted up on the hillside. Its Latin name came back to me: *strix*, *strigis* — and that's the noise it made, *strix-strix-strix*, jabbering across the valley.

The last to leave the pool, we swam slowly towards the far end, to where an awning from the hotel dipped down towards the surface of the water, like the mouth of a vast anaemic fish.

Pitigliano is built upon a promontory between two rivers that have cut deep fissures into the soft stone on either side. The town is built on foundations laid by the Etruscans, for whom twin rivers had a sacred significance. Their tombs, for the most part simple chambers, are cut in the sides of the gullies, and new ones are frequently discovered by the local archaeologists.

During the late middle ages Pitigliano became a refuge for Jewish families fleeing north from the Papal States, this being the southernmost fringe of Tuscany. They were given various privileges by the local barons, which were endorsed by the Medici, and finally by the grand-dukes of the house of Lorraine. Their synagogue, founded in 1598, is one of the oldest surviving synagogues in Italy.

I was there to check out a brutal story.

On our previous visit, a family outing, five years earlier, we had arrived late and wasted the morning and afternoon examining the old Etruscan road down to the valley floor, and as many of the tombs as we could find. We ended up back in Pitigliano again, wandering around desperately looking for a place to eat. It was only with difficulty that I persuaded the keeper of a trattoria to give us a quick plate of pasta and a salad.

It happened that I asked the owner of this little restaurant how it was that so many of the crumbling houses seemed to be for sale, with signs in German, giving telephone numbers in Stuttgart and Berlin. I could imagine the owners, alternative and actorish, a bit like us.

'Ah, *Signore*,' she said, 'there were such a lot of houses for sale, after the Jews had been taken away.'

Shocked silence.

'Such a tragic thing,' she said. 'A misfortune, a disgrace for us all. Pitigliano was full of Jews. Full! And in the war they took them all away.'

If anything she looked complacent, fanning herself with a menu and longing to give details.

'I have nothing against the Germans,' she said, 'all very good and generous people, especially the young. A terrible thing — but maybe it was not their fault.'

I suddenly disliked this bearer of bad news. Upset, I rose and paid and left, which was embarrassing, as the woman had reopened her kitchen as a special favour.

Superficially I checked out the story at the local bar while waiting for my womenfolk to catch up with me. It was true that many of the empty houses had been bought by Germans — those brothers in the federation of Europe with whom I had identified an hour before. 'But, *Signore*, they are now obliged to sell, as the core of rock on which Pitigliano is built is crumbling. In five or ten years, unless we get help, the outer walls will fall to the bottom of the valley, and most of the outer ring is owned by these *stranieri*.'

'Why,' I said, sipping coffee, 'how very unfortunate for them!'

Revenge through crumbling masonry. Hmm. We left an hour or so later, but the story stayed in the back of my mind like an itch. Everything about it seemed too pat, and most of all my own volatile reactions. From time to time I would inquire whether or not there was any truth in the story. The answers were circumstantial but grim. This had been one of the few places in Italy where the Germans had been successful in destroying a whole community. God knows how many had perished.

And so, on this fresh day of early spring, I was back in Pitigliano to talk to a man whom I took to be one of the few survivors, Signor Umberto Calò, owner of a small haberdashery in the main square, opposite a shop for domestic appliances.

I arrived early on purpose so as to examine the state of the synagogue, which I had heard had been totally abandoned by an apathetic town council.

It was hard to recognize the little town, it was so much more cheerful since my last visit. Washing no longer hung from one side of the narrow streets to the other. Well-dressed children out of school squabbled for tuck at the main bar, the site of my original researches. When they had left I offered an old man coffee, and listened to his reminiscences of working in Germany with the American army. From his pocket he took a huge wallet of photographs, and I admired his younger northern self standing by a tank in the snow, and his expired ID card with the bald eagle printed on it in blue.

I longed to ask questions, but in the end I merely complimented him on how much neater and more cheerful the town looked than when I was last there. And as I left, I asked directions to the synagogue. Number 13 Vicolo Manin.

The houses there were no different from the rest of the town, though perhaps quieter. The street number of the synagogue had been cemented into its baroque portals, perhaps recently. Cast-iron gates screened off the little blind alley from the road above, and cats with their eyes tight shut enjoyed the early afternoon sunshine.

The building was on the edge of the town, but I was glad to see fresh pontoons and planks about it, indicating that it was being restored. To the left a minuscule *piazzetta* ended in a wall set on the very rim of the steep cliff on which the town stood.

Jackdaws turned and squabbled in the air. On the other side, across the dip, small kitchen gardens carved by hand went up the steep slope.

Inside the building I found quantities of pigeon feathers in a clean and freshly plastered room. I deduced that the building had been half restored, with now a pause for thought. The proportions were square and handsome, with a good light. There were four plaques painted on the wall, the most legible one commemorating the presence of His Royal Highness Pietro Leopoldo, *nel 13 di Marzo 5533*, and a quotation from Isaiah xxxiii in Latin and Hebrew.

For an hour or so I walked about, enjoying the good impression that Pitigliano this time made on me. There seemed to be a lot of building going on; perhaps the Common Market had given some donations. There were no signs in German that I could see.

Signor Calò was expecting me; I had had no need to wait until three-thirty precisely. The minute I walked in he said that he had prepared a document for me, and with muscular fingers tapped seven sheets into a neat rectangle. The history of the Jewish community in Pitigliano, as far as he had been able to establish it.

I sat there for twenty minutes, while customers came and went, buying small items for mending clothes. At one point a young couple came in, the girl engaged in a petit-point embroidery depicting two eighteenth-century lovers under a tree, with a Greek temple in the background. She needed some black and yellow. As she chose the colours, her massive boyfriend suppressed a yawn.

I took out pen and paper and extracted the bare facts which interested me.

The most prosperous time for the Jewish population, according to Signor Calò, was in the mid seventeenth century, when they numbered five hundred out of a total population of three thousand. By the time of the unification of Italy in the last century, this had halved. Another dip took place after the First World War, and by 1938, when Mussolini's racial laws were implemented, the community had shrunk to about fifty persons. The reasons for this decline lay in the gradual easing of difficulties for Jews in the larger cities after the unification of Italy, and in the economic stagnation of Pitigliano itself. Parents would send their children to Acquapendente or Grosseto or Latera for schooling, and later they would stay there to work.

Between customers, we talked. He was not from Pitigliano himself, he said. He lived here by accident, as he was courting a local girl there, and when Italy fell out of the war he received a telegram from his parents in Florence saying he should not come back.

We talked for a while about the synagogue, its roof, its need for repairs, what the *Comune* said and what the Belle Arti said. It took time to work round to discussing the persecution of the Jewish population of Pitigliano during the war.

Signore Calò was not an embittered man, it seemed to me, and the facts that emerged were low key. There was ample warning before 1938, and even afterwards. Some of those fifty who still lived in the town in 1938, perhaps as many as half, had escaped by 1943. When things became very bad some of those who remained had been hidden by the local peasants and farmers. Some even managed to hide in the town itself, in the Etruscan tombs with which the rock of Pitigliano is honeycombed. Even those who were caught had a certain amount of luck. They were kept for a long time in a camp at Grosseto, and sent to Germany slowly, in alphabetical order. Which was a disaster for the Caro family, but the Servi family survived. At least, that branch . . .

'If you are talking of extermination,' he said, 'it seems to me you are missing the point. Many of those who were persecuted were eventually also taken and killed. That was certainly a terrible thing to happen. But don't forget that many Pitiglianesi themselves suffered during the war. Many were killed in an allied bombardment when the front passed through. In a physical sense, that was the greater tragedy. No, the real disaster was not physical. The real disaster was the destruction of the relationship between the Pitiglianesi and the Jewish community in those five years after the racial laws were passed.

'I come from Florence, and there it was possible to bypass most of the rules. You could sit in a bar, go to the cinema, and it was unlikely that anyone would report you. Here it was different. Pitigliano had a Fascist *Podestà* who made sure that the racial laws were severely executed. It was impossible to ignore them. And, after a while, there was a change in the Pitiglianesi themselves.'

An old lady came in, seeking to replace one lost button. The shop was small and full of chests and boxes and drawers, and tins held together by rubber bands.

After she had gone I said, 'I suppose that the remoteness which made Pitigliano a secure place in the fifteenth century made it more vulnerable in our own. If it only took one man . . . I suppose he was trying to ingratiate himself down in Rome by showing his enthusiasm.'

Signor Calò seemed indifferent to this speculation.

'You see,' he said, 'in a sense the qualities the Jews in Pitigliano acquired, which made them so different, would probably have been lost in any case. There are not many documents to go on, unfortunately. However, I have formed an impression of what their life must have been like. I think that during the day there was nothing to chose between the Jewish citizens and any of the other Pitiglianesi. It was afterwards, when they shut up shop, that their other life began. They would meet in the school – I mean the scripture school – and sit around for hours talking about the Torah, arguing one way and another. That was their real pleasure in life. With letters to other communities, arguing obscure points . . .

'Once, when I was in Jerusalem, an old rabbi asked me where I came from. And when I told him, he beckoned me in, and showed me a whole correspondence he had had with the rabbi of Pitigliano. He told me what a vigorous, argumentative congregation they were. Now that,' said Signor Calò, 'was a quality which would probably have disappeared in any case. Even without the war and the persecutions. The population diminished, became distracted. Which of them would have had time these days, in the big cities to which they went, for all that other life? So maybe it was inevitable . . .'

To overcome a sadness which seemed to be accumulating in him I said what a pity it was that some patriot had not taken a pot-shot at the *gerarca* who had behaved so monstrously. Slowly, he smiled. 'Well,' he said, 'it's such a long story.'

I insisted he tell it.

'As I mentioned, after 8 September [i.e. when Italy abandoned the German alliance and surrendered], I was here in Pitigliano, and my father wired me some money and told me not to come back to Florence. What could I do? I asked about in the piazza, and of course the local gossip had it that a band of ten thousand partisans were in the woods above Manciano, faithful, loyal, well-armed, etcetera. So I took the bus, went to Manciano and asked to join them.

'I was very young at the time, but even then it seemed to me that it was difficult for them to organize anything at all. They spent all their time in arguing. Soon we were tipped off that the Fascists were coming with a lot of German troops, so we were told to move away. "Why can't we fight them?" I said. "We are ten thousand, and have arms from the allies." Do you know how many we were? Twenty-eight! And how many guns? Seven, each taking different ammunition.

'Two of our band were Russians – and that's another story. They had come back with one of the few Italian divisions which had returned from the Russian front. These soldiers happened to be in Manciano when the armistice took place, so some of them took to the woods, and with them, these two Russians. Terrible men! They were always drunk. We had to go everywhere with those Russians, as they were much too dangerous to leave by themselves.

'Every now and again we would try to destroy the bridge over the valley below Pitigliano, which would have been a fine military move, and would not have killed anyone. So we took dynamite from the mines, and tried to blow it up. But none of us knew how to work the stuff, and each time something went wrong. In the end we ran out of explosive and it had to be bombed by the allies. It was on that raid that some idiot of a Fascist started shooting at the planes with a sub-machine-gun, so one of them turned round, came back, and bombed Pitigliano for good measure, and a lot of Pitiglianesi were killed . . .'

Signor Calò sighed.

'Eventually we decided we would try to shoot this head of the Fascist party in Pitigliano. A symbolic attack.'

'Did you know,' I interrupted, 'that he was the one behind the persecutions?'

'I did not think of it at the time. I don't think that that would have made any difference, at any rate not to me. Good people and bad people exist everywhere, and it is not necessary to go around shooting the bad ones. Perhaps we are all both good and bad. But anyway, we decided to do this thing, and so one evening, when we knew there was a big meeting on, we broke into Pitigliano – there was a curfew, and the town was closed – and attacked the Casa del Fascio. Only there was nobody there!

The meeting had been cancelled! At which point it would have been a good idea to slip away, no? So what happened? One of the Russians took his machine-gun and shot the portrait of Mussolini which was there, hanging on the wall. At which from the other end of the village came a Fascist calling out "To arms! To arms!", so we shot him too. You know,' he said apologetically, 'there were seven of us and it was hard to miss.

'A little later this Russian tried to rape the daughter of one of the peasants who were protecting us, so he was put up against a wall, and that was that.'

Feeling more good-humoured, Signor Calò turned towards another customer. Then he invited me out to the local bar. What was the point of having a shop as modest as his, he asked me as he locked up, if one couldn't nip off to the corner bar every now and again? The lost buttons could always wait.

'To think that after the war they gave us each a citation,' he said, 'for our glorious heroism.'

Signor Calò was smiling. I was glad that the sombre moment had passed. He bought me a drink, offered an ice-cream, insisted on paying. It was his town, he said; I was his guest.

'There is not so much one can say about Fascism,' he told me in a conciliating manner, as if I were the one to have bad dreams. 'It was just one group of poor people running round with sticks to beat up other groups of poor people. It's a long time ago now. And after such an age is over, who wants to ask any questions?'

Thus, very lightly, he touched one of my deepest convictions, that in extreme situations, only chance divides the role of the torturer from that of his victim. But of this, to him of all people, I could not speak. He seemed a man of great evenness of soul, and I did not wish to disturb him.

The bar filled slowly as the evening gathered round, the young well-dressed and full of intrigue. And so we talked about life in the woods. And from the woods, we moved to bandits, of which the Maremma held many, one of the last having been shot in 1926 or thereabouts.

'They were supposed to rob from the rich and give to the poor,' said Signor Calò gently, 'but as far as I can make out, they just robbed.'

23 · ETRUSCANS

The Etruscans believed that the world was an insubstantial reflection of some drama in the sky above. Fretfully they would look upward, waiting for secret signs to be revealed, in the flight of birds or the movement of wind in the trees; or merely sensitive to the pearly belly of cloud, at that moment, early in the year, when so much seems to be active up there, compared with the large areas of forest underneath, poised between the black of winter and the first feeble greenery of spring. Each year as the winter loses its grip I become conscious of their presence. The changing quality of light acquires some emotional charge, before being transmitted as another kind of energy into the earth below.

I am obsessed by a trace memory like a recurring nightmare concerning the demise of the Etruscans.

The Emperor Augustus, bringer of peace, stands with his officers outside the city of Perugia watching the town burn. Perugia was the last big Etruscan city to oppose the authority of Rome, and is now in the process of being sacked. Night falls; time passes in silence. The faces of the soldiers are occasionally lit by distant flames. These are men used to extreme military measures and are apparently unmoved by the slaughter. Then one by one the officers sink to their knees, pleading for mercy for the town. They are, among the members of his staff, those of Etruscan origin.

I am unable to trace the origin of this apparent eyewitness account of the sack of Perugia in 40 BC. It must come from childhood histories of Rome. Like so many fragments to do with the Etruscans, it is not so much evidence, as an image. I do not need to be told that it is apocryphal.

That many civil servants of the early Empire considered themselves Etruscans is, however, true. Maecenas, the famous patron of the arts, was one of them. Virgil was proud of his Etruscan background, while celebrating in Latin the creation of Rome. Their grandfathers had been coopted into the Roman orbit in 89 BC, when Roman citizenship was offered to most of the Italic tribes of the peninsula. Those towns or tribes which refused the offer and made resistance were harried during the civil war of Marius and Sulla by every army that happened to pass them by. From the Roman point of view the siege of Perugia was a domestic disturbance rather than a foreign war. The loyalty of those officers on their knees in front of Augustus was not in question.

The elimination of the Etruscans was one of the more successful genocides of modern times. It worked, not because it concentrated upon the physical elimination of a group of people defined as an Etruscan race, for the Pax Romana was not interested in genes. It was the cultural identity of the Etruscans which was destroyed. After the sack of Perugia Augustus made it illegal to speak the language. By the reign of Claudius a mere fifty or sixty years later, the emperor himself was one of the few still able to speak Etruscan. His many books on the subject, written as an antiquarian and a critic, did not survive the middle ages, for who could be interested in a language which was no longer spoken, even by scholars?

Because we are dealing with a case of genocide, the historical questions the Etruscans raise attract all kinds of obsessions more relevant to our own century than to theirs. Where did this race come from? Did they arrive all at once as an invasion, from Lydia, as some of the ancient texts suggest? Or were they indigenous, descending from the so-called Villanovan culture? Was their society strongly hierarchical, based on slavery? Was their decline self-sought? Was the Etruscan race decadent? Were they a race at all?

In whatever language we phrase these problems, ghostly echoes from our own age haunt them. And the questions settle inside each other like Chinese boxes. If there was no invasion, then the Etruscans must have been indigenous; and if they were indigenous, then their language may have been one of the oldest in Europe. The language of the Cyclops in the *Odyssey*. The language of Cro-Magnon man.

If there is one thing which seems to me undoubtedly true about the Etruscans, it is that we do not have enough evidence to generalize about their culture.

We have the 'Mummy of Zagreb' — an Etruscan text written on linen which was subsequently used as binding-tapes for an Egyptian mummy brought back to that city by a tourist. We have the 'Liver of Piacenza', a piece of bronze found by accident, shaped like a sculpture by Henry Moore and representing a pig's liver, with hints for sorcerers inscribed on its face. And we have the 'Tile of Pyrgi', inscribed with a short text in both Etruscan and Phoenician, the one unfortunately not quite a translation of the other.

All these have considerable romantic appeal, but they hardly give a full picture of the cultural achievements of the Etruscans. If just one book or one major work of art were to turn up, our entire view of the Etruscans would be revised. To make any evaluation of their literary worth today, for instance, is like trying to re-create the text of *Bleak House* using a junkshop of Victoriana and an excavated segment of Highgate cemetery.

Funerary inscriptions, pots, small sculptures, some fine terracottas which are now in the Villa Giulia in Rome – the evidence is so thin, yet the works which we see in museums are immensely attractive. Even scholars who dislike the Etruscans are forced to respond to the strange energy that their objects exude. We learn just enough to *think* we dare say something. More than almost any other hermetic people, the Etruscans encourage reverie which spills over into history. They obscurely reflect our own faces, against a background of the bright sky above.

Six miles south of our house in the direction of Siena lies a seventeenth-century villa, the decorations of which have remained untouched for two hundred years. The shutters of the *piano nobile* are seldom opened, to preserve for a few years longer the damask walls bleached pale by the sun. Short horsehair beds by the wall are still protected by rococo *baldacchini* – ornate frames of wood covered with hanging silk. Light has devoured the pliability of the material, which hangs in shreds like paper streamers. Everything is of such fragile beauty that almost immediately you beg for the shutters to be closed again, to save this sleeping world for a few years longer.

I first went there twenty years ago to examine the wallpaper of an upper bedroom, hand-printed in Paris in 1780 in a factory established by Marie-Antoinette. I had no idea that the owner of the house, Ranuccio Bianchi Bandinelli, was also one of the finest Etruscan scholars of his generation.

'Perhaps these things should be restored,' I said, gently fingering a curtain.

'For the love of heaven,' he replied, 'if we had ever had them restored, they would have died years ago. I count it a blessing that none of my ancestors were rich enough to afford improvements.'

He took us round, ignoring what must have seemed the callousness of unknown tourists tramping through. *Invadente* would be the appropriate Italian adjective; 'invasive', on a small scale. Idly I took down from a shelf a book on Etruscan mirrors published just after the First World War and amply illustrated with steel engravings. I became excited to see how close they were to the etchings Picasso made in the 1930s for Vollard, illustrating the *Metamorphoses* of Ovid.

From there, we went on to discuss the Etruscans, and incautiously I expressed my enthusiasm for their sculpture.

'Name one work,' he said fiercely.

Well, I thought, what a tiresome old die-hard. So I mentioned the so-called Sarcophagus of the Newly-Weds, in the Villa Giulia in Rome.

'We shall see!'

And took me to a bookshelf, chose a volume, leafed rapidly through.

A slight, feathery doubt hatched and fluttered behind my eyes. Raising my face to the library wall, where one gap marked a row of twenty-two identically bound books, I saw on the back of each B. Bandinelli, and quailed.

'What a beautiful book,' I said, to change the subject.

He became confidential, happy, like a boy at school with a stamp collection.

'It *is* a beautiful book,' he murmured, 'and it took me forty years to write.'

It was Bandinelli who suggested that with the Etruscans one could practise a kind of 'aesthetic' archaeology. Most historians hitherto had argued that they placed their towns on hilltops that were easily defended - unlike the Romans, who chose sites in the plains which were strategic economically rather than militarily. Bandinelli pointed out that Etruscan sites frequently consisted of twin hills separated by a stream, one hill for the living and the other for the dead, and that therefore one could search for two beautiful adjacent hills, and then start looking around for shards.

For about six months I became very excited about this theory, and scoured the countryside for new Etruscan sites. I ended up with about four. One day I took Vittoria around to see them all.

At the last of my sites, on the back road to the kiln of Urbano Fontana, between Poggio San Polo and Castellina, we stood quietly on a small hill looking at the sky, before scrabbling around on hands and knees for bits of terracotta in the *albarese* shale dumped there by peasants in centuries of clearing the fields.

We found very little. But undaunted, Vittoria looked around at the horizon. She pointed out that north-west of where we stood we could see the Etruscan tombs of Castellina, and almost due east, the large hill above Radda which is surely an Etruscan site – pieces of tile and crockery surround the ragged troughs left by moto-cross bikes. The Etruscans, she said, enjoyed keeping within sight of each other.

'I think that very probably you are right about all these sites,' she said. 'You are certainly right about Radda, as there are shards of terracotta there to prove it. But unfortunately for you, all the literary sources indicate that this was a very poor part of Etruria, and the poor,' she said, 'are boring.' She waited a second or two until I had registered shock, then smiled, very bright-eyed. 'From the archaeological point of view, I mean.'

Bandinelli did much pioneering work on the Etruscans, identified many new sites, set up criteria by which they should be excavated, established a central library for collating material, and did some fine excavation on two or three sites himself. But he was foremost a philhellene, and he would always come to the conclusion, after a year or two of immersion in Etruscan culture, that whatever was good in it was taken from Greece. In his last book he went to the extreme of suggesting that any Etruscan work of superior quality must *per forza* have been made by a Greek craftsman who happened to live in Etruria![59]

Bandinelli expressed a prejudice which was essentially humanitarian. He felt that only in Greece had there been a modern sense of freedom and creativity based upon a unique feeling for the role of the individual, and that historically this takes Greek art and culture into a superior sphere. Of course he was usually right in maintaining that there was no individual piece of Etruscan sculpture or painting for which there is not a finer and earlier example to be found in Greece. The problem which worried me was that this constant confrontation with Greece, to the detriment of the Etruscans, missed some point about their own particular qualities. Why did the comparison always intrude?

A peculiar incident punctuated the life of Bandinelli. When Adolf Hitler visited Benito Mussolini in Rome and Florence in 1938, for an amicable cultural tour, Bianchi Bandinelli was chosen to accompany them as translator and academic guide. Needless to say the job was as remote as possible from Bandinelli's interests. However, these requests are sometimes very difficult to refuse.

He managed to keep notes on the meetings, and after the war he published them. Hitler, he said laconically, appreciated art 'as a hairdresser who thinks he likes music, and becomes progressively more excited the higher a tenor sings'.

In the baths of Caracalla, Hitler halted in front of a palaeo-

Christian sarcophagus, and made an improvised speech of mounting hysteria. Christianity, he said, destroyed the Roman Empire through its weakness and decadence. Evil influences such as these should be eradicated. In artistic terms, Christianity was like the Expressionist movement in painting, 'which I have banned in Germany'; or like Bolshevism, 'which will also destroy everything, unless it is itself destroyed'. At this point the speech became an inarticulate hymn of hate against the Bolshevik menace. This close physical contact with an insane argument I believe coloured the rest of Bandinelli's life.[60]

I never met Bandinelli again, and he died before I could take up with him this question of the Etruscans' originality. But it happened that one of his most distinguished old pupils was Vittoria's formidable aunt, the Director of Monuments, who lived in the over-restored villa at Bagno a Ripoli. Curious about both the villa and the aunt, I finally arranged to see her.

I found that the inside was quite as austere as its brightly plastered exterior walls – done with marble dust, she told me, with the colour mixed into the lime, like fresco. The great lady invited me in very cordially, with an air of being professionally good about interruptions.

On the wall of the front hall hung a magnificent gilded picture frame, containing nothing. It was a house of ideas, not loot.

At length I found myself in front of a large pile of grey files of ministerial documents tied with their attractive linen ribbons and set in columns upon a truly Olympian desk.

I spoke for about five minutes. I said that we did not know enough to generalize convincingly about the Etruscans. With such a premise, it followed that any theory about their origins, social structure, achievements, could in certain circumstances merely act as a catalyst for the fantasy of historians. Ranuccio Bianchi Bandinelli, caring passionately about human liberty, thought that in this respect the Etruscans were in some way inferior to the Greeks. Could one connect this analysis with the experiences of his own life? Most particularly, with his reaction against Fascism? Could he have been inspired by Mussolini's praise of the Etruscans for their innate Italian virtues of 'realism', as opposed to Greek 'idealism', into some prejudice against them?

For answer, she covered her face with her hands.

This simple gesture made me doubt, not for the first time, my natural talents as a historian.

She stayed like that for ten or fifteen seconds, calming herself. Then she straightened and said, 'Of course, you can say what you like. I accept the justice of the accusation that historians tend to build views on too little evidence, especially when it comes to the Etruscans. It is also true that Bandinelli preferred the Greeks to the Etruscans and that his later work sounds almost bitter in this respect, I don't quite understand why. As to being influenced by contemporary politics, it is an interesting idea, and I am sure that if you work at it you will be able to find some quotations or evidence to substantiate it. But,' she said with a smile, 'please don't.'

The land occupied by the Etruscans was recognized by the Romans to include the area circumscribed by the Arno and the Tiber rivers, and therefore embraced much of northern Lazio together with modern Tuscany. The sites covered by D. H. Lawrence in *Etruscan Places* were for the most part in Lazio, and thus outside my area, but I need to discuss his book all the same, because what he says about the Etruscans is important.

Lawrence possessed a genius for going somewhere for two days, and having enough to write a book about it by the morning of the third. His visit to Etruscan sites lasted from

Wednesday, 6 April 1927, until the following Monday. From what he saw he produced a series of travel articles which were assembled into a book by others after his death. Had he lived, he would probably have rewritten it – but still, *Etruscan Places* works perfectly well as it stands.

Most certainly Lawrence used the Etruscans as his archetype of a perfect society, where creativity is a kind of natural overflow of the overwhelming forces of life:

> The clue to the Etruscan life was the Lucumo, the religious prince. Beyond him were the priests and warriors. Then came the people and the slaves. People and warriors and slaves did not think about religion. There would soon have been no religion left. They felt the symbols and danced the sacred dances. For they were always kept *in touch*, physically, with the mysteries. The 'touch' went from the Lucumo down to the merest slave. The bloodstream was unbroken. But 'knowing' belonged to the high-born, the pure-bred.
>
> So, in the tombs we find only the simple, uninitiated vision of the people. There is none of the priest-work of Egypt. The symbols are to the artist just wonder-forms, pregnant with emotion and good for decoration. It is so all the way through Etruscan art. The artists evidently were of the people, artisans. [61]

Lawrence thus subscribes to the idea that Etruscan society was highly stratified, held in check by a religion firmly in the hands of a Lucumon or Priest-King. Where he adds peculiar touches of his own is in the concept of transmitting knowledge by 'bloodstream', by 'touch'. Then there is the suggestion that the civilization is waning: 'there would soon be no religion left'. And then unexpectedly, in view of the impression he gives of a strict hierarchy, he suggests that the tombs were painted by a free, 'thoughtless' artisan (rather than artist) class, not much supervised by the priests.

Concerning the continuing preoccupation, shared by Bianchi Bandinelli and others, as to whether or not the Etruscans owed everything to the Greeks, Lawrence is magnificently brusque: 'It is useless to look in Etruscan things for "uplift". If you want uplift, go to the Greek and the Gothic. If you want mass, go to the Roman. But if you love the odd spontaneous forms that are never to be standardized, go to the Etruscans.'[62]

In his perception of these qualities he variously describes as 'carelessness', 'thoughtlessness', Lawrence is remarkably close to the contemporary Italian artists who in the late twenties looked towards Etruscan art for inspiration: Campigli, perhaps Carrà among the painters; Arturo Martini and Marino Marini among the sculptors.

Arturo Martini said that the attraction of the Etruscans was that they made their sculpture 'like bread'. This beautiful image seems to me Lawrentian in feeling, and indeed the strikingly straightforward pages which Martini wrote about sculpture are closer to Lawrence than to any Italian writer of his time.

The Etruscans in all their ambiguity appealed to Mussolini and the Fascist leadership, who saw in them an opportunity to promote an extreme version of Italian nationalism. The Greeks seemed to imply that there is another, ideal, world lying behind that of mere appearances, and their philosophy and mathematics as well as their art hint at this other perfect identity. But the Etruscans remained down to earth, and in this sense a worthy ancestor to the 'realism' of the Florentine Renaissance: or at least so this thesis runs.

Either the artists took the argument seriously, or else they profited by the chance to escape from the pressure of the Fascist regime by absorbing one of the more imaginative messages from the Minculpop. Or perhaps the quirky, slightly violent straightforwardness to which Lawrence was also sensitive was perceived by others at the time. At any rate, there was a definite 'Etruscan period' in Italian art between the wars.

All this turned sour after 1938, when the Fascist racial laws began to be seriously implemented. The Etruscans suddenly became, as it were, contaminated by their inclusion in certain racial arguments. Some fine artists became extraordinarily bitter, just before the war. 'Today sculptors cannot do anything more than re-work some variation on a theme the ancients have already checkmated,' was how Martini felt about sculpture at the end of his life. In a sad and beautiful book he argued that whereas painting had developed its own 'vernacular', sculpture was like Latin and Greek, '*una lingua morta*', a dead language. Sculpture was 'as sad as a seed laid on marble, remote from any chance of coming to life.'[63]

Lawrence's view of the Etruscans has the virtue of being intensely visual:

> On a fine evening like this, the men would come in naked, darkly ruddy-coloured from the sun and wind, with strong, insouciant bodies; and the women would drift in, wearing the loose, becoming smock of white or blue linen; and somebody, surely, would be playing on the pipes; and somebody, surely, would be singing, because the Etruscans had a passion for music, and an inner carelessness the modern Italians have lost. The peasants would enter the clear, clean, sacred space inside the gates, and salute the gay-coloured little temple as they passed along the street that rose uphill towards the arx, between rows of low houses with gay-coloured fronts painted or hung with

bright terracottas. One can almost hear them still, calling, shouting, piping, singing, driving in the mixed flocks of sheep and goats, that go so silently, and leading the slow, white, ghostlike oxen with the yokes still on their necks.

And surely, in those days, young nobles would come splashing in on horseback, riding with naked limbs on an almost naked horse, carrying probably a spear, and cantering ostentatiously through the throng of red-brown, full-limbed, smooth-skinned peasants. A Lucumo, even, sitting very noble in his chariot driven by an erect charioteer, might be driving in at sundown, halting before the temple to perform the brief ritual of entry into the city. And the crowding populace would wait; for the Lucumo of the old days, glowing ruddy in flesh, his beard stiffly trimmed in the Oriental style, the torque of gold round his neck, and the mantle or wrap bordered with scarlet falling in full folds, leaving the breast bare, he was divine, sitting on the chair in his chariot in the stillness of power. The people drew strength even from looking at him.[64]

I have to confess I find this writing incredibly attractive. When I dream of the Etruscans, which I do quite often, my dreams are Lawrentian. Stiff, highly coloured figures engage in vaguely threatening behaviour, ultimately aimed at me. I wake, sweating.

Analysis risks sounding pedantic. You balk slightly at the use of words such as 'careless' or 'clean' but accept them temporarily. You might hesitate a moment at his stark and simple view of the peasant, the noble, the Lucumon. Oh well, you say. By the time you read through to the end, you are bludgeoned by unsubstantiated metaphor. As a vision, it works. Once you have experienced it, as a vision, it is almost impossible to go back to the beginning and start doubting.

Lawrence in fact continually uses imaginative material as if it were factual. He tells us that the Etruscan peasants were 'red'. They may have appeared red in the tomb paintings, but this is surely an idiom to do with paint, not life. To state as a fact that the Etruscans were red destroys the elementary difference between objective reality and imaginative re-creation of it.

We believe it because in reading Lawrence we are not dealing with history, but autobiography. In this case Lawrence has not distorted a fact, so much as obliterated the distinction between himself and the Etruscan artists who are in a sense his predecessors.

On the penultimate day of his tour of Etruscan places, Easter Sunday, 10 April 1927, Lawrence was in Volterra. His visit coincided with a reception in honour of the new *Podestà* of the town, one Colonel Carraro.

The role of *Podestà* had existed in Tuscany since the twelfth century. It arose from the need to appoint a dictator in those city-states whose internal politics had reached maximum confusion. About the only credential required of a *Podestà*, apart from looking good, was that he should *not* be a citizen of the town he was invited to govern. Desperate measures, in other words. This institution was revived by the Fascist regime as a means of appointing provincial governors from Rome, rather than having them elected locally. The undemocratic hand of the central government.

Because of the presence of Colonel Carraro, Lawrence found it difficult to find a room, get a meal, move around the town, enter the museum, and he grumbled about the decadence of modern Italy in a way which might superficially be taken as anti-Fascist. The natives, instead of welcoming Lawrence with appropriately 'clean' and 'carefree' gestures, were presumably in front of the town gate knuckling their foreheads, as the new official, ruddy of complexion and with his shirt unbuttoned, was staring straight ahead in a pose of appropriate solemnity.

It occurs to me that the Lucumon described by Lawrence in the passage just quoted is *seated* in his chariot. Is it possible that Lawrence is thinking of a Bugatti? Surely it is Colonel Carraro who is 'sitting in his chariot in the stillness of power . . . Then a few words – and the chariot of gilt bronze swirls off'?

When Lawrence wrote up the quick tour in the following weeks, can he have seen no connection between his fantasy describing the return of the honest rustics to the Etruscan village in front of the noble Lucumon and the feast in honour of Colonel Carraro?

In the old days one would call such coincidences the *Zeitgeist* or spirit of the times. It is hard to be more precise. Bandinelli in later life was as far from Fascism as is humanly possible for a man to be. On Lawrence's contacts with Italians, Fascist or not, his biographers are vague. Of the Etruscans, the evidence is so thin that it is anybody's guess how they arranged their society. It's a question of insufficient evidence. None of the characters concerned effectively comes into focus.

24 · MURLO

Gassato means excited, full of fizz. With the excitement that can only come from not having settled the year's income tax, and only two days left for the debt to be paid off and in the post, we grabbed our coats after lunch one nice spring day and drove south through rain and sun to visit Etruscan ruins.

I was teaching Vittoria to sing 'Only You' as the three of us scuttled out to her car. A clutch of international phone calls had convinced Maro and me that in spite of our retired life and innate natural modesty we were still a definite pin on the world map, a small flag still waving.

The landscape in spring acquires a sudden violence. The oaks shed the blackened leaves that have clung all winter and instantly replace them with green freckles. The walnut planted in the back garden with Vittorio Fosi when first we came had attained its unique moment of oestrus and was dropping small bronze umbrellas all over the garden.

Vittoria sang well, really into the swing of it, as she drove beside the bed of the Arbia. The scuffed row of self-seeded acacias and poplars by the river had been cut for the first time in years and were stock-piled near the road in one long arsenal. The vines had an inch or two of tightly rolled green tissue, a branch of fifty leaves all in one small leaf, with a tense air like the frozen photograph of an explosion. The messy flowers of the poplar trees had fallen, their leaves just past the phase when they are small, sharp and bright orange.

We turned left at the quarry of wet marble under a duvet of cloud. The plastic factory where Giovanni lost a piece of finger looked dormant, the bakery was shut. Then a small cliff studded with the giant shells of extinct oysters, the shore of a long-dried sea. After the turn the landscape changes, with fewer stones to be assembled into the retaining walls of the fields, more silt from erosion and from the bed of the vanished sea. Here, large areas of winter wheat were gradually maturing. The dripping heavens gave us the sensation of being underwater. I could identify with extinct Precambrian dolphins.

Past Montaperti and the condominium built by the saintly politician. Maro, dozy in the back seat, wondered how wet the Etruscans got when it rained. On the larger hills the wheat was streaked with lines of darker green by the passing dispenser of chemical fertilizer.

A tangle of mad peas on stilts by the other great condominium, just south of the Superstrada. Broad beans starting to bend under the pods, and fresh squares of new seedlings. Behind them, a symphonic field of mustard surrounding an old brick chapel cut like a rose diamond. We turned left again just before hitting the ring road round Siena, and drove through small hills past the stacked wood of the timber merchant's where I buy supplies for future sculptures.

Lightning flashed to earth on Monte Amiata, southern Tuscany's Mount Fuji.

Rain continually wears down the clay hills of the *crete senesi*, causing deep fissures. Every three or four years the fresh layer of tarmac on the roads becomes punctuated with serrated lines, and whole segments of road sink at the corners. The clay soil is laid over its hard rock base like a thick piece of material, and like material it is unstable. The little brick villages south of

Siena shift gently as on a slow liquid. The houses are patched and repaired over centuries, showing segments of new brick-work already spattered with lichen.

Round the edge of this basin of unstable silt is a harder ring, and on the first sharp ridge of this is Murlo. A gulley behind the town contains a feeble stream coming down from the hills, rock clearly visible among a scrubby vegetation that includes tall gorse bushes and a few ferns. Not far away there was a clear view of Monte Amiata sunlit in a gap in the cloud.

Hawthorn blossomed in the hedgerow, just like England. There were large areas of wild borage, the bread of bees, flowering in the gutters. Rain from a dark patch of cloud was visible far over on the left, streaking more faintly towards the ground, like brushstrokes. Blackbirds flew by the side of the road. The blackbirds have made a real comeback in the last decade.

Just outside Murlo we passed a house like a haunted vicarage, with a vast horse chestnut in full flower. Asking a very deaf local for a direction to the museum, he pointed to a murky little town upon a nearby hill, as remote as a tower in a dirty fresco. We drove up and parked beneath the walls. Then we walked along a path circling under the battlements in a lucky dry moment of this low afternoon of showers, admiring the kitchen gardens.

We found the little museum of Murlo in the old stronghold. In a calm entrance like a dungeon a young girl with bleached hair watched what happened inside the museum on a closed-circuit TV while she sold the visitors tickets and postcards.

We went from room to room, reading the placards, looking where we were told to look.

A placard told how the Etruscans made walls of clay and wattles, or sometimes just of clay. I examined the three drawings carefully to understand their technique. Etruscan houses were built of wooden uprights with mud walls between them, and a roof of terracotta tiles. They rarely used stone or brick with cement in the Roman style. Their ruins are transient, their architecture, as far as we can tell, was unambitious. We know what they built chiefly from the interiors of tombs in Cerveteri, where the visitor can look up at a stone ceiling which mimics the original wooden beams.

The site of Murlo is important for one extraordinary find. Upon the roof of a building which may have been a patrician household, or else perhaps a small shrine, stood a series of upright terracotta figures wearing large, almost Mexican, hats. If they had not been found right there on the site, no scholar would have believed they were Etruscan. Murlo acts as a warning to experts: how can we tell what the Etruscans were really like, when so much was destroyed, and when every new find completely alters all our preconceptions? No scholar, no artful faker, could ever have imagined that such sculpture was theirs.

All three of us knew the seated gods well, having visited a specialized exhibition in Siena two years previously. As we looked at everything else in the museum of Murlo, for the most part in silence, a feeling of frustration gradually accumulated. Drains, and a few heads taken from moulds; the contents of the cases seemed disappointingly thin.

We squabbled briefly about the composition of the terracotta used in the pots. Maro said it was a scruffy local mixture. I was not so sure. I wanted the aggregate to contain exotic mixtures, marble dust from the quarries of Carrara to the north, and black sand from Lake Bolsena in the south, so that when outside again I could sniff the air and imagine the trade routes winding among the hills in opposite directions. They were too poor to go to all that trouble, said Maro. The informative placards tended to bear her out.

We came out vaguely unsatisfied, wanting more. The guidebook seemed to exude the same feeling, as if its authors had gone through all the layers of love, obsession and eventual remorse which come over those who desire too much of the past.

Below the city wall, beyond the straggled caper bushes growing out of cracks, there were two or three superlative kitchen gardens. A lemon tree grew straight out of the ground, and there were lettuces the size of footballs. Maro started talking about a microclimate, and we looked up as if expecting to see its edge somewhere in the gorse-covered hillside opposite.

By and by we came across an old man leaning on a gate, so we asked him these important horticultural questions. Microclimate? He looked puzzled. You usually have to bring in the lemons, he said, but I make a basket against the frost, and sometimes I cover it with gorse, sometimes with plastic. From time to time they die, he said, looking cheerful. The winter of 1985 was a bad one, when all the olives went.

Then he took us into his little garden and showed us every single lettuce, with footnotes about the favourites of his large, dispersed, but happily oft reunited family. Some of the bolting, fuzzy ones – lettuces, not family – looked remarkably ornate; vertical cathedrals of emerald green in a ladle of black earth.

Soon the conversation turned to Etruscans. Surprisingly the old man had a great deal to say.

It was not Professor Bandinelli who recognized the site at Murlo, but Professor Neri, a local teacher who happened to be a friend of Bandinelli. They were cutting down the wood, and all these shards emerged. Professor Neri called Bandinelli, and at first he would not come, so he took some of the shards down to Rome, and the findings were published.

'Mind you,' said the old man, dropping his voice and stepping nearer, 'my father told me that once a golden calf was found, and a hen with golden chickens – not there on the hill, but down in the valley.' But we resisted the impulse to hare off after treasure, and got him to talk about the site of Murlo itself.

'There is another site up there they never finished excavating,' he said. 'When they were digging for a well, up there, near the big pine on the hill, they heard a booming noise under ground, and came across masses of burned terracotta, which we thought was the old Etruscan kiln. An Englishwoman lives there now. Her son goes to Florence to study. She likes my wine. Not as much as the German archaeologist who comes every year. I can take her into the cellar and she drinks straight from the plastic tube I shove in the demijohn. It's so funny! She sent me a globe from Vienna. It has a little house in it, and when you turn it upside down, the globe is filled with snow.'

So we went to visit the English lady who lived on the hill, and found her surrounded by dogs. She knew nothing about the kiln, but was cautiously polite, as long as I found no Etruscan site on her land, thank you very much. The view was magnificent. South, Monte Amiata, and north, the towers of Siena, in what looked like a straight line from where we stood.

She directed us into the woods, to put us on the right path. We took the dogs, silent and well behaved.

From time to time Maro would stoop to the ground after some plant, and I had to tell her not to nick the nice lady's euphorbia. Geraniums, she said, bottom still in air. Vittoria and I came to a halt. The dogs looked from one to another as Maro dug around in the dirt with her fingers.

'*È bassa la terra,*' said Vittoria, looking at Maro's rump and repeating ironically an obscure remark the old man had made when Maro said how fit he looked, from working his garden. Acquiring merit by bending low.

As Maro stooped for plants, I prodded the ground with my toe for shards, but none were interesting.

'I would like to walk, to see something,' said Vittoria. 'I am cold.'

The path through the woods was long and faintly obsessive. Scrub ilex, juniper and spindly oak hemmed us in at a height of three or four metres, obscuring the view. Someone had stapled a cardboard arrow from time to time, drooping now in the damp air. It was like a maze.

After quite a while we heard sheep in the distance. We came across their rearguard, and they turned their mask-like faces to look at the dogs. No sign of a shepherd.

'He is using his sheep,' said Vittoria, 'to warn him if people come near. While he looks for Etruscan gold.'

'Or perhaps he was scared off by Matthew's rabbinical hat.'

The sun was peeping below the cloudy muffler above our heads, which apparently did not reach entirely to the horizon.

We decided to give up the search for the dig, and then Maro came across the site as we were walking back. Part of the wood had been cleared, and was chewed here and there across a large front. A smudgy layer of charcoal two or three feet down indicated traces of the fire which had destroyed level F. Otherwise nothing. After twenty years, and the largest Etruscan building in Tuscany, just this lonely spot and two or three interesting pieces in the museum.

The old man had told us that we would find a few holes filled with water, and he was right. The archaeologists had covered up again after they had finished, for protection. It was a dig camouflaged as not a dig.

'A north London bomb-site,' I said, 'for those old enough to remember them. What a paradise for wild flowers they were!

Daffodils in spring, and a special tree we called the bomb-site tree, which had its leaves on feelers.'

I came across a huge heap of discarded tiles and pot-handles and other rubbish from the excavation. Excited, I examined what I could, hoping to prove my point about the aggregate.

Roof tiles for the most part, not too highly fired, not completely vitrified, but still two thousand years old. To my disappointment the clay was rough local stuff, full of impurities and with holes like small caverns where the clay had been too thin to hold. There were fragments of old powdered brick in it; the aggregate did indeed seem nothing but brick and quartz. There were many quartz lumps interspersing the outcrops of rock we had walked past. But there was an interesting red sheen to one or two of the tiles that looked like a kind of oxide glaze.

'Steal it.'

The voice of temptation in my ears. Vittoria's.

'Oh, I was planning to, don't worry. I must find out about this red glaze.'

'Steal one piece for me too, then I can analyse it,' she said.

'Why can't you steal your own?'

She seemed amused. Indeed, as I frowned down at her, king-of-the-castle upon a heap of ancient tiles, she seemed extraordinarily fresh, almost childish. Perhaps she enjoyed the fact that the site was not hers.

'If I steal from a site, I will never have an academic job, anywhere. If I want just one small piece, I would have to fill out papers, many many papers. Permission from the Sovrintendenza ai Monumenti, then stamped by the university, with a file for my department. The Ministry of the Interior. The signature of the *Signor Ministro l'Onorevole Tizio*. It is not possible. It is a pity, because maybe we could start a programme to analyse the terracotta of all the Etruscan sites. Maybe it would be interesting. Maybe we could find out something about transporting sand from Lake Bolsena, as you believe.'

'But if I steal, and give it to you, would it not be receiving stolen goods?'

'I am sorry?'

I explained about the gentle crime of receiving. I regretted having done so. Her face clouded over; she was thinking of the interdepartmental ramifications.

We walked back together, following Maro, who was not interested in holes or tiles and had gone on ahead. The day was building up to a harmony of deep blue with sidelighting, after which it would get dark quickly.

After about five minutes we discovered we had taken a wrong turning. What seemed to be another grander excavation turned out in fact to be a gravel pit filled with some kind of rusty ferrous shale and pebbles. I stopped there for a while, with the panting dogs and Vittoria fussing about with her foot, momentarily curious. With eyes half closed I could imagine I was actually within a tile. The colour was right, and some of the gravel was light and dark, mixed pepper, just like the terracotta.

I wanted so much to tell Vittoria something, now that we were momentarily alone, but I could not remember what it was. I sat on a rock to recover, and one of the dogs nicked my bit of Etruscan roof. I started to follow but then let him alone. Perhaps he'd take it back to the mouldy old heap.

I was annoyed to find Vittoria laughing at me. So I quickly asked about her lover.

She replied in Italian. For some reason she refuses to talk about emotions in English.

How could I permit myself, she asked. Of what interest would it be to me?

I told her I cared what happened to her and that she could

always be assured (I smiled) that my interest was totally disinterested. She could count on me.

Bah!

By this time I was really curious. I insisted on hearing some sort of an answer. The timing of my question might have been prompted by the dog, I said, and for that I apologized; but seriously . . .

He was a man of great responsibility, Vittoria told me. She spoke cautiously, smoking abruptly and seldom looking me in the eye. She seemed wary of giving a too intimate reply, as if I were some schoolmaster or parent to whom only a little truth should be given, with a deceitful smile. She reminded me that he had these considerable responsibilities at home. His extremely religious mother, and his neurotic sister. 'Mad as a mare' was her expression. The fact that his mother was a widow meant that he was the only man of the family, therefore they were in a sense his dependants. And she and they could not stand each other, she said. So much so that after that first terrible meeting three years ago in Turin, they had never met again.

Vittoria told me I could never imagine how right-wing an old Torinese family might be. Or what sad houses . . .

'A sister? You are unable to marry him because of a sister?'

She looked at me. I was seated on a heap of stones as I did not wish to inflict my height on her while we talked of intimate things. More calmly I told her I found it surprising that a man would sacrifice his future because of an obstinate mother and disagreeable sister.

On the rim of the quarry looking down at us, the dogs waited motionless for us to move. High against the setting sun they looked black and sinister, pointing towards us in unison.

'Perhaps you are right,' she said. 'Perhaps he is too weak to leave his family. But you do not understand everything about

Italy, even after all these years. It is not unusual to have this kind of responsibility to your own family. It is not necessary to think that he is weak, if he takes these obligations more seriously than his own relationships.'

She told me that she could only see him for a certain hour of the day.

I did not understand.

In a way, she said, this was not such a bad thing either, given her own character. For though she, Vittoria, was capable of working night and day for months on end, nobody in their right mind could say that her life was in any way ordered. It did her good to be obliged to be ready, with the flat tidy, for the afternoon of every other day.

I got up and walked to the nearest patch of remaining daylight, at the edge of the gravel-pit. She followed.

I asked what he was good for.

She ignored the crudeness. As far as she could tell, she said calmly, he was very good at playing cards. Bridge, poker. Very nearly professional standards.

I snorted.

She told me that this too was training, of a kind. He had peculiar characteristics. He had a great capacity for noticing things, remarkable peripheral vision, an excellent memory. He read fast, spoke well. When he came to see the site in Sicily, he noticed something that had escaped the team, and he made them rewrite a paper they were preparing because he said there was an unnecessary repetition in the argument.

With most of the world darkening rapidly and the sun setting behind us, the far side of the valley fifteen miles away was picked out in minute detail by the extraordinary last light.

I asked her if she planned to marry and have children.

She told me it was unlikely. She sounded amused. She said that her lover desired to leave no trace of himself behind.

A deep sigh overcame me, so shattering that it seemed to rise from the landscape, rather than from within.

'Many years ago,' I said, 'there was an inland sea here. I think we are probably standing upon some shore of it, all these pebbles and stones having been worn smooth by water at some time. But here in the valley must have been water. For some reason it is an image which occurs to me frequently, and at night when I sink down to sleep, I imagine all the beasts in that water, all sorts of extraordinary Precambrian –'

'*Pliocene*,' she said, pronouncing the word in Italian.

'What?'

She did not reply, but taking my arm led me away.

Finding the road again, I was surprised to encounter, from time to time in the mud, the print of a naked foot. Looking closer I disentangled a dog's footprint and Maro's superimposed.

It hardly rained as we drove home. With the warmth and the wet weather the buds were visibly breaking out into leaves as the young green trees became more ambitious.

25 · MONTECAPRAIO

It was five months before I saw her again. She had been to the Middle East somewhere on a dig, and had now come back to see her family while the sun burned down on her companions still in the desert. She seemed jittery, but it was hard for me to tell what ailed her. She phoned me to say she needed company on a peculiar quest, and so I went.

Southern Tuscany in late summer acquires the texture of velvet bleached over the years by the sun. After the wheat is in, the land is ploughed, and the ploughshare glazes the damp clay as it passes, giving the milky air a flicker of reflected light that carries for miles.

Dozy in a field beneath the battlements of Montecapraio, an almost defunct town surrounded by fat stone walls like flaky bread, Vittoria improvised some monologue about a late Renaissance dictator. The cicadas whined their one-note hurdy-gurdy. She smoked too much. The fields curved in and out like interlocking bones. It was hard to find a soft rock or patch free from spiky stubble in this neglected ditch that had been so often filled with bodies in the late middle ages.

The view extended across the entire Val di Chiana to the ridge of hills above Assisi and Cortona. So why compete with cicadas? I listened to the sound of her voice as one might listen to the mechanical patter of a piano when an incompetent musician is playing. The keys clicking, the dampers thrumming out, the digital transmission of nerves expressing some inner voice that lies behind the music.

I have noticed that Italian girls are often as secretly conventional at thirty as they were openly revolutionary at twenty. I took her fretful body-language to mean that Vittoria was approaching a nest-building phase of her life. After the revolutionary sit-ins in the Bologna riots of 1977 at fourteen, after the alternative feminist commune in Milan – which ended with a corpse rotting in an unopened room – after the macrobiotic all-night café where she never got paid, we were down to this: a spoiled off-stage man past forty who had to be weaned from his mother.

As to her career, she now admitted that the move of sending her thesis to her professor's great rival had been suicidal. She was a *dottoressa* at last, yes indeed, but now she had to make amends, she said, or leave. What these amends might be, she would not say. Kow-tow in the crowded piazza? Ritual sacrifice in print of some much-loved theory? Some horizontal exercises of a certain kind upon the sandy desert floor? In Italy, all were possible.

Vittoria had convinced herself that she was a victim of the Evil Eye. I decided after much thought that I approved of this. She loathed indecision in herself, and I remembered that long ago she had gone through a frighteningly bad moment merely because she had found herself unable to chose between two courses of action. It was much healthier, on the whole, for her to see her difficulties as having been imposed upon her externally by malignant enemies.

Il Mago di Montecapraio – the two m's went well together – was the most famous healer in south Tuscany. His name, or nickname, was '*Il Riccio*', which can mean either 'Curly', or 'Hedgehog'. I had been looking for an excuse to meet him for years – which perhaps explains my tolerance towards Vittoria's descent into fears which I would otherwise laugh at as irrational.

She looked at her bare watchless wrist and announced that he would be back now. So we walked over the dry clods and climbed back into the citadel to see. A bar run by his niece gave word where he might be. Il Riccio had no phone, took no appointments, asked no fees. You caught him like the wind.

The *Mago di Montecapraio* lived in an extremely modest house beside a bakery, in a narrow street behind the town hall. At one end of the street were the battlements of a decayed Aragonese fortress. At the other the town drifted away into the valley.

His tiny car, which we had been told at the bar down in the piazza to look out for, was outside his front door. In the back, onions and a goat's skin. We rang, and instantly his head appeared above us, bald, eyes almost white as we looked vertically upwards.

The chestnut door opened with a noise like a carpenter bee, and we went in. We walked quickly up a dark internal staircase, urged on by peremptory noises above. My hands encountered framed prints or drawings on the walls as I steadied myself in the dark. My forehead momentarily touched the small of Vittoria's back.

Vittoria was already explaining things when I got to the top. She had been there before, three years ago. She had some difficulties. Her life was not going well . . . This was her friend, she said, an English writer, who might write about him in a book to be published in England.

This was not the best thing she could have said. Against the light I could not see him well, but he gave the impression of a small man filled with ferocious energy. He made sweeping gestures with the back of his hand as if to shoo us away. He spoke fast and loud and I had difficulty in catching the words though the gist was perfectly clear.

He was busy. His cousin was ill. Soon he would go to the hospital to see her. He did not remember Vittoria, denied that he had ever seen her. The hospital had strict visiting hours and soon he should go. He was often asked for interviews by journalists, but had had a bad experience and wanted nothing to do with them. His was a sacred calling; he did not work for money, he needed no publicity. He was not a charlatan like certain quacks one saw on the television, advertising their powers and guaranteeing a cure. Nobody can give such guarantees. If he were to do such a thing, his powers would vanish.

My eyes, growing used to the light, took in a brown face with grey eyes and a small white moustache.

That he had a certain reputation, had effected certain remarkable cures, he said, was well known. But it would be useless to try to explain what he did, how he achieved his results. It was dangerous even to inquire into certain things.

I was desperately looking for a place to sit down, if need be on the ground. The sitting-room was incredibly small and I was much too large for it, for him. But Vittoria and Il Riccio were waving at each other, almost dancing as they talked, between me and the formal table with its dun cloth and flowerless greenery and large ashtray of blue cut glass.

The last thing he wanted, he said, was people writing articles about him. Journalists always got things wrong, chose the spectacular where there was nothing abnormal or supernatural. Writers did not understand the problems! Doctors were something else. He had good relations with doctors. Up at the hospital he could come and go as he pleased, the doors were always open for him. He was a personal friend of Professor So-and-so of Bologna, president of the Institute of Parapsychological Research, who was always welcome. But if we thought we were doing him a favour by writing about his work, we could take our hats and go.

I managed to slip between them and sit down.

Vittoria, making placatory noises, said I wouldn't write anything without his approval. I joined in for the first time, saying I was far more interested in getting her, Vittoria's, problems solved than I was in writing articles – which incidentally was true.

Up at the hospital they were expecting him, and he should be there already. They knew him well up there, because if a patient of his was ill, genuinely ill, he always recommended seeing a real doctor before trying anything else. He was certainly not competing with the medical profession! If something could be cured by medicine, why then he himself would take medicine, and he pointed to two or three small flasks on the sideboard, standing in line with miniature liqueur bottles of the same size and shape.

On the other hand, if a patient of his had to undergo an operation, he liked to be there to participate. He was known to do this, and he was welcome there. He worked in tandem with the surgeon, often making video recordings of operations, for his own satisfaction. It was one of his passions, he said, meaning his hobby. He would take up his equipment, his camera and lights – not that one needs more light in an operating theatre – and switch them on and stay until the operation was finished.

Last month he attended a friend of his who had to have a tumour, as large as a child's head, removed from his stomach. After two hours the surgeon asked him how he felt and he said 'Fine', because he, Il Riccio, had no heart at all. A heart of stone is what he had.

'That is not true,' said Vittoria. 'Nobody believes you when you say these things. You have a tender heart, otherwise you would not dedicate yourself to others in the way you do. You have a tender heart, but strong nerves, and that is how it should be – a soft heart within a hard shell.'

Through a pebble-glass wall, I could see a tiny kitchen, with pans hanging on the wall and a magnetic rod for knives.

Bit by bit Il Riccio seemed mollified by Vittoria. He sat down at last opposite me, and she on my right, and when he placed his fat hands on the table a formal relationship seemed to click into shape between his hands and the large blue ashtray between us.

The sitting-room was crowded with an extraordinary amount of clobber. By the wall near the stairs, shotguns in slings hung from wooden pegs, on which were also a few strings of boar-tusks, a cartridge belt, an old leather bag. Cartridge boxes on a low black chest. Above the guns, a framed photo of the Alps.

Next to this a large glass-fronted cabinet filled with expensive crockery, mainly modern hand-painted cups from Richard Ginori in Florence. The glass front was faceted, and engraved with wild flowers.

'As for my powers,' he said, suddenly turning to me, 'I can see by your face that you do not believe in them. Luckily for you it does not matter whether you believe or do not believe. All you need do is observe, and see that they work. How they work, I cannot tell you, because I do not know. I do not ask. All I know is that they are there.

'For instance,' he said, to Vittoria now, 'if you were to be in an interesting state [meaning pregnant], then I would be able to tell you, even if it were only as of five minutes. And if you came back three months later, I would be able to tell you the sex of the *piccirillo*, in writing!' And he slapped one hand in the other, to make the point.

A quick cock of the head, as if listening for something.

'Belief in the *aldilà* [hereafter] or in the supernatural is not necessary. It is not necessary to ask so many questions about things which come from Heaven. I myself am a good Christian. I have an excellent relationship with the *Reverendo* of this village, and I am a personal friend of the Bishop of Arezzo. But certain things it is better not to know. What need is there for belief? Either it works, or it does not work, and that is all there is to it.

'I have a wife, two sons aged forty and forty-five. I have grandchildren, nephews, nieces. I shall not tell you how many we are when we all meet. They have all seen me working, all their lives, and what do they understand? Nothing! They understand nothing at all. They look. I explain. I show them; it is so obvious! But they cannot feel how it works, and without the instinct that comes from the emotions it is useless to explain, to demonstrate. Even my wife thinks that it is all without sense. Imagine! I have worked like this for fifty-five years, ever since I was a child, and still she doubts.

'So if you are pregnant, I will write it down on a piece of paper and you will keep it, and in seven months' time you will see if I am wrong. And if I am, you will bring me back the paper and show me. Bring it, otherwise I shall not believe you.'

'I do not think that I have that problem,' said Vittoria, perhaps a little sadly.

Certificates and photographs of various kinds. A veterans' reunion, with snaps of grinning survivors tucked into the frame. Parchment honours with red embellishments of Sienese curlicues that from a distance looked like dragons.

'It would be difficult for me to be pregnant,' said Vittoria, 'but I have a great deal of confusion here' — she tapped her head — 'and a need, you will understand, to clarify certain things.'

Photographs of relatives with infants, in small gold frames. Clocks. Quite a lot of clocks, of the kind that strike the hour firmly, one after the other.

Il Riccio seemed to see her for the first time. A sort of arcane confrontation took place between them, Vittoria hesitant, Il Riccio momentarily like a bull about to charge.

'I remember you now,' he said. 'But you look so much better than last time! You surely don't need anything that I can give you? I only need to take one look at you to know that you are perfectly capable of facing your life.'

'Truly . . .' said Vittoria.

'Well,' said Il Riccio, 'I can cure running sores that the doctors have given up, both the kind that weep and the kind that are dry. I can cure the gout, the abscess, the herpes.' (The words he used sounded ancient, like words from Bocaccio or Dante.) 'If your mouth puckers and turns sour so that you are ashamed to smile because it is painful, and you cover your face with your hand, I can cure it. I can cure styes in the eye in two days only. If you come on Friday, on Sunday you can go to church, and anyone can look you in the face.

'I can cure many of those diseases which strike one' – he pointed a finger straight down – 'but first you will have to show me what you have, to see if I can cure it or not. And should you feel shame, I would say, "Am I not a doctor too? You have come all this way, and show shame?" In my youth perhaps I abused my position once or twice because I wanted to see a certain woman naked. Perhaps even doctors do that, for they are human too. But now a naked woman for me is just a figure without clothes, with some hair down there between her legs.'

'I have another problem,' said Vittoria. 'I cannot tell you even what it is. I feel confused. It could be love, or it could be something to do with my work.'

'Do you have enemies?'

She hung her head. It seemed clear that she thought she did.

Deaf though Il Riccio occasionally seemed if Vittoria or I tried to speak, he heard his wife's soft step upon the stair and turned to meet her. He greeted her with a list of insults with which she was evidently familiar. A wife so old (he said), so fat and incapable, so empty of healthy appetites, that if you were to take her and divide her into three wives, a third each in age and weight, why then you would be doing him a great favour. For we are all pigs in our family, he said proudly, and have certain desires and needs. And in the air he seemed to hold between finger and thumb something large and round and shiny, as if it were his own imagined testicle.

She was pale and older than her husband, moving with difficulty. Listening to his speech she looked tired but faintly amused.

Stepping behind him as he made this speech she went straight into the kitchen to prepare his instruments of divination, and it occurred to me that many of the more incomprehensible stories of the last hour must have been filling in time, waiting for her to appear.

'Come,' he said.

We went into the kitchen. I hovered uselessly in the background, wondering if perhaps this was going to be a private session, but he seized me by the shoulder and sat me down opposite him, at the far end of the kitchen table, Vittoria on his right, while his wife stood behind us.

'So you think you have the Evil Eye? Or that there is a spell on you?'

'Or just envy,' said his wife gently in the background, 'it all comes to the same thing.'

A blockboard table with cheap tin legs, covered by a red plastic tablecloth, with interlacing flowers. Upon this surface, in front of the Master, Il Riccio's wife placed a large glass containing about two inches of water, with an inch and a half of olive oil floating on top. On the oil, a small aluminium ring with a cotton wick, and three spikes the size of nails protruding from the ring, the ends inserted into three round segments of a cork, to make the little island float.

This lamp, Il Riccio lit.

Between him and the lamp his wife now placed a plain white soup plate filled with water. He never stopped talking, about the cures he would effect (don't believe him, said his wife) and the adventures he had had (if only, said his wife), while simultaneously he made Vittoria write down her name for him on a small perforated pad which had evidently been used many times before, in the same circumstances. One could read the impression of previous names indented in the blank page, in crude letters.

In mid-sentence, he suddenly grabbed Vittoria's left forearm with his right hand. She tried to draw back, but he held firm. Silence.

Very gently he approached the surface of the water in the soup plate with the thumb of his left hand. He seemed to be listening for something. The thumb touched the surface. It seemed as if the water had gone up to the thumb rather than the thumb descended to the water.

Well, he mumbled, you have told me the truth about your name, and there seems to be nothing serious . . .

His wife handed him a glass of water, which he drank quickly. As he had not called for it, I assumed this was some part of the ritual, rather than mere thirst. A libation of some kind.

Il Riccio placed the piece of paper with Vittoria's name under the wrist of his left hand, with the thumb very gently touching the side of the plate. Then he placed the index finger of his right hand in the oil of the lamp, removed it again, and with great care allowed one drop to fall upon the surface of the water in the plate. Quickly wiping his finger, he took hold of Vittoria's forearm as before and stared intently downwards.

The drop of oil hesitated for a moment on the surface. The refracted light of the little candle (his wife had switched off the kitchen light and the place was quite dark) formed a pretty geometrical shape.

'The cross,' said Il Riccio. 'Do you see the cross?'

In leaning forward to see better, Vittoria moved the table, and with a slight spasm the drop of oil split into three droplets, which seemed instantly to shy away from each other.

The three small particles certainly behaved very oddly. The larger one seemed to have turned black, and whereas it had kept still, the two smaller drops seemed overcome by frenetic activity. The black drop moved towards Il Riccio, and then slowly went back towards the centre of the plate. The two other particles seemed to chase around each other, while attempting simultaneously to rejoin the dominant black drop, which moved more slowly.

At a certain point the two smaller drops hesitated, stopped. The black drop then advanced on them and very gently reabsorbed the pair of them, at which point the oil turned golden once more, and the cross faintly reappeared.

'I do not see this as a physical problem, also because I feel your physical state is good. There is no doubt that you are in a confused state, not at ease with your soul, filled with dark thoughts. Only when you are reunited with the wayward part of yourself will you find peace.'

Very surreptitiously, Vittoria sighed.

'There is definitely a wicked spirit over you, but this we can easily remove.' So saying he took some salt from a small dish and sprinkled it on to the drop, which instantly fragmented itself into a fleet of small sparkling boatlets on a turbulent inland sea of miniature waves.

'The confused soul,' he said, 'left the two smaller figures and descended – you saw – to the bottom of the plate. When it returned, it was able to absorb into itself any turbulence it found in its path.'

'You saw nobody else?' Vittoria asked.

For a long time Il Riccio just looked at her, apparently unaware that he still held her arm in his sturdy hand.

'If there is someone,' he said gently, 'from whom you wish to escape, you will need to bring me a piece of his clothing, which he has worn within the last twenty-four hours, and a piece of yours. And, if it is possible, some hairs.'

He made a brief nod to indicate from which part of the body these hairs were to be taken.

'I can either bind you together, or make sure that you will gently separate, distance yourselves from each other. But in either case, it is essential for you to be certain what you want.'

In the background his wife shook her head, as if to say, 'To think that there are still people in this world who believe this rubbish.'

He made a fine show of refusing our presents, which were only a bottle of Vin Santo and some biscuits to dip into it. Once risen from the table, his mood of sombre concentration vanished and he became as chatty as before. He showed us his poem, the one he had written for the poetry contest the year before, in the voice of the last local brigand. Showed us photographs of the event. Gave me a photocopy of it to translate into English, having apparently forgotten his antipathy to writers. Showed me the parchment he wrote in honour of his wife, for their golden wedding. Pointed out the silver cups, gestured contentedly at the row of ticking clocks . . .

Fifteen years ago I was in love with Vittoria, for two hundred yards, on the back road from Radda to Greve.

Spring. The abandoned field by the mill was filled with dog-roses and, 'What fireworks!' I said as we drove past. We were in a rush to get my elder daughter's photograph embossed within its dark passport, with the raised letters, the tactile values, the dry stamp of the late British Empire.

Vittoria was in the front seat, daughter was in the back. I looked at the roses exploding, and at Vittoria. We smiled.

My extraordinarily powerful infatuation survived one other brief glance, which stilled in my brain the image of her two hands neatly folded upon her lap. Mute, lit by spring sunshine. Still, where every other thing was rattling along the main road.

I shall keep this fragment with me for ever. The bones of her wrist, and above the wrist one thin line denoting some absolute frontier between her hand and the rest of her body. But most of all the self-containment of one hand gently within another. Fine skin stretched slightly over the bone, whiter briefly among thin muscles like a lizard. Flat fingers, if the hand is opened.

She runs across the floor of some cocktail party in Milan for the classic urban greeting, the quick buss on the cheek, the formal inquiry concerning health. And unknown to anyone I check her wrist for its unique line, my forefinger as she takes my hand touches the bone. For me it is a talisman. If this can survive, so can the rest of the world.

We went back down to the *piazzetta* and sat for a while in the bar to think it all over.

'It's not love is it?' I asked. 'You did not bring me all this way just because of love, did you?'

Vittoria was amused.

'Like all good prophets, Il Riccio just edges you towards what you want to know,' she said. 'In fact I understood instantly everything that happened in the plate, better then he did. It was as if I had already seen this happening. It was all clear to me! I could have predicted how the oil was going to move. It was as if I had seen it before in a dream.'

'Oh. And so what was it all about?'

'I would never tell you, not even if I were to be struck dead.'

I felt ashamed for her, this spasm of inhuman rejection.

The waiter brought us two ice-creams in a little wire stand.

'The cross was just refraction, wasn't it?' I said when I had recovered a bit. I needed a neutral touch. 'The drop of oil on the water was turned into a little lens, and the single candle projected through it . . . '

She nodded, as if I had said something too obvious for words. She took her ice-cream and said, in the voice of a girl reciting at school, '*Gesù Giuseppe e Maria, se c'è il malocchio portamelo via.*' ('Jesus Joseph and Mary, if there is the Evil Eye then take it away.')

'You don't need to be very powerful,' she said, 'for the *malocchio*, you know. Anyone born at seven months can do it. Even my mother can . . . '

I felt I was being very stupid.

'Will you please just tell me what I ought to have seen, and what it was all about?'

A waitress came from inside the café and yelled across the piazza at a group of boys. One moved off to his bicycle.

Vittoria went on licking her ice-cream. Eventually she said, more to herself than to me, 'When he lifted his thumb from the plate, before he started, I saw a little halo there. You did not? Ah! You did not! Immediately I saw that halo, I knew I would be all right.'

The boy took his bike and rickety went up the street, ducking into an arch halfway along. I had the impression that he wasn't going to do what the waitress told him to.

'And you want to know, eh? Well, I shall tell you. I think if my doctorate has been given by the enemy of my professor, I should go to see this new professor, no? Maybe he would like to have me. I cannot make love to my actual professor! But on the other hand I know so much about him. He has not always been correct, you know, in everything he has done at the site.'

'Careful,' I said.

'I am always careful. You do not know me if you think I am not careful!' She laughed. It sounded mischievous and irresponsible. 'And if I do not find a solution here in Italy, I will go to see Cavalli Sforza in America. He is very brilliant. He is making these theories based on genetic archaeology, which here in Italy they do not like, but it is very interesting. And then I could go to Chicago, where they have offered me something.'

'Chicago?' I said incredulously, 'you have an offer from the Chicago school and you didn't tell me?'

'My English is not very good.'

I don't like being teased indefinitely; I called the grumpy waitress over to pay.

Vittoria was very cheerful in the car driving back.

However tactfully I tried, it was impossible to get any information about her lovers out of her. Having finally made me curious, she gave nothing back. Complacent at having made me witness to some mysterious rite, she explained neither what I had seen nor the reason why she had chosen me to see it.

Listening to her humming at my side, on the long drive north towards Siena, I felt deprived. Had I really taken her to the local *mago*? For whom, for what? Did she really believe that love was a spell woven off-stage by some unknown malignant personage? That could be made to come and go by saying spells over dirty underwear? That could be murdered by dripping oil on water?

What was to become of her? I worried about it. I worried more about her than I worried about my own family. My own daughters, ten years younger than Vittoria, were more able than she to make a long-term plan and stick to it. And thinking thus casually of age, and time, I fell to brooding about the incomplete semi-paternal role I was manoeuvred into playing with her, or freely chose.

On the drive back, it seemed to me that my fingers around the wheel looked like the closed legs of a boiled crab. To me, the Latin lover is a tomcat whose only acceptable mode is asleep in the sun. The phase of wailing neck-biting followed by complacent indifference – very frequent in Vittoria's life – strikes me as rock bottom in terms of human communication. Except, being English, I would never dare say as much.

And if ever her face turns to mine with a smile, a certain laziness, an echo of that moment on the Radda road, far from being flattered thus to be beckoned forward once more, I say yet again No. And in so doing I feel yet again the whole peninsula slip gently away.

26 · FINALE

Hemp wicks in hot wax bowls shone on the low wall, far enough from the dry shrubs not to cause a conflagration. Stare hard at one flame, and the villa became a series of insubstantial panels, catching the light at differing angles like scenery parked in the wings when the stage is empty.

The black smoke from the candles moved in pointed wedges like the dark cypresses above them, only faster and smaller. Within each flaming bowl the shiny surface of the wax destroyed all sense of scale. Beneath its tense surface small specks seemed to move by their own propulsion while the boiling wax itself appeared still. My eyes shunted their equipment: the cornea flickered, the iris snapped. You might be in a darkroom looking up at a negative of a row of dark trees in sunlight, backlit by the safety-bulb.

I turned momentarily back to the parked car, where Carla was checking her face in the mirror. Maro, Franco and I waited, and we approached the villa arm in arm, in unison. Noises from the garden drew us in. The harsh wrought-iron gate had the look of Maurizio of Lecchi, *circa* 1969 – a good year for gates, though not entirely appropriate for a seventeenth-century villa.

A marquee had been set up to one side. Well-dressed guests obscured the edges of a long table covered in white, with rows of glasses set formally as if for a wine-tasting. The Stucchis were there already, and those northerners whose interrelationships I had yet to disentangle, though we could greet each other by name. I touched my wayward hand to throat and waist and crotch in a quick check that all was seemly. All the Italians were carefully dressed. Our host had a dark silk tie, and a small lapel rosette. I seemed to belong to a minority of the tieless, and felt naked.

Beyond the wine-tasters the vineyards went up and down the hills, incised by a huge fork on the background of black velvet. The scarred face of the villa was freshly plastered, and cars from the cities of the northern plain lined a sunken car park just below the level of the land. A floodlight transformed the upper branches of the great pine into a cathedral. Leaning badly, the tree was wired to its neighbour for support, suggesting that acrobats might appear any moment above our heads.

I was welcomed by our host and complimented him on his compassion towards the tottering pine, a tree I had known for years. His smile became fractionally warmer; I do not enjoy cutting down trees, he said.

A spotlight masked by a clump of lavender touched the surface of a fresh lawn, at the far end of which light from the blue pool filtered upwards towards the cypresses. By a mock-seventeenth-century changing-room, a towel in the half-light lay forgotten on the back of a park bench in the English style. Nothing too ostentatious! Further still, among the decayed baroque statues, a fence of green wire gave just a hint of the empty tennis-court beyond.

I moved on, unsure how to continue. Drinks for the thirsty – oh yes. I bowed. Then I turned towards Carla, who was standing with the wife of the new owner to the left of a saint on a plinth in a soft sandstone that is quarried behind Vicenza. The feet of the statue seemed to stand upon their shoulders. His toes were bony; their necks wore pearls.

They were discussing the advantages of buying property in Eastern Europe. I could add nothing to that, but was able to talk of the beauty of the Charles Bridge in Prague, where I have never been, and of the latent sadness of our brothers in the east. Someone had told me that the cobbled streets had remained un-repaired since the fall of the old Habsburg empire. In Prague – or was it Kiev.

'What you do,' said our hostess, smiling, 'is create a holding company in East Germany and pay in dollars.'

'Ah,' said I, 'the old trade routes across Hungary. How good that they will flower again by cash rather than by the sword! Trieste, the Veneto – why you are closer to the Slav world up there where you live than you are to us down here.'

Leaning forward, I reminded her that Udine was only five hours from Brno by car.

And while I stood there doing my best, a kind Italian whom I did not know asked permission (*'con permesso'*) to turn down the collar of my summer jacket. I stopped, momentarily shaken in my middle–European discourse, and he made that strange gesture with two parallel hands, as of surrender. 'Unless your collar is up on purpose,' he said.

For some reason – perhaps half a glass of white wine had already gotten to me – this gesture of politeness struck me as infinitely kind. The first social move of this nice man, I thought, was to infringe the barrier of my personal space, my shell of protective air, and he did so without breaking the rules of Italian formality, those ritual hand gestures of permission and apology.

We moved away from the marquee, where the voices were growing louder. I yearned to confide in this useful stranger.

'I have just been offered what seems to me to be a lot of money to write a book,' I said, 'which is something I have never done before. I am very much disturbed.'

I noticed his own suit seemed to be made of a silk so ancient that it had acquired the quality of hand-made paper. An heirloom. Such material you inherit, you do not buy. I looked at his face, muscular, lined, faintly sardonic.

'What sort of book?'

We walked sideways into the darker patches of the lawn.

'Well, the theme is Tuscany. But in effect I can take it to include anything that strikes me, concerning this . . . ' I gestured to the pines, and beyond the pines the ripening vineyards, the far circle of enclosing hills.

'I am at the stage of elimination,' I said. 'I know what I cannot do. I cannot write a detailed history; and something without detail, a quick total sketch, can be done better by others. I loathe talking of food, restaurants, hotels, timetables, itineraries. I thought I would take just one or two events in the remote past, or even from my own life here, and cover them well, leaving the readers to fill in the gaps.'

'*Giusto,*' said my new best friend, smoother of crumpled jackets. 'Your logic is impeccable. It so happens,' he said, looking down, 'that I have to face this problem (which is essentially one of determining the parameters of a certain action, no?) almost every day in my work. I direct a large industrial organization which is highly diversified, continually changing its direction . . . '

We walked over beautiful shadows in the grass, like soft barbed wire.

' . . . all the progress in industry over the last ten years has been in the perfection of organizational structures rather than the invention of new materials or techniques. Inventions! When one thinks how many electric machines were already invented in the last century . . . '

The daughter of the house came towards us across the lawn, dressed in brief sequins, walking slowly, like a dancer who appears to be fractionally behind the beat.

' . . . to establish vertical systems according to an intellectually perceived strategy is insufficient. There has to be continued communication laterally between the various levels. The whole challenge is to remain elastic, flexible, at any given moment. Still, this discourse . . . '

'No, please! I am very interested.'

Some ghost of a conversation with Saskia's Greek teacher at the Liceo Classico came back to me, the feeling of being devoured by a subordinate clause.

'What I intended to tell you,' he said at last, summing up, 'is that in my job, I have acquired over the last two or three years a kind of image, an interior paradigm. It goes like this. Let knowledge, *va bene*, be an apple. The totality of knowledge is concentrated in this round, single fruit. Now evidently it is not given to any man to be able to devour the whole apple – '

'Any more than Adam – '

'Exactly! *Bravo*, you have understood me immediately. Adam and Eve had no more than a quick bite before, *fuori*, they were kicked out. We who live outside Eden for ever have two choices: we can burrow into the apple like a worm, or we can slice across it with a knife. The worms are the specialists. They have no view of the whole picture, but what they see before them they can thoroughly digest. Those who do not munch, as it were, those who slice, can only have a detached or bird's-eye view – but at least this view covers a whole section of the apple, which permits them to make certain deductions.'

'How wonderful! And what happens,' I asked, 'if the knife slices through a worm or two?'

The captain of industry, the straightener of bent collars, shrugged.

'It happens frequently,' he said. 'It is a good age for knives.'

Then, to show he was not as ruthless as I might expect, he smiled and said, '*Scherzo*, I am joking, of course. I intended merely to say that your own plan for a book is not intrinsically wrong. Precise tastes of the apple in various very specific places, within an overall structure that could give a very good idea of the whole.'

Suddenly, over his shoulder, at the corner of the villa where the candles ended and electricity dulled by parchment took over, I became aware of Vittoria, arriving in a small group of guests all in a bunch.

I was shocked to see that she had cut off her hair and permed the residue into short sharp curls. A public declaration that she was a girl longing for a new identity.

Standing alone for a moment on the grass I felt the presence of some unusual event, future or past, I could not tell. A huge moon began to rise above the hills, weeping slightly in the moisture that thickened slantwise along the curve of the earth.

As I prepared to meet her, however, a waiter came between us carrying a tray of white wine. I recognized in him a colleague from the village band, all togged out in white gloves and gold buttons on ironed cotton. I could not let him stand there without a greeting, if only – 'What, you here too, and all in your best, eh?' A bridge of sorts over one of the many odd chasms of the evening. And by the time this was over she had disappeared, absorbed by the statues, flesh and stone, of the ever-sculptural young.

The guests started to move forward to their tables.

Obscured by shrubbery and the plumage of summer visitors, I lost sight of the members of my various families. In these situations I tend to identify with the inanimate fixtures in the background, leave the scramble for a chair too late, and become the lone invading presence among a small table of unknowns.

Five wine glasses, six pieces of cutlery: the evening was serious. I held out my hand, to my left, to my right, and was ignored.

What was this emotion that so consumed me all of a sudden? Moral anxiety? Adrenalin? Alcohol? Overdose of newspapers at a time when the world seemed ferociously active? Why was I so overwhelmed by this sense that History was out there, galloping past, leaving me like a walking sack of guts on the periphery?

Polite noises came from my mouth. 'My Italian is good. Thank you. Yes, we have been here for many years.'

The meal was ornate and well-made. The improvised Tuscan waiters served a vegetable soufflé usual to the north, and Foffo as he served me whispered that in the kitchen they had brought their own cook. He sounded respectful, or shocked, I could not tell which. I fingered the beautiful glass of extraordinary thinness, and only became aware of the conversation towards the end of the meal.

'Huge, I tell you, and totally black. The stuff of madmen! And that he should ask me, of all people, to buy a fake Gucci bag . . .'

They were talking of the *vucumprà*, the Senegalese and Malian street-vendors who were cluttering the centre of Florence. The word is southern, Neapolitan, I think, and means 'you-wanna-buy'. Not a complimentary epithet for a fellow man.

It was a busy time for illegal immigration in Italy, and I tend to identify with all immigrants and refugees on principle.

'Have you noticed it's always the same Gucci bag?' said a light-voiced gentleman opposite. 'It seems to me possible that they have the same source of supply, throughout Italy. It leads one to think that perhaps they are already in the hands of the *criminalità organizzata*. Surely they have come to some arrangement? How else would they get to Italy, if not by fishing boat to Trapani, or to the islands? Or perhaps to Mazzara del Valle, with the smuggled tobacco and hashish?'

In these circumstances, to be obliged to be serious about the wine can be a blessing. As you gather your thoughts, you tip your nose into a glass, inhale, look very thoughtful, and prepare for the next round.

'The waiter at Rivoire's this afternoon said he thought they should all be rounded up and sent back to Africa. If this kind of tension were to increase, it would not be amusing.'

'*Divertente*' was the word used. Diverting. Distracting from the harshness of the day-to-day.

I felt I ought not to let him get away with it. In the candlelight it seemed to me his face resembled a button, with shiny holes for eyes.

'In a household composed entirely of refugees,' I said, 'whether Armenian or Jewish or Lebanese – '

'Lebanese! But have you not just told us that you are English?'

'The extended family of *fuoriusciti* who live in my house, descendants of those who believed that when things became difficult, you should pack a bag, not load a gun . . .'

The blond lady of fifty was looking at me with curiosity, at such a fiery beginning.

'The newspapers are very confusing,' I said, sobering up and assembling an argument properly. 'They talk about "another black stabbed at Novoli", for instance, but when you read the article, the "black" turns out to be called Ahmed ben Ali. I have no idea whether this confusion is conscious or not, but surely there is a difference between the north Africans from Morocco and Tunisia, who are and always have been mixed up with the drug trade, and are regularly stabbed, and the new wave of blacks from Senegal or Mali, who are culturally non-aggressive. And aren't, so far, mixed up with drugs.'

One of the gentlemen opposite nodded as if I'd said something very sound.

'How complicated life has become in Tuscany,' said the lady.

'Think of gradual erosion of arable land in Africa! The great water basins like Lake Chad drying out. Compassion on the poor peoples of the interior is surely what is needed. What hope is there for the continent to become self-sufficient, hocked as it is to its back teeth to the World Bank? At the woodyard below Siena, the African hardwoods cost less than the local pine, they are so desperate for hard cash.'

They exchanged glances among themselves, but were prepared to be polite. The man with button eyes said that perhaps there was some misunderstanding: he personally was for a compromise.

I asked what choice did they have, but to move? Ours, I said, was to become an age of mass migration. There were a million or more new souls a year in Egypt alone! Whole peoples were about to shift across the face of Europe. Maps with arrows would appear in the newspapers. It was inevitable, I said, that Italy would become a channel along which a huge number of people would soon be moving.

I was faintly bored as I said all this, and listened to a nightingale by the pond up in the wood. The evening was becoming cooler, the sound echoing as if the brain had suddenly cleared of cobwebs.

'But how serious you are!' said the blond lady opposite, and it was true that I was forgetting the cardinal rule of these occasions, to retain a light touch. Oh, that Italian politeness, descending from the *ancien régime*, that consists of talking of food, or the sun, or the ripening grapes, the burgeoning produce of weather and ease! For a brief moment I listened to the ebb and scatter of other conversations, and indeed they were all light, like shingle on the beach.

'In a sense,' I said with a charming smile, 'you could argue that tourism also is a kind of mass migration. This phenomenon which annually crushes the country, differing from other migrations only in that it is temporary – '

'And brings money, instead of – '

'Like birds. The arrival of swallows at Easter can be compared to the arrival of German tourists at Rimini or Riccione. And after the summer they go away again. Except they don't lay eggs and breed!'

The lady opposite told the company I was '*spiritoso*'.

'Add to that the Easterners who are our brothers, who will surely begin to migrate here now that the frontiers are breaking down. And may they be welcome! They too are Europeans, and in our European Federation is our only hope!'

'I would have thought . . .' (The gentleman was wiping his mouth to give sentence.)

'Already at the railway station in Siena the Polish girls have arrived, according to the best friend of Foffo over there.'

This last remark was so arcane that they demanded a footnote.

Intimately I told them that Rodolfo, *detto* Foffo, was my companion in the ranks of the village band. Surprise! Village band, and an Englishman playing in it! Glances at Foffo dressed as a waiter in the middle distance, now circulating with the wine. A great master of the *flicorno*, I told them, and uncle of a very disruptive infant whom he teaches and who is really quite talented. And what, they asked, is a *flicorno*. Ah, said I, it's an instrument which looks like the fossil of an extinct cuttlefish cast in bronze, and in the full score under Cesare the bandleader's beady eye, it is called '*flic*', ha ha.

At this party, it seemed an odd relationship to declare to my puzzled table. Perhaps it would have been better to keep silent.

'Foffo,' I went on, 'at the last rave-up of the band last June, brought along this slight crazy cousin of his, whom I happened to sit next to, just as now I am sitting next to you. This massive man asked me if I'd discovered the Polish girls down at the station. "*Le Polacche*", he insisted, had arrived about three months ago and taken over the pitch formerly occupied by the Senegalese girls – who incidentally were inevitably asked by their lovers to "do it as you do in your country", indicating God knows what fantasy on the part of these cash-paying Latin lovers, ha ha.'

My audience at this point ceased to give me the benefit of the doubt. The general conversation broke up into individual chess pieces, with only the blond lady momentarily left with ears for me.

'And so,' I continued, 'one can imagine a series of migrations, the first symptom of which is the arrival of a bunch of whores. Following the whores, the pimps, who obviously have to make some sort of a deal with the local traders. Thus it is that the Common Market is to be created from the very bottom upwards – bottom in two senses, ha ha – and we can begin to feel really integrated when at the back of platform five at Siena station we at length see the beautiful wenches of Azerbaijan.'

'You a historian?' said Vittoria. 'Matteo the great social analyst? Don't make the chickens laugh!'

She had risen up suddenly behind us – a drastic intervention. Oh, take it from the top, conductor, and let's try that one again.

'It's a perfectly valid theory,' I said, panicking, 'based on personal observation, and a careful assessment of selected newspaper articles.'

'Gossip,' she shouted, 'is all you are interested in, either of you. Not even gossip, but *malizia*.'

'Has Maro . . . ?'

'I get on fine with Maro. Don't try to interfere with that relationship! It's you! Who gave you permission? What makes you believe you have any capacity to derive a theory from facts? What have you ever given me but quick theories for

344

every fact I've told you, and if I add another fact you don't agree with, you invent another theory, instantly, just like that?'

'Right,' I said *sotto voce*. 'Keep moving.'

'What do you understand of – ?'

'Child,' I said, 'let us reason a moment. I hope I know the distinction between gossip and, say, historical argument.'

'Do you think this man' – Vittoria was definitely shouting now – 'has the training, the dedication, to talk about any kind of standards? Standards! When he is nothing but a man who piles shit on canvas and smears it around. A real – a pile of – '

It seemed a good moment to rise and take Vittoria by the elbow and lead her away from the table, where her attentive public was showing restive signs. Four faces were unfolded expectantly upwards at us as, tripping and bumping, we moved towards the centre of the grass. Four faces fixed in their smiles like pale flowers expecting rain from the black sky.

'Leave me alone,' she said shaking a shoulder under my nose, her ridiculous new curls about as attractive as cold cuts of boiled ham. 'I do not want you in my life.'

'I am not in any way *in* your life.'

The others turned back to their own conversation, relieved at last to recognize the signals of a private dispute.

'*Smettila.*' Her favourite word. 'Leave me alone. You have no need to arrange . . . My life – '

In the moonlight, her face turned black and crackled like scraped acquatint.

'What makes you think I can depend on you in any way? In what way do I need to rely on you? What can I trust you for?'

Thus at the still core of the grass verge, surrounded by lit tables at which the guests continued their modulations among the white tablecloths, I stood and listened to a speech which she had carefully prepared, now tattered by alcohol, but still deeply felt.

Distracted, I concentrated on observing how she stood. Square-cut like a wrestler, feet parallel, the opposite from her cajoling, convincing pose, when she reverted to feet at right angles in a ballet position. Her mouth was open. Her face was very clear in the moonlight. Her forehead seemed wrinkled, slightly leathery. Her teeth were clean.

Weight, in a sense, overcame all other feelings as I listened. Phrases became discards of marble, as in the medieval torture where criminals were executed by being crushed by an accumulation of stones.

Weight, so that by drooping to listen the more carefully, I became bored, and imagined myself hung there from a clothesline or rope that came down vertically from the acrobat's wire between the pines.

By and by I found myself alone. I straightened up (with what a sigh), and felt flakes of rust falling from unused internal organs around my heart. I looked up at the large moon and found it too shiny, in its wilderness of stars.

I could see her down by the tennis-court and I knew that sooner or later I would have to walk across the lawn to speak to her. But first it seemed courteous to return to the table, pretending that nothing had happened.

The blond woman to whom I had been relatively rude briefly took my wrist.

'You are trembling,' she said.

'I am sorry, I – '

'Please! There is nothing for which you have to apologize. On the contrary, I feel I should explain something, as I feel our remarks about the Africans in Florence might have given you a wrong impression . . .'

Once, I remembered, at just such a party as this, Vittoria had grabbed me from behind as I was sitting down so that my hands were pinned behind me. By some contortion I was able to find her pliable knees, from which my fingers began to creep upwards, confident that the unhingeable nature of my shoulders would make it impossible to get further than the soft flesh of the inner thigh, that my libidinous gesture was doomed to failure, when '*Smettila*' I heard in my ear – practically within my head – meaning 'Stop it'. I was amused. With her arms around my neck, what does she hiss all sibylline and serpent-like (such a serpent-like word, too), but '*Ssstop it*,' while to the rest of the world her body-language said, '*He's mine.*'

Narcissism, Maro said about this particular incident, with the detached omniscience of our long and peculiar marriage. Narcissism on her part, and on mine. Hers, to show her capacity for a passion she was incapable of feeling. Mine, the desire to present some truly masculine front to the hinterland of Latin lovers, who were less demonstrative, though evidently more effective. In short, Maro saw immediately that we were both entirely possessed by an imaginary public.

'Signora,' I told the woman opposite with tears in my eyes, 'I am truly touched that you have gone to the trouble to explain that you have no prejudice against our Senegalese brothers, and surely the misunderstanding was mine . . .'

But my reaction to her kindness was too late. She had passed the moment of the *vucumprà* and was, it seems, recounting something which had happened to her in Ireland, but I could not tell. With great attention I observed a diamond ring she was wearing. My eyes went from the tennis-court to the cold fiery centre of her fingers. I could see Vittoria and her fake curls down there, nodding intensely within a shrub of arms and legs, with an occasional flash of a sequin to balance the far more explosive flash of the moon within the vast facets of Granny's old rose-cut.

There might be some kind of tug-of-war in all this, I thought. A question of who was to cross the spiky close-cut lawn first. There was no question but that we would have to have it out.

347

After the meal broke up I returned to stand under the drooping pine, with which by now I had some kind of identification. And as the pine and I leaned there in parallel, I was joined by Chiara Paradiso. 'What! You too!' Etcetera. I felt unable to talk of Handel or castrati just then, the only subjects we had in common, but launched instantly into a long rambling discourse about my feelings for Vittoria. I was glad in the moonlight to see little of her face. When she replied at last she became, as it were, the reasonable voice of my own conscience.

'I have never learned what it was that governed her emotions,' she said, 'even though I lived with her for three years, when we were at university. Perhaps she does not even know herself.'

The young in the far shrubbery were tangling like maggots, only beautifully dressed. Slightly swaying here and there but still overcome by a top-heavy elegance, she of the sequinned bottom looked up towards the house from time to time, perhaps waiting for a parental command.

What is it that makes the young so beautiful? What terror do they hold for the early middle-aged? Their eggshell eyes slant as in a fresco by Giotto, their bodies are tight with chained energy, however innocuous or domestic their upbringing. Indeed, the more insipid the background, the healthier the bodies, and with health the frightening implication of an explosion to come, unwanted, unsought.

'I mean why?' I said. 'Why now? Why me? What could be more permanent, less malevolent, than this fidelity of mine to an experience which after all never took place? It's ridiculous! More than ten years ago. From what great weight of my affection did she feel obliged to free herself? What could be more innocuous than a little love spread over a long period of time?'

A snigger came over her. I saw a small cloud of cigarette smoke hang for a moment in the moonlight, and she coughed.

'Is it possible,' said her amused disembodied voice, 'that you also are totally ignorant of your own feelings? Of yours, let alone hers?' She started to laugh, laughing while smoking, coughing, still laughing, shoulders bobbing and head down. A dancing human trunk, and two dark wedges of hair.

'How is it,' she said, 'that my friends are so ignorant about their own emotions, when they spend all their time analysing them?'

Some bleary fireflies pursued a residual affair at the head of a row of vines. Chiara's head momentarily blocked my view of the tennis-court behind.

'That you love your wife, everyone can see. That Vittoria wants nothing more from you, enjoys very much the power she has, is equally obvious, no?'

Her voice was ironic and assured. There was something in the way she held her cigarette that seemed intelligent.

'What on earth more could either of you want?'

As I listened, my eyes fixed on an Englishman behind the wire, where the children were dancing. A young Englishman so appalling that he made me ashamed that the English should ever have been made welcome in this place. Tall, much too tall, very pale, with mousy tousled hair stiff with dried chlorine, trimmed badly by the man himself. No tie – so rude at a formal party like this – heavy dun trousers of a fashion the French might call *éclat merdeux*, smeared with darkening souvenirs of food and drink, bound by a belt ripped from the corpse of a dead guardsman. No shoes. I hate a man who dances barefoot.

The noise of the music was faint. The beat was like a millwheel turning.

And such a dancer. Could he dance? No, he could not dance. He merely took up more than his natural room in telling the world he was dancing. He kicked a hole formal in the Italians, who innocently applauded while he dominated a whole segment of the tennis-court, scattering with his jabbering feet little eddies of powder from its bituminous surface. His body said, 'I am an Englishman bent on enjoying himself, and I shall break the leg of anyone who comes near.'

At my age the difference between the past and the present becomes intangible. I have my doubts about my reactions to either. Is this the common experience of exile, either enforced or chosen? A defect intrinsic to me? Acquired by experience? Or is it Tuscany, where the past is so palpable?

A flash at the bottom of the garden: a photographer's, perhaps. Then the distant rollerskate of thunder. A cool wind came slowly over the valley, disturbing the pines, sounding more powerful than it was when it reached our faces.

Down near the tennis-court, Vittoria was talking to the girl with sequins. They seemed to be very absorbed. The distance across the garden seemed at last too far for me to get up and check.

That's how it is with emotions, isn't it? At one moment, they plough you under. Next, you can't remember what made you feel that way. You stumble from one apology to another, and with incredulous looks they say, 'But nothing happened. Surely you exaggerate?'

As I watched, Vittoria placed her arm around the girl's neck. Easily, the gesture was reciprocated. Their heads joined and became one head.

Thunder again, a little nearer.

The weather tends to break towards the end of August. The equinox approaches, and the earth changes trajectory in its ellipse around the sun. The clouds pile up on themselves, and then the rain comes down. Something to do with the change of direction, as we continue on our way.

NOTES

3 · SAN GIUSTO

1. *Le lettere di Michelangelo Buonarroti*, ed. Gaetano Milanesi, Florence, Le Monnier, 1879, p. 489.

5 · SERAVEZZA

2. Caio lent me *Marble in the World*, G. Conti and others, Società Edizionia Apuana, 1986, which has much interesting information on the working of marble in the Carrara district in both the ancient and modern periods. For marble in the ancient world in general, *Marmora romana*, Raniero Gnoli, Edizioni dell'Elefante, 1971, is a classic. *Carrara cave antiche*, Enrico Dolci, Ed. Comune di Carrara, 1980, describes all the surviving traces of Roman and medieval workings in the quarries near Monte Altissimo. All of which is enough to convince me that no trace of Michelangelo, no carving left in some secret unknown lode, remains to be discovered up there by further research.

It would be difficult to trace which piece of sculpture comes from which mine. The *Pietà*, which Romano thought was carved from Seravezza marble, was in fact commissioned by Cardinal Jean Bilhères de Lagraulas in 1497. The marble was obtained from Carrara in 1498, long before the Seravezza mines were reopened. The *Moses* is a more likely candidate, but Frederick Hartt thinks that Michelangelo started work on the piece in 1515, which is again too early for Seravezza (*Michelangelo*, NY, Harry Abrams, 1969, p. 156).

The marble for the lost columns for San Lorenzo, however, certainly came from Seravezza. To look for the quarry which provided the lost columns for a facade of a church which Michelangelo never started is a fairly arcane approach to his work, surely. But incompleteness is a quality one has to keep constantly in mind when contemplating his work, an exercise of the imagination, in a sense an act of utmost respect.

6 · MICHELANGELO

The most accessible selection of Michelangelo's writings translated into English is Michelangelo, *Letters and Poetry*, ed. G. Bull, Oxford University Press (World's Classics), 1987.

Gaetano Milanesi, ed., *Le lettere di Michelangelo Buonarroti, edite ed inedite, coi riccordi ed i contratti artistici*, Florence, Le Monnier, 1879, is a more complete edition of the letters.

For the contracts with artisans: Lucilla Bardeschi e Paola Barocchi, *I riccordi di Michelangelo*, Florence, Sansoni, 1970.

Condivi and Vasari exist in many editions. I used Ascanio Condivi, *Michelangiolo Buonarroti, rime e lettere precedute dalla vita dell'autore*, Florence, Barbera, 1858; Roma, Biblioteca Nazionale, 1933. And Giorgio Vasari, *Le vite de' più eccellenti architetti pittori, et scultori italiani da Cimabue insino a' tempi nostri* (1550 ed.), Einaudi, 1986. The conversations between the merchant d'Ollanda and Michelangelo, quoted in part in Holroyd, *Michel Angelo Buonarroti*, 1903, are also essential primary sources.

The quotes which follow come from *Le lettere*, ed. Gaetano Milanesi, op. cit.

3. To Domenico Boninsegna, 2 May 1517, from Carrara, ibid., p. 383.

4. To Pietro Urbano, March 1518, from Pietrasanta, ibid., p. 385.

5. To Domenico Boninsegna, March 1518, from Seravezza, ibid., p. 386.

6. To Berto da Filicaia, August 1518, from Seravezza, ibid., p. 394.

7. To Pietro Urbano, 20 April 1519, from Seravezza, ibid., p. 403.

8. Michelangelo Buonarotti, *Rime*, ed. G. R. Ceriello, Biblioteca Universale Rizzoli, 1954.

A whole book could be written about this one poem, which is in a sense the guiding prayer of what sculptors have called in this century 'direct carving', i.e. letting your imagination discover something that is intrinsic to the materials, rather than imposing on them a preconceived idea.

'*Concetto*' in the poem seems to mean both 'image' and 'intention', in the sense that Michelangelo, looking at a block of stone, imagines the form it will ultimately produce, and which he *intends* to produce. '*Soverchio*' means 'cover', and suggests that the piece of sculpture strains at the surface of the stone, before the working hand strikes it free.

Then and now, the poem was considered to have a Platonic or Neoplatonic flavour. Michelangelo looking at a stone calls to mind a philosopher looking at a table and imagining an ideal table behind the physical presence. But there are difficulties. The moment that the sculptor takes his chisel and works, the ideal recedes leaving an imperfection behind it – a real table, by association, rather than an ideal table.

Michelangelo as a young man lived at the court of Lorenzo de' Medici, and had ample occasion to overhear classical scholars discussing Platonic ideas. It is possible that this poem intuitively creates a parallel between creative processes and philosophical processes. This does not make it a philosophical idea. It remains a metaphor.

In spite of this, in philosophical terms the poem obliquely uncovers the possibility that there might exist a gap between what a work is and what it intends to portray. For this reason it is also an early and important statement about one of the key philosophical problems in representational art.

9. I am thinking especially of a lecture which Professor Edgar Wind devoted to the incomplete quality of Michelangelo's sculpture, which made a great impression on me when I was at university. Edgar Wind said that we are conditioned to prefer the unfinished work to the finished, because of the accumulated decadence of our destructive and fragmentary century. We have arrived at the point, he said, eyes bright behind twinkling spectacles, when the sketch is preferred to the masterpiece, the fragment to the finished work, the shard to the pot, the discarded limb to the complete statue. This fact seemed to give Professor Wind infinite satisfaction, as if the achievement of a new aesthetic was a valuable result springing from the rubble of all the beautiful European cities bombed during the last war.

It is an important point to make, but it tells us more about the taste of our century than about Michelangelo. Henry Moore used to suggest that Michelangelo purposely left his works unfinished, for aesthetic reasons. Both these arguments are really an imposition of a modern sensibility upon the facts. In the twilight of the Accademia the Michelangelos suddenly metamorphose into Henry Moores. This is not the way to understand the sculptures in the terms of his own time.

7 · VIAREGGIO

10. Byron had been a member of the Carbonari, the Italian patriotic revolutionary association, from early in the century (Byron, *Letters and Journals,* John Murray, 1973–80, vol. 9, p. 23). In the Romagna he armed a subgroup of these called the Americani, who used his house for storing arms and ammunition (ibid., vol. 8, p. 47). He wrote an account of all these conspiracies and gave it, as he was setting off for Greece, to a Venetian friend called Mengaldo, who promptly burned it as being compromising. It is highly probable that all this revolutionary activity was noticed and reported by two secret services, those of Austria and of the Papal Curia in Rome. (See Iris Origo, *The Last Attachment*, John Murray, 1971, pp. 14–17.

11. L. Marchand, *Byron, a Portrait*, John Murray, 1971, p. 236.

12. Byron, *Letters and Journals*, op. cit., vol. 9, p. 149, 26 April 1822.

13. ibid., vol. 10, p. 11.

14. John Hunt, Leigh's brother, published a poem by Byron that was critical of the monarchy, and was prosecuted for it. Sensibly, Murray had kept out of this, but for having refused to publish the piece, Byron had called him a 'sad shuffler' and a 'dirty fellow' (ibid., vol. 10, pp. 26, 58).

15. ibid., vol. 10, p. 34.

16. ibid., vol. 10, p. 69. Also: 'In general I do not draw well with Literary men – not that I dislike them but – I never know what to say to them after I have praised their last publication. – There are several exceptions to be sure – but they have either been men of the world – such as Scott – & Moore &c. or visionaries out of it – such as Shelley &c.' (ibid., vol. 9, p. 30).

17. Edward John Trelawny, *Records of Shelley, Byron and the Author*, Penguin Books, 1973, p. 166.

18. John Taaffe in a report of 1826, published in *The Journal of Clarissa Trant* in 1925. Quoted in Richard Holmes, *Shelley, the Pursuit*, Quartet Books, 1976; Penguin Books, 1987, p. 729.

19. Holmes, ibid., p. 789.

20. Trelawny, op. cit., editor's footnote on p. 313.

21. Anne Hill, *Trelawny's Strange Relations*, printed privately, 1956, p. 5. Byron said of him 'if we could but make Trelawny wash his hands and tell the truth, we might make a gentleman of him'.

22. Trelawny, op. cit., p. 165.

23. Byron, *Letters and Journals*, op. cit., vol. 9, p. 202.

24. Origo, op. cit., p. 106.

8 · BEES

25. The patent which Langstroth took out on his movable-frame hive expired before beekeeping became a major industry, and he died a poor man – though of course worshipped by his colleagues in the profession. Comparing two photographs of him – one in youth, passionate and hungry, the other in old age, serene and saintly – suggests that he was satisfied with this pinnacle of esteem. 'To know that I have been of service in putting such an important industry on solid foundations is worth more to me in my old age than silver or gold.'

David Garnett gave me his copy of *The Dadant System of Beekeeping*, Hamilton, Illinois, 1920, and I read with great fascination *The ABC and XYZ of Bee Culture* by A. I. Root (founder of the A. I. Root Company and author of *Gleanings in Bee Culture*), Medina, Ohio, 1972. Besides being full of practical advice, this is also an indirect cultural history of an important component of rural life in the United States.

The works of Karl Von Frisch exist in various editions, of which I read *Bees, Their Vision, Chemical Senses and Language*, Cornell University Press, 1971.

9 · SIENA

26. *Inferno*, xxix, 121–3. Let it be said that Dante said horrible things about the Pisans, the Genoese, the Aretines and almost any other Tuscans one can think of.

27. Giovanni Antonio Pecci, *Relazione distinta delle quarantadue Contrade*, Siena, 1723. His list describes the games as being '*di Gladiatori, di Giostre, di Bufalate, di Pugna, di Caccia di Tori, e d'altre bestie feroci, colle quali combatteranno i Giovani più coragiosi*'. Pecci was a lawyer and antiquarian who wrote an interesting account of Sienese history: *Memorie storico-critiche della città di Siena*, Siena, 1755.

28. The best edition of the *Commentaires* of Blaise de Monluc is that published by Gallimard/La Pléiade, 1964.

There are two manuscript versions of the work, one much longer and more embellished than the other. It is not absolutely clear how much help Monluc had with the embellishments, and the story of the Sienese women is one of them. It appears in works by other contemporary writers, but there are sufficient small details in Monluc's version to make it seem authentic.

The song the Sienese women sang as they went down to the ramparts was perhaps by Laura Ciuoli, and it is probable that it still exists in a manuscript version by Pecci, somewhere in the library in Siena. I was unable to trace it, as Pecci left a vast mass of unsorted material. There were many women poets in Siena at the time. See *Miscellanea storia senese*, V, 1898, p. 38.

29. The story of the football-playing Spaniard comes not from Monluc but from a Sienese historian who wrote an account of the siege based on his diary. Alessandro Sozzini, *Diario delle cose avvenute a Siena dal 20 luglio 1550 al 28 giugno 1555*, new ed., Florence, 1842.

30. Pietro Leopoldo, *Relazioni sul governo della Toscana*, edited by Arnaldo Salvestrini, Firenze, Olschi, 1969, vol. 1, pp. 21–2.

31. The rule of Pietro Leopoldo in Tuscany still arouses controversy among historians. There are two possible readings: one, that he was a liberal and democratic ruler who was unfortunately removed to Vienna just at the point when he was about to introduce to Tuscany a liberal constitution, with elected representatives. The other, that he was an intelligent reactionary seeking to bypass the towns and the politically conscious classes (such as they were) by creating a link between an efficient bureaucracy and a happy, contented and above all *quiet* country gentry. See A. Wandruszka, *Pietro Leopoldo: un grande riformatore*, Firenze, 1968. C. Francovich, 'La rivoluzione americana e il progetto di constituzione del granduca Pietro Leopoldo', and F.

Venturi, 'La circolazione delle idee', both articles in *Rassegna storica del Risorgimento*, Fasc. II–III, aprile–settembre 1954.

32. *Relazioni*, III, 203.

11 · MONTAPERTI

33. *Inferno*, Canto XXII, ll. 1–9. I used E. Moore's edition (OUP, 1894). The Italian editions are not consistent in spelling and punctuation.

34. ibid., Canto XII, ll. 73–82.

35. ibid., Canto XXI, ll. 92–6. Caprona was a castle belonging to the Pisans, taken by a joint force of Florentines and Lucchesi in 1289, and this passage is taken as evidence that Dante was present when the garrison surrendered.

36. See Gaetano Salvemini, *Magnati e popolani in Firenze dal 1280 al 1295*, Florence, 1899.

For the battle of Montaperti, a good guide is Cesare Paoli, *La battaglia di Montaperti*, Siena, 1869, and his edition of the *Libro di Montaperti*, the entire muster records of the Florentine army, captured after the battle.

For a note on both these historians, see note 50 (Chapter 13).

For the later quotations in this chapter I used the Sienese chroniclers Domenico Aldobrandini and Niccolò Ventura, published in *Il primo libro delle istorie sanesi*, Marco Bellarmati, Siena, 1844.

Also Giugurta Tommasi, *Dell'historie di Siena*, Venice, 1625.

The Florentine chroniclers are Marchionne di Coppo Stefani, *Storia fiorentina*, and, always useful, the *Cronica*, of Giovanni Villani, which is still in print in Italy.

37. Tommasi, op. cit., vol. I, p. 327.

38. *Inferno*, Canto IX, l. 128 and *passim*.

39. ibid., Canto X, l. 36.

40. ibid., Canto x, l. 81.

41. ibid., Canto xxxii, ll. 70–112.

12 · POGGIO A CAIANO

42. This and the quotations which follow are taken from Jacopo da Pontormo, *Diario fatto nel tempo che dipingeva il coro di San Lorenzo 1554–56*, ed. Emilio Cecchi, Le Monnier, 1956. (There are many other editions.)

13 · CAREGGI

43. The great nineteenth-century historian Pasquale Villari describes the incident with a melodramatic emphasis indistinguishable from the mood in the paintings in the front hall at Careggi. 'Then Savonarola stood up, appearing to grow in stature as the dying Prince shrank fearfully in the bed. Savonarola said, "You must restore Liberty to the people of Florence" (Pasquale Villari, *La storia di Girolamo Savonarola e de' suoi tempi*, Florence, Successori Le Monnier, 1887, p. 160), in *Commentationes Joannis Pici Mirandulae*, 1495–6.

14 · FIRE

44. Papal brief of Alexander VI, early March 1498. There was a private threat to excommunicate the whole city of Florence, which would have placed the goods of Florentine merchants all over Europe at risk.

45. Villari, op. cit. This and the following quotations are extracts from the *Pratiche* of the Councils, in the appendix of Villari, ibid., vol. ii, p. 143.

Roberto Ridolfi, *Vita de Girolamo Savonarola*, Angelo Belardetti, 1952; Sansoni, 1974.

While working on the chapters covering Florence, Dante and Montaperti, and later on the chapters on the Medici and Savonarola, I made a curious discovery.

A direct personal line connected the historians whose work interested me most, for Pasquale Villari, who wrote about Savonarola, was the teacher of Cesare Paoli, who wrote about Montaperti. And Paoli was in turn the teacher of Gaetano Salvemini, who wrote about the clash between nobles and populace in thirteenth-century Florence.

Pasquale Villari was a young follower of De Sanctis in the revolution of 1848 in Naples; after its failure he was forced into exile in Florence. There he dedicated himself to historical research, producing works on Savonarola, Machiavelli and the city of Florence, based on a knowledge of the documents (many of which he traced himself) which is as yet unsurpassed.

The opposite of a detached academic, he took part in many political debates involving Naples and the South, was a deputy in the early parliaments after the unification of Italy and, in 1891, became Minister of Education.

Cesare Paoli, his pupil, remained more detached from public life, working in the University of Florence for many years, where he had great influence on more than one generation of pupils. His political ideas entered into the classic tradition of Italian liberalism, as one might expect from the grandson of Pasquale Paoli, the great Corsican patriot and freedom fighter of the late eighteenth century.

Salvemini wrote his *Magnati e popolani in Firenze dal 1280 al 1295* when he was twenty-six, and it represents an interesting Marxist interpretation of the struggles inside Florence during that period. His books thereafter dealt with more recent topics – the French Revolution, a study of Mazzini, political parties in nineteenth-century Milan – after which he became in effect a contemporary historian, whose life was wholeheartedly dedicated to opposing Benito Mussolini. He was one of the founders of *L'Unità*, a left-wing Socialist newspaper which later became the official paper of the Italian Communist party; in exile in England after the assassination of Matteotti he co-edited *Non Mollare!* ('Don't Give Up'), the newspaper dedicated to resisting Fascism.

The attraction of these historians is that their history is passionately felt and emotively expressed. This is not to suggest that their works are biased, or that they altered or suppressed facts, for these are historians of extraordinarily high professional standards. But their ideas are clearly 'interested', as one might say in any Latin country. These historians found their vision of the past deeply entwined with their sense of the present, so that their books became part of the continuous history of their country.

46. For a discussion as to how many works of art were destroyed in the Burning of the Vanities, see Ronald Steinberg, *Florentine Art and Renaissance Historiography*, Ohio University Press, 1977. Also Villari, op. cit., vol. II, pp. 421–2.

Vasari says that Lorenzo di Credi and Fra Bartolomeo were overwhelmed by Savonarola, and destroyed many works in the fires. But Vasari was very pro-Medici, and perhaps therefore took a dim view of Savonarola.

The *Vita latina* of Savonarola says enthusiastically that Donatello burned some statues.

One should perhaps take into consideration what a marvellous occasion the Burnings were to clear out of the studio all the works that hadn't quite come off . . .

47. Lorenzo Violi, *Apologia*. The relevant extract comes from Villari, op. cit., vol. II, p. lxxiv.

Violi was a lawyer skilled in shorthand, who took down many of Savonarola's extempore sermons. His *Apologia* is a memoir of Savonarola, written as a dialogue between two speakers, Didimo and Soffia, which explains the hesitancy of a language half written, half spoken.

48. Giorgio Vasari, *Le vite de' più eccelenti architetti, pittori, et scultori italiani, da Cimabue insino a' tempi nostri* (1550 edition, with notes), Einaudi, 1986, p. 478.

49. The fragment is dated 2 November 1499, some eighteen months

after Savonarola's death. Quoted in Steinberg, op. cit., and Roberto Ridolfi, op. cit.

50. Savonarola died in 1498, Botticelli in 1510. The average number of works per year in the last twelve years of the painter's life is slightly higher than in the years that came before – bearing in mind that the dating of Botticelli's work is unusually difficult, and many works have been lost (Gabriele Mandel, *L'opera completa del Botticelli*, Rizzoli, 1978).

Most scholars discuss the influence of Savonarola upon Botticelli's work, usually with reference to *La Calunnia*, in the Uffizi, and *La Derelitta*, in the Rospigliosi collection in Rome. The question is a very personal one. For myself, the only Botticelli which has made me think instantly of poor Fra Girolamo has been the *Agony in the Garden*, in Granada, with its extraordinary image of a fence of sharpened wooden stakes separating Christ from the sleeping disciples.

It would require another whole chapter to discuss Savonarola and Michelangelo. Condivi, in his *Life of Michelangelo* (1554), said: '. . . he has read with great attention the Holy Scriptures, both the Old Testament and the New, and the works of those who studied them, such as the writings of Savonarola, for whom he has always had a great affection, keeping always in mind the memory of his living voice' (Roma, Ed. Biblioteca Nazionale, 1933, p. 112).

Condivi knew Michelangelo better than Vasari did, and presumably witnessed the marvellous spectacle of Michelangelo imitating the way Savonarola spoke, fifty years after the Friar had died. (Vasari stole the story for the second edition of his *Lives*, saying that Michelangelo had 'heard his voice from the pulpit'.)

On 26 February 1497 Savonarola gave a sermon which, to me, has something in common with the way Michelangelo wrote about art. Somewhere at the back of it lies a struggle with Plato, and with God, and with a feeling that the whole pursuit of art is both sacrilegious and doomed to failure. The language is abrupt – perhaps there were some artists in the crowd below who caught the attention of Savonarola and caused him to improvise this tangent.

The theme is the vanity of anything that gets in the way of the contemplation of God. In this case, philosophy:

> Every imperfect thing depends upon one more perfect, and if that itself is imperfect, it depends on another more perfect, until one reaches the precious thing; and if that itself is imperfect, then it is not the first. For the first is absolutely perfect; and that which is absolutely perfect is absolutely good – therefore God, which is the prime mover is perfect, *ergo* perfectly good. *Item in omni genere est dare unum primum.* Light enters: the first light; colour enters: the first colour. And among many kinds of goodness, the first good: for God is the first good, *ergo* he is absolutely good.
>
> How pleased with himself was the philosopher! Do you want to see his pride? See that, even knowing that God was the highest good, why did he not love him? They did not reason as they did for love of God, but in order to show that they were men of great knowledge, for human honour and glory. Their intellect went upwards to God, but their love was devoted to themselves. *Et sic evanuerunt in cogitationibus suis, dicentes se esse sapientes et stulti facti sunt.* That's the real motivation behind philosophy! But let us leave the argument for a while and I shall show you a better one later.
>
> Do you want to see how vain was this knowledge of the philosophers? They say that the magicians of the Pharaohs *defecerunt in tertio signo*; that they spoke, *id est*, in the goodness of the Lord. Do you want to see that? And they say that every painter paints himself. He doesn't paint himself as a man, because he makes images of lions, horses, men and women who are not himself, *id est*, according to his idea [*secondo il suo concetto*]; and though these are different images [*fantasie*] from the painter who painted them, they are still all according to his own ideas. Thus the philosophers, because they were proud, described God by fantastic exaggerated means, and because of their own excellence,

in that they thought themselves wise, they said that God did not lower himself to human affairs; because if he were mixed in these human things, he would appear to them to be corrupted by it. Take those two great minds, Aristotle and Plato . . .

Edizione nazionale delle opere di Girolamo Savonarola, ed. Angelo Belardetti, Roma, 1955, vol. 1, *Prediche sopra Ezechiele*

51. For example: 'Moral good, in a word, has a power to attract, towards itself. It is no sooner seen than it rouses the spectator to action, and yet is does not form his character by mere imitation, but by promoting the understanding of virtuous deeds it provides him with a dominating purpose.' Plutarch, 'Life of Pericles', in *The Rise and Fall of Athens*, translated by Ian Scott-Kilvert, Penguin Books, 1960, p. 166.

16 · MACCARI

52. I should offer a translation of this word, but it is difficult. It means 'wild' or 'savage', and has both the connotation of 'the wild man of the woods' and also, probably, a subliminal reference to the 'fauve' movement of painting in France – also difficult to translate.

53. *Il Selvaggio*, 19 July 1924.

54. Marcello Piacentini was an eclectic architect much influenced by late Roman models, which he carried over into many public works during the Fascist period – the age now tactfully called '*anni trenta*' by Italian historians. The Palazzo di Giustizia in Milan is easily seen, and a masterpiece; so is the Piazza della Vittoria in Genoa. Arches are punctuated by square windows set between them, in an unusual mixture of open and closed spaces. In a sense, Piacentini's revival of classical models has itself been revived in the Post-modern movement.

55. *Il Selvaggio*, 15 May 1933.

56. ibid., 30 November 1934.

57. ibid., 30 December 1932.

20 · PORCUPINES

58. I presume that the Guelfs and Ghibellines painted the native white iris, *Iris florentina*, on their shields. This flower is extremely rare today; in fact, I do not remember ever having seen one in the wild.

The wild iris I refer to in this chapter is *Iris pallida dalmatica*, which was introduced into Tuscany (and, incidentally, Provence) in the eighteenth century, for use in the perfume trade. This iris had become 'wild' over the years only in the sense that hardly anyone takes care of them any more.

23 · ETRUSCANS

59. Works by Ranuccio Bianchi Bandinelli:

Enciclopedia dell'arte antica classica (with G. Becatti), Roma, 1953 onwards;

'Arte etrusca e arte italica', article in the *Enciclopedia italiana Treccani*, 1963;

L'arte romana nel centro del potere, Milano, Feltrinelli, 1969;

Etruschi e Italiani prima del dominio di Roma, Milano, Rizzoli, 1973;

L'arte etrusca (intr. M. Torelli e L. Franchi dell'Orto), Edizioni Reuniti, 1982.

60. The chapter 'Visits to Hell', in Ranuccio Bianchi Bandinelli, *Dal diario di un borghese*, Il Saggiatore, 1962.

There is also a very interesting introduction by Bandinelli to *La politica culturale del nazismo*, by Hildegarde Brenner, Bari, Editori Laterza, 1965 (a translation of *Die Kunstpolitik des Nazionalsozialismus*, Hamburg, 1963).

In the original cryptic notes that Bandinelli kept of the meeting with Mussolini and Hitler, he used as pseudonyms for them the names Marius, because it began with an M, and Sulla, 'because of the feminine ending'! Perhaps the reference to these two great rivals of the late Roman republic indicates a subconscious wish that Mussolini and Hitler would end up foes rather than allies.

The *Diario* has many interesting incidents. Bandinelli had also met the ex-Kaiser Wilhelm, whom he compared to Hitler.

'Everything I told him [Hitler] was repeated, but completely deformed and adapted to some preconceived idea of his ... the Procrustean bed of Nazi ideology with, simultaneously, an innocent desire to catalogue everything exactly. The same mentality, infantile and fantastic, I had seen years previously in the Kaiser.'

Why did Bandinelli make no attempt to assassinate the monsters when he had the chance? It was a question to which he gave much thought, both before and after meeting them. He refrained, partly because he 'belonged to those social classes which have demonstrated by now on too many occasions how they ignore the guiding forces of history'. And because he thought that 'perhaps it was not the function of a single individual to stand in the way of the historical process . . .'

61. D. H. Lawrence, *Etruscan Places*, ed. G. Kezich, Olive Press, London, 1986, p. 85.

62. ibid., p. 65.

63. These and the following quotations are from Arturo Martini, *La scultura lingua morta*, ed. Mario De Micheli, Jaca Book, 1982. I wish I could write more about this wonderful sculptor, but I have no real excuse to bring him into a book about Tuscany.

66. D. H. Lawrence, op. cit., p. 94. Lawrence cheated a bit in pretending that his reaction to Etruscan objects was a series of spontaneous primary experiences. His ideas about the origins of the Etruscans, for instance, which he describes as if he had received an inspiration while lying on the beach and looking at the sea, in fact sum up one of the books he had read. He prepared himself thoroughly before the visit by studying books before the visit and photographs after.

He is known to have read George Dennis's *The Cities and Cemeteries of Etruria*, 1848. (This is the classic work on Etruscan sites.) and Pericle Ducati's *Etruria antica*, 1925, which represented the latest research on the subject at the time Lawrence was writing. And he asked his mother-in-law to send from Germany *Etruskische Malerei* (Weege, 1921). He also had a series of Alinari photos of the tomb paintings.

For a discussion of his use of published material, see the postscript by Giovanni Kezich to the Olive Press edition of *Etruscan Places*, op. cit.